MIKE LOOKS BACK

MIKE LOOKS BACK

*The Memoirs of Gardner Cowles
Founder of Look Magazine*

Published by Gardner Cowles ● New York

To Mother,
the greatest influence
on my life

CONTENTS

INTRODUCTION

I am privately printing these memoirs for the benefit of my children, grandchildren, and a few of my closest friends and business associates. I feel some of the unusual experiences in my life should be recorded before my memory slips away.

I started writing my memoirs about a decade ago, but the end result never seemed quite right. Finally, I turned to Chris Welles, a seasoned and highly successful author. He substantially improved what I had written, but it still did not seem to me to be a book which I should inflict on the general public. Hence, my decision to print it only in a limited edition.

Nothing would have been turned out except for the persistence of my able Executive Secretary, Martha Stephens. She kept after me month after month, year after year, to get my memoirs in some kind of written form. She has been my able right-hand for more than thirty years—advising me, counseling me, and helping me through my somewhat checkered publishing career. I am deeply in her debt.

William Arthur, who served with distinction for many years as *LOOK*'s managing editor and editor, shepherded the book through to publication and deserves my heartfelt thanks, as does Will Hopkins, *LOOK*'s last art director, who designed the book. Earlier, Belle Sideman and Doris Doland Lynch helped enormously. I am grateful to all of them.

GARDNER COWLES
Spring, 1985

PREFACE

"I've always had a lot of fun out of life."

When I first read those words toward the beginning of a draft of Mike Cowles's autobiography, I didn't give them much thought. After all, most of us, looking back on our lives, like to think we've had a lot of fun.

But when I reflected about it in helping to prepare the draft for publication, I realized that, in writing about companies and corporate executives for the past twenty years, I had met few people who were really having fun. Most seemed so busy seeking money, power, recognition, and all of the other common fruits of business success that they had little if any time for fun other than a few rounds of golf. They seldom seemed able to get around to pursuing a diversion or other activity simply because it might be intriguing, amusing, or pleasurable.

No one could ever make that criticism of Mike Cowles. His career in publishing has been certainly full and complete—from its early days when he was a reporter and later managing editor of his father's *Des Moines Register* to the thirty-four-year lifespan of *LOOK* magazine, which he conceived and presided over as publisher and editor in chief. This memoir provides engagingly contrasting accounts of small-city newspaper publishing in the early part of this century and big-city magazine publishing in the latter part of the century.

But Cowles made time for an extraordinary array of extra-curricular adventures. Perhaps the most notable was accompanying Wendell Willkie during his 49-day around-the-world trip in 1942 at Roosevelt's behest to reassure our allies of our determination to defeat Germany and Japan. That trip included meetings with Joseph Stalin, Charles de Gaulle, the Shah of Iran, and Chiang Kai-shek.

Those are only a few of the world figures with whom Cowles has had relationships ranging from brief encounters to, as in the case of Willkie, life-long friendships. They include a long list of presidents: Hoover, Roosevelt, Truman, Eisenhower, Johnson, and Nixon; numerous international personalities such as Nikita Khrushchev, Conrad Adenauer, Winston Churchill, Haile Selassie, Jawaharlal Nehru, Eva Peron, and the Duke and Duchess of Windsor; and such celebrities as Jacqueline Onassis, Rita Hayworth, H.L. Mencken, Marilyn Monroe, Charlie Chaplain, and Hedy Lamarr.

Cowles's accounts of these individuals form an especially rewarding portion of this book. At heart, he is a journalist as much as a businessman, with an eye and ear for the revealing personal detail and the illustrative anecdote that provides insightful glimpses into a person's character. A particularly arresting example is a vignette of Herbert Hoover during the 1932 campaign: a man so depressed about his virtually nonexistent chances for reelection that, to get him out on the stage for a campaign speech, his wife had to implore him as he sat slumped with his head in his hands, "Herbert, be a *man!*" In many cases, Cowles's impressions go beyond or against the common public image. The Marilyn Monroe and the Jackie Onassis that emerge from these pages, for instance, may surprise even those readers who assume that nothing more could remain to be said about such exhaustively publicized figures.

Cowles's appetite for adventure has extended beyond encounters with luminaries. A pilot, he has had a lifelong passion for aviation that has entailed many years on the board of United Airlines and one of the first transatlantic flights from Germany to the U.S. aboard the Hindenburg in 1936—a year before the dirigible crashed in flames while attempting to land in New Jersey. And one must mention that adventure of having four wives, two of whom are deceased. All remained his friends. (His divorces were always duly covered by *The Des Moines Register*.)

Yet few of the anecdotes Cowles offers about himself are as revealing as his experience with what was called the Cardiff Giant: a stone figure of a man more than ten feet tall that was buried in upstate New York in 1868 by a tobacco farmer as a hoax, the idea being that when the giant was discovered it would be seen as the petrified remains of a Biblical race of giants. The hoax was spectacularly successful. After the tobacco farmer confessed to the prank—to the great embarrassment of experts who had attested to its authenticity—the Giant enjoyed a long life in circus exhibits. Cowles had followed the Giant's exploits with what he calls "boundless fascination bordering on obsession," due in part to the fact that it had been fashioned from stone quarried twenty miles from Fort Dodge, Iowa, near where he was born. When the Giant eventually came up for sale, Cowles bought it for $4,500. Installed in the den of his house and set off with theatrical lights and posters from its more glamorous days, the Giant served for many years as perhaps the ultimate conversation piece.

Even Cowles's business life can be seen as a series of projects that were adventures as much as they were ventures. After serving with *The Des Moines Register* and *Tribune*, he came to New York in the middle 1940s to build his own empire. Though undertaken officially in the pursuit of profit, it seems apparent that the motivation behind many of the numerous publications he launched was just as importantly the feeling that putting them out might be fun. Among many examples: *Venture*, a travel magazine with the first three-dimensional cover; *Quick*, a very small-sized news magazine that might have proved a potential rival for *Time* and *Newsweek*; *Flair*, an innovative arts magazine; the *Suffolk Sun*, a newspaper serving the eastern end of Long Island; the *San Juan Star*, Puerto Rico's first English-language newspaper which won a Pulitzer Prize in its first year; and, of course, *LOOK*, the product of an abiding interest in photojournalism and his primary obsession for many years.

Perhaps because Cowles was stirred by more than strict bottom-line calculations, many of these publications eventually failed. But their legacy remains. *Flair*, a hopelessly impractical venture edited by Fleur Fenton, his wife at the time, employed elaborate graphic designs that were years ahead of their time. Art directors still talk reverently about it, and copies of its dozen issues are prized collectors' items. *LOOK*, doomed by the same unfavorable mass magazine economics that also led to the demise of *LIFE* and the *Saturday Evening Post*, was widely acclaimed during its later life for its ground-breaking reporting, photography, and art direction. I know only too well that it provided stiff competition for *LIFE* and the *Post*, for I worked as an editor at both publications.

Despite the setbacks, which he is not chary of chronicling in detail though they could hardly be termed fun, Cowles's business career was far from a financial failure. Cowles and his brother John originally put $500,000 into what was called the Look Corporation. Later renamed Cowles Communications, Inc., it made numerous profitable acquisitions. Many, including *Family Circle* magazine (one of the largest-selling women's magazines), a Memphis television station, and some Florida newspapers, were sold in 1971 to the New York Times Co. for Times Co. stock constituting a 22 percent interest in *The Times*. That proved an excellent investment. When Cowles Communications was liquidated in 1982, some $200 million in cash and other assets was distributed to shareholders.

Mike Cowles's publishing achievements certainly loom large in any assessment of his life. But as his autobiography demonstrates, his life was far richer. Other business leaders would do well to peruse the memoirs of a man who was eager to take risks though the return was more likely to be psychic than fiscal, and who knew there was much more to a business career than making a buck.

CHRIS WELLES

5

GROWING UP
IN IOWA

1

When I was a day or two old, my father Gardner Cowles took a good look at me and announced, "He looks like an Irishman. Let's call him Mike." Although I was christened Gardner, Jr., the nickname has stuck throughout my life. Why I, the third son and last of six children, was named Gardner, Jr., I don't know. If I was ever told, I don't remember. To my friends, family, and just about everyone else, I am "Mike." Even today half of my mail comes addressed to Mike or Michael Cowles. After my father's death I dropped the Junior. When my only son, Gardner III, was born we began to call him "Pat" to perpetuate the Irish whimsy.

My father's ancestors actually emigrated from Scotland and settled in upper New York State where my grandfather, William Fletcher Cowles, was born in 1819. He became a Methodist minister and since ministers in the Methodist Church were transferred frequently in those days he moved westward from one pulpit to another through Missouri and Iowa until he settled for a while in Oscaloosa, Iowa, where my father was born.

I have no recollection of Grandfather Cowles, who died in 1899 before I was born. But I was told by my older brothers and sisters that he was a patriarchal figure right out of the Old Testament, tall, spare, stern, with a booming voice and a long, gray beard that descended to his waist. He ruled his God-fearing Methodist household with an iron hand and was equally imperious in church. Although many members of his congregation supported slavery during the pre-Civil War years—slave running was common in nearby Missouri—he vociferously advocated freedom for blacks. Like Abraham Lincoln, with whom Grandfather was friendly and whom he supported for President, Grandfather argued that the nation could not endure half-slave and half-free. When he preached on the subject, his divided congregation sometimes turned into an angry mob and he needed the protection of armed guards.

My father was born in Oscaloosa on February 28, 1861, just two months before the start of the Civil War. Less outgoing and gregarious than Grandfather and initially quite shy, my father nevertheless inherited or more likely picked up Grandfather's firm belief in such virtues as honesty, self-reliance, self-improvement, hard work, and thrift. These virtues were necessities as well. Grandfather had little money of his own and his family learned to subsist on a budget of $1 per person per week, which had to cover all necessities. My father later recalled, "At an early age, I knew that I would never have any money given to me, that I would never be helped to get jobs and that it was up to me alone if I succeeded in business."

Beginning when he was very young, Father always had a job when he wasn't in school. At Grandfather's decree, he and his brothers initially worked on farms in the summertime. Later, Father held such jobs as pasting strips of paper on cards of buttons in a dry goods store and folding copies of a local newspaper. While he was in college, he spent one summer traveling from farm to farm in Southern Iowa selling maps of the United States and trading religious literature (both Catholic and Protestant) with farmers for food and lodging. During one vacation, he worked on a survey crew planning a railroad route in Iowa. Between his junior and senior years, he earned $75 a month helping to build the Union Pacific's Oregon Shortline from Portland east into Utah.

Grandfather's migratory ministry made Father's college years equally peripatetic. He attended three Iowa Colleges: William Penn, Grinnell, and finally Iowa Wesleyan, where he received his B.A. and M.A.

The geographical diversity of Father's employment and educational experiences provided him with an extensive if informal education in the state of Iowa that would prove invaluable during his later career as a newspaper publisher. But following graduation from Wesleyan in 1882, he initially decided to become a school superintendent and landed a $720-a-year post in Algona, a small town with a population of 900 in the prairies of northern Iowa. Shortly thereafter, he convinced the school board to let him establish a high school-level course in instruction. As his assistant for the venture, he chose a young elementary school teacher by the name of Florence Call. She was the daughter of Ambrose Call, a prominent Algona banker whose family had founded Algona, and the former Nancy Henderson, whose family had settled in Algona after a journey from Ohio by covered wagon. After a brief courtship, my father and Florence—whom he called Flora—were married on December 3, 1884. I was born on January 31, 1903, the youngest of six children, three boys and three girls. My mother at the time was forty-two years old.

Ambrose Call was a strong believer in education for women as well as men, and my mother was among the first women graduates of Northwestern University in Evanston, Illinois. She majored in art and her interest, or more precisely passion for art continued throughout her life. She devoted herself to developing cultural and artistic institutions in Des Moines. Her children became deeply involved in artistic pursuits. My brother Russell became a professional painter of considerable repute.

My father operated in a quite different world. Always restless and ambitious, he realized soon after his arrival in Algona that his horizons extended far beyond educational management. Within a year, while continuing as superintendent, he purchased a half interest in *The Algona Republican*, a weekly newspaper, and began running its business affairs. The move provoked a blistering page-one editorial attack from Harvey Ingham, the feisty, opinionated owner of the competing *Upper Des Moines*. Calling for Father's ouster as superintendent, Ingham wrote that a new man should be appointed who was "old enough not to be attracted by side speculations and smart enough to only try to do one thing at a time." Despite the assault, Father not only held on to the two jobs but became fast friends with his assailant. The two men later went on to become lifelong business partners at *The Des Moines Register*, the core of my family's communications empire.

Soon after buying into *The Algona Republican*, Father had a bitter disagreement with the other owner. He sold back his interest and went into business with Ambrose Call. With Father's help, the Call-Cowles firm substantially expanded its mail contracting business. At the time, hundreds of small Midwestern towns were not served by railroad lines, and the federal government accepted bids from private companies to provide wagon and horseback mail service. Soon Call-Cowles had more than thirty routes in Iowa, Kansas, and the Dakotas.

Father also got into the business of arranging loans for farmers who were transforming the wilderness of northern Iowa into fertile farms. That led into banking. He came to control ten banks and became president of the major bank in Algona. It was said that Father's net worth during his Algona days eventually reached the then extremely impressive figure of $200,000.

Father's political involvements were expanding as rapidly as his business ventures. Inheriting an interest in public affairs from Grandfather, he soon became active in Iowa politics, whose tumultuous and often chaotic machinations were then closer to European politics than the U.S.'s now relatively staid two-party system. In 1899, at the age of 38, he was elected to the Iowa legislature. Two hectic terms were enough for him, but his close association with Republican party affairs lasted far beyond his career as an elected official.

Father's friend Harvey Ingham, meanwhile, had left Algona to become editor of *The Des Moines Register and Leader* in the state capital. After a year, Ingham was in trouble, and the paper was losing ground to competing newspapers. Ingham knew he needed both Father's capital

9

and his business acumen. In 1903, he and Ingham acquired the paper for about $110,000. The deal required a major portion of Father's financial resources—and a great deal of fortitude as well. As his obituary in *The Des Moines Register* noted, "He jumped overnight from banking to the then hazardous business of newspaper publication. His savings were placed in pawn and it appeared for a time that he had lost in one turn of pitch and toss the careful accumulations of half a life-time."

With that purchase, publishing became Father's consuming interest. The following year, when I was a year old, he moved our family south to Des Moines.

FATHER AND HARVEY INGHAM

My father and Harvey Ingham, at first glance, seemed an unlikely team. Father was reserved, cool, and, in his political views, conservative and Republican. Ingham was gregarious, genial, warm, and, in his politics, liberal, a reformist, and a frequent supporter of Democrats. But the two men were alike in perhaps more important ways. Both came from similarly austere pioneer Iowa backgrounds. Their fathers were high-principled and strong-minded mavericks who did not shrink from espousing unpopular causes. They were both college educated, a rarity in those days, and intellectually curious. And they had enormous respect for each other.

Their individual talents were perfectly complementary. Father was the quintessential business manager, who delighted in the minutiae of circulation and accounting. Ingham was the quintessential editor who delighted in rooting out the news and advocating ideas.

The Register and Leader's most pressing problems were financial and managerial. The paper was losing money and its circulation turned out to be much lower than Father had been led to believe: only 14,000 against claims by the previous owners of 32,000. While the paper was widely known and respected in Iowa, its influence, due to poor management, was fading. Staff morale was low and sinking while turnover was high and rising. Though it was the city's only morning paper, it faced stiff competition from three afternoon papers, *The Capital*, *The News*, and *The Tribune*.

A tough and demanding perfectionist, Father tightened and reorganized the newspaper's financial systems and practices. He scrutinized every penny of operating expenses, checked and approved every bill before it was paid, and signed every payroll check. To eliminate costly collections of overdue subscription bills, he cancelled unpaid subscriptions—some had been delinquent for several years—and ordered that subscriptions would be accepted only on a cash-in advance basis. Despite vigorous protests, he told clergymen, who used to receive the paper free, that if they wanted to keep getting it they would have to pay like everyone else. He was equally tough with advertisers. Most publishers were afraid to press major advertisers whose bills were in arrears. But Father directed that if an advertiser had not paid for last month's ads the paper would not accept any more advertising from him. Though this policy certainly cost the paper some linage, Father believed that in the long run the paper would benefit from an enhanced reputation for prudent business management.

He refused to acquiesce to a number of dubious financial relationships then common between newspapers and institutions they covered. Shortly after taking over, he learned that the paper was secretly on the payroll of a major railroad company. He immediately terminated the subsidy.

Circulation was perhaps his greatest love. "It does you no good in a business way just to put out a good paper," Father once told an editor friend. "You also have to go out to sell it." It was true, as one observer noted, that "Iowa was practically virgin territory for a newspaper circulation genius." Most communities in the state were served by small weeklies and, to a much less extent, by out of state papers. The reach of the Des Moines papers extended barely beyond city limits. No newspaper, weekly or daily, even remotely served the whole state.

But it took a genius to make *The Register and Leader* fill that void. While Ingham gave increased space to state-wide news, Father, drawing upon his experience as a map salesman and mail hauler, developed new and often innovative delivery techniques. He became such an expert in railroad schedules that without checking a schedule he knew where every train in Iowa was supposed to be at any given time, day or night. He became an ardent advocate of highway construction and improvement. Because the postal service did not operate on Sundays, he organized an elaborate system of carrier boys to deliver the Sunday paper. He turned the carrier boys into salesmen as well by giving them a commission for every new subscriber they recruited.

Merely getting the newspaper to subscribers was not enough. He was a great believer that reading a newspaper was a habit and that a publisher should nourish that habit in every possible way, particularly by getting it to readers on time. "A good newspaper promptly delivered can scarcely shake off the subscribers with dynamite," he once said. He tried to make sure that the time the paper arrived on the doorstep of each home would not vary more than five minutes from one day to the next.

These circulation strategies paid off quickly. By 1906, circulation had doubled to more than 25,000. By 1908, the figure was over 31,000.

Circulation growth translated into a surge of new advertising. This allowed Father to be more selective about the advertising he accepted. When he took over the paper, he had been shocked by the numerous full-page advertisements for miracle cure-alls of every conceivable ailment. He was just as disturbed by the numerous ads for beer and

11

liquor. Both Father and Ingham were non-drinkers and active in the temperance movement. (After he reached 75, Father relented a bit and occasionally would have a cocktail before dinner, which he called his "medicine.") Though nearly a third of the paper's display advertising consisted of medical and alcohol ads, Father and Ingham wanted to get by without them.

They were provoked into a decision on the matter during a city election campaign. After *The Register and Leader* editorially supported the move, a delegation representing liquor interests called on my father to protest. Unless the paper changed its editorial stance, they said, they would withdraw their advertising. Their threat came too late, my father told them. He was canceling their advertising as of that day. The paper announced that it would refuse "to enter into contracts to print liquor or questionable medical advertising."

(Many years later, when the fervor of the temperance movement had long since become just a memory, my brother John and I tried to talk Father into changing his mind. But when we put clippings of liquor ads from other papers on Father's desk, he told his secretary, "You needn't bring those ads to me anymore. Tell the boys that I throw such ads in the wastebasket." Not until 1970 did the Cowles papers in Des Moines resume taking ads for alcoholic beverages.)

Though motivated by moral principle, the ban on liquor ads was good business. It was roundly applauded by Iowa's powerful "dry" forces and produced another round of circulation gains and of advertising increases that more than made up for the loss.

The Register and Leader's financial prosperity, engineered by my father, provided maximum latitude to Harvey Ingham's activities as editor. With Father's support, Ingham was a pioneer in the new trends that were reshaping American journalism in the early 1900's, especially the separation of news coverage and editorial opinion. In most newspapers at the time, fact and opinion were so thoroughly interwoven in news columns that it was difficult if not impossible to separate one from the other. Father and Ingham assiduously sought to avoid slanting the news and to make the paper's reporting as complete and accurate as possible.

On the editorial page, meanwhile, Ingham had free reign to express his liberal views that were at sharp variance with many if not most of the paper's readers. Yet he was a true opinion leader in that as time went on his views found ever stronger support in the community. He railed against racism, opposed war as savage and futile, supported organized labor and the interests of the underprivileged, viewed with alarm the abuses of big business and entrenched wealth. Though the Middle West was overwhelmingly isolationist, Ingham was a confirmed internationalist. He was a free trader and an opponent of high tariffs. Even in those days, he believed that the world was shrinking and that world problems affected the United States as well. In all his years as editor of a provincial

12

paper, he always thought in terms of the world as a whole.

While Father shared many of Ingham's internationalist views, his position on most domestic issues was more conservative. Yet he always accorded Ingham complete editorial freedom and, further, encouraged the widest range of opinion and expression in the newspaper.

Under the two men, *The Register and Leader* became more and more prosperous and powerful. In 1908, Father acquired the ailing afternoon *Tribune* for less than $30,000. Though its circulation was only somewhere around 6,000, the move gave Father an afternoon outlet, which enabled *The Register and Leader*'s presses to run fulltime instead of remaining idle much of the day after printing of the morning paper overnight. And it provided a valuable Associated Press afternoon franchise. As *The Register* and *The Tribune* grew, the less well-managed competition languished. Father acquired *The News* from Scripps-Howard in 1924 and *The Capital* in 1927, both of which were absorbed by *The Tribune*. As his newspaper empire grew, Father gained national recognition and became a director and trustee of banks, colleges, and hospitals. In 1932, the year of the banking crisis, he was appointed by Herbert Hoover to serve as director of the Reconstruction Finance Corporation.

My father lived in Iowa all of his life and to the end participated in the management of his papers. By the time he died on February 28, 1946, his eighty-fifth birthday, *The Register* and *Tribune* had achieved a circulation of 350,000 daily and 425,000 on Sunday—remarkable figures for a city of 162,000. It was said that the papers were read by half the people in Iowa. *The Washington Post*, one of the numerous publications that mourned his passing and heralded his achievements, commented:

"He operated his paper on the assumption that the people are interested in honest, competent and unbiased reporting and independent editorial comments. The theory by which he was guided was, in his own words: 'The more honestly a paper is conducted the more successful it will be.' His experience goes a long way toward providing the soundness of that view."

My brothers and sisters and I knew Father must have been doing pretty well with *The Register and Leader* because around 1910 or 1911 he built one of the most elaborate houses in Des Moines. Set off by a dozen manicured, rolling acres and beautiful old oak trees, it became the subject of much gossip and probably derision when word got out that there would be nine bathrooms in the mansion, including a powder room for guests on the ground floor, a toilet for the help in the basement, and a bathroom in the servants' quarters at the back of the third floor. Few houses in town, even those owned by the wealthiest families, could boast of more than one bathroom.

In our home evening meals were called supper and were served around six o'clock. On Sundays, however, the big meal of the day was "dinner," served after church, usually at one o'clock. It invariably consisted of delicious fried chicken, mashed potatoes, peas or beans, a salad, and ice cream. It was my duty to pack the home freezer with ice and turn a crank for about forty minutes while the cream hardened in its container in the center of the freezer. Sunday school, for me, was a period for marking time until I got to that ice cream machine. The machine was supplied by a horsedrawn ice wagon which used to make daily deliveries except Sundays. Kids all over town used to jump on the back of the wagon to sneak chunks of broken ice to suck.

George Timothy, our black chauffeur, was a good companion and mentor, and it fell to his lot to have me on his neck a good part of the time. The things that children are always afraid to ask their parents or even their brothers and sisters, I used to ask him—and George was pretty earthy and explicit about giving me the answers.

He also taught me to shoot craps and I used to lose most of my very small allowance in crap games with him. Somehow, I never did master George's trick of throwing the dice to increase the chances that they would always come up seven or eleven. I used to hope that sooner or later I would overcome the temptation to shoot craps, but I've surrendered to it. I once broke the bank in a casino down in Cat Cay—off the Florida coast—for about $30,000 when I was visiting with the Roy Larsens very early in *LOOK*'s career, and once you've done that you never see a casino anywhere in the world without thinking, "Well, I did it once, I can do it again." And you keep trying.

Our yard man also intrigued me. Since there were no power lawn mowers then, he spent entire days mowing the extensive lawns. I sometimes could not take my eyes off his face. Most of his nose had been bitten off in a saloon fight and the gruesome repair job was a far cry from the wonders of plastic surgery today.

After supper, my parents and I used to retire to the upstairs sitting room adjoining their bedrooms. Father usually played solitaire and Mother read aloud. When I was very young I was permitted to listen to her reading only until nine. Later I was allowed to stay up until ten o'clock. Mother loved reading aloud and she went through many of the English classics including such favorites as *Lorna Doone, A Tale of Two Cities,* and *Bob, Son of Battle.* My father would sit quietly at his solitaire game in his Herbert Hoover-style high stiff collar. I am not sure he listened to Mother's reading as raptly as I did, but I do know she cast a spell of magic and serenity that I have never forgotten.

Des Moines may lack some of the glamor and excitement of the large East Coast metropolises, but as one of the most important cities of the Midwest it was often on the itinerary of touring dignitaries. And as a son of the most important publisher in town, I was often able to observe these celebrities close up.

When I was about five years old my father and a few other men invited

14

Billy Sunday to Des Moines for a week-long revival meeting. Each evening during that week I was taken to one of those sessions. Since Father was one of the sponsors, our family was always seated in the front row on the stage of the temporary tabernacle erected for the occasion. One evening I fell sound asleep stretched out on the floor. As he jumped and pranced from one end of the stage to the other in his typically dynamic performance, Billy Sunday came down hard on one of my fingers. Much to my father's chagrin, I let out a howl that unfortunately only temporarily diverted audience attention from the more spiritual matters.

Many years later, when I was managing editor of *The Des Moines Register* and *Tribune*, Aimee Semple McPherson came to Des Moines to hold a week-long revival meeting in the coliseum. Aimee's manager, with whom she was living, was an adept promotion man who spent much time in the news room of *The Register* and *Tribune* wheedling publicity for Aimee's meetings.

One day I invited him and Aimee to come out to my house for coffee or a drink after the session. As they climbed into my car they were in the midst of a fierce argument over the meeting's format. The order of hymns, prayers, and sermon had been carefully designed over the years to stimulate audience fervor and produce the maximum outpouring of fiscal generosity. The collection on this particular evening had been below par, and Aimee's manager was blaming a change that Aimee had made in the schedule of events. Aimee heatedly disagreed. The two of them fought it out all the way to my house.

I had invited four or five couples to meet the famous evangelist. Among the guests were Henry and Ilo Wallace—the Henry Wallace who later became Secretary of Agriculture and then Vice President under Franklin Roosevelt and, later still, an unsuccessful candidate for the Presidency. Henry was a great agricultural scientist but, as it turned out, not a very able politician. One of the curious facets of his personality was his deep interest in religions—all religions. An authority on all the important religions of the world, he prided himself on the fact that he knew the Bible backward and forward. As he sat talking with Aimee McPherson, Henry quoted a passage from the Bible. Aimee promptly corrected him.

"You aren't quoting it correctly," she said.

"But I am," Henry said. "I know the Bible better than you do."

With that Aimee turned to me and said, "Get me the family Bible." After some difficulty I finally came up with one. Without hesitation Aimee turned to the correct chapter and verse and read it to Wallace. Much to his embarrassment, she was right and he was wrong.

McPherson, of course, was not exactly held in the highest regard in more sophisticated ecclesiastical circles. She comported herself somewhat like a nightclub entertainer and was recklessly undisciplined in her personal life. But if her confrontation with Wallace is any evidence, it should be noted that she certainly knew her Bible.

I grew up next door to the Wallace family. Henry A. was the son of Henry C. Wallace, Secretary of Agriculture under Harding and Coolidge. One day when I was about ten, my Boy Scout troop excitedly lined up on Henry C. Wallace's lawn to greet President Taft who was arriving for a visit. After shaking hands with each little boy, Mr. Taft was led upstairs to the guest room. When the President, an enormously heavy man, sat down on a rocking chair to remove his shoes, it collapsed and he fell flat on his back. Mrs. Wallace gasped in alarm. Some of the Boy Scouts who had tiptoed upstairs for another glimpse of the President giggled out loud.

A trim figure was not at the time a requisite for political activity. Another quite fleshy figure of the era was William Jennings Bryan. Once, when he was Secretary of State under Woodrow Wilson, he came to Des Moines to deliver a lecture. My father brought Mr. Bryan home for dinner and my mother went to great lengths to serve a typical Midwestern dinner—chicken, mashed potatoes, peas, salad, and ice cream with chocolate sauce. Mr. Bryan not only ate every course the first time round, but eagerly accepted seconds on most of them. We had hardly finished our meal when my father said that they would have to leave for the coliseum where Bryan was to make his speech. Bryan turned to my mother and asked if she would make up a sandwich for him to take along. Flabbergasted, my mother nevertheless went out to the kitchen and fixed a generous sandwich which she wrapped in newspaper, waxed paper not yet having been invented. I remember bringing the sandwich out to him. Bryan thanked my mother warmly and put the sandwich into the tail pocket of his frock coat. He then offered an explanation for the request. He was constantly on the move, making speeches in small towns all over America. They usually took place in the evening, and by the time the talk was over he would be very hungry and restaurants would be closed. And so, he told us, he made it a practice always to carry a sandwich in his pocket.

Physical heft not only was not a liability for Bryan but it may have been an asset, at least insofar as it contributed to the power of his voice. Bryan's oratorical talents have been widely written about. Less well known is the fact that Bryan would have had little need for the elaborate electronic amplification that sustains most modern-day politicians. William Jennings Bryan could and did address six hundred farmers on a cornfield and make every single farmer hear exactly what he was saying—even when the wind was blowing.

For all my attachments to Des Moines, I knew when I made my first trip to New York that that was where I wanted to live eventually. I was about twelve at the time. Until then, my only experience away from home had been a month at a Wyoming dude ranch one summer and a trip to the San Francisco World's Fair. The morning after we arrived in New York, my father gave me a five-dollar bill and told me I could spend the day in Coney Island—alone! He didn't see any reason why New York would not be just as safe as Des Moines and thought the trip would be a good experience for me. My mother was terribly upset but said nothing. I set forward by subway and arrived safely after an interminable underground and eventually elevated ride. It was as though I'd conquered Mt. Everest. A strange city, alone among strangers on that long underground ride—a new self-confidence surged through my timid soul. I spent the five dollars recklessly, continuously riding the shoot-the-chutes until the money and the seat of my pants gave out.

My mother was sick with worry when I returned to the hotel at six o'clock. But her anger did nothing to dampen my enthusiasm for New York. For me, it was love at first sight. Years later, one of the reasons I wanted to start *LOOK* magazine was because I knew not only that it would give me a national stage—which I was cocky enough to want—but also that it would eventually bring me to New York.

When I was fifteen, after ten years in Des Moines public schools, my parents told me that I was to be sent to Phillips Exeter Academy in New Hampshire. After that, it was anticipated I would go to Harvard. I would be following in the path of my older brother John, four years my senior, whom I worshiped and tried to emulate when I was growing up. His influence on me had been and would continue to be tremendous.

Though my oldest brother, Russell, the painter, had gone to Dartmouth, my father was quite insistent on the educational path to be followed by his two younger sons. The reason was more than our fraternal closeness and the obvious scholastic merits of the two schools. Father happened to be a second cousin of Thomas W. Lamont, the well-known senior partner at J.P. Morgan. They shared a common Scottish ancestry to the extent that the Cowles family was entitled to use the Lamont plaid. Father had enormous respect for Lamont and since Lamont had sent *his* sons to Exeter and Harvard, Father felt that was the most appropriate course for John and me.

Relations between the Cowles and Lamont families remained very friendly for many years. Thomas' son Corliss, who was a class ahead of me at Harvard and who would become an eminent and quite controversial teacher and author, befriended me shortly after I arrived in Cambridge and invited me to spend the Easter holidays at the Lamonts' home in Englewood, New Jersey. It was the most elegant house I had ever seen.

The visit gave me an opportunity to observe Corliss' father. The routine that Mr. Lamont, Sr. followed in commuting to the office continues to fascinate me every time I think about it. When he arose in the morning, he would put on a dressing gown and, thus attired, would

17

be driven immediately by his chauffeur to his yacht, which was moored on the west bank of the Hudson River. On board awaiting him would be his barber, his manicurist, and one of his secretaries. As the boat cruised down the river, Lamont would have his shave and shower and enjoy a leisurely breakfast. He then would glance through the morning papers and perhaps dictate a letter or two to his secretary. By this time the boat would be docking at the Battery and Lamont would conclude the routine with a brief walk from the end of Wall Street to the famous Morgan corner at Broad and Wall. (Less regal commuters in those days before the construction of the George Washington Bridge and the Holland and Lincoln tunnels had to make the trip across the Hudson by ferry.)

Considering that I was a rather shy boy from Des Moines with little if any knowledge of the ways of Eastern society, Corliss was very solicitous and kind. He managed to get me invited to various debutante parties. Unfortunately, though, I had only one tuxedo and one rather frayed evening shirt. When I came downstairs all dressed for the first party, the Lamont butler took one look at my shirt and declared, "That will never do. Come with me." The butler, whose name was Metcalf and who more or less ran the Lamont household, led me back upstairs to a huge closet almost the size of a room. It was incredible, less a closet than a men's clothing store: shirts, socks, underclothes, suits (business as well as evening) in all colors and sizes.

My bewilderment must have been apparent to Metcalf. The Lamonts, he explained, constantly entertained bankers, businessmen and political figures who very often did not bring the right clothing with them. From this private Brooks Brothers Costume Co., Metcalf was always able to supply the proper attire, whatever the size, fit or occasion. For me, he selected a brand-new evening shirt, suggesting I throw away my old one. He then dismissed me as suitably dressed for a party evening at the Lamonts.

Many years later in 1945, when I moved to New York, Thomas Lamont called one day to invite me to lunch at the Links, one of his clubs. He asked about my father and then quickly came to the reason for the invitation.

"If you've moved to New York for good there are some important things you must do to get started," he said. "You must join a few good clubs, for example. This one, the Links, and the River, to begin with. I will arrange for that. Then Tommy (his older son, who was also a Morgan partner) will get you a membership at the Racquet Club. And you don't need any help from anybody to get into the University and Harvard Clubs."

I was bowled over. It was true that I hardly knew a soul in New York except for a few old acquaintances and friends from my Exeter and Harvard days. But Lamont at the time was unquestionably the preeminent banker in New York and had no special reason other than his

18

friendship with my father to be concerned about me. Yet true to his word and to my amazement, I was elected to the Links, River, and Racquet Clubs within just ten days. The incident illustrated Lamont's vast power and prestige—as well as the more human qualities beneath that awesome exterior.

A PARENTAL BRIEFING

Before I left for Exeter, I was summoned to the upstairs sitting room for the traditional parental briefing. Father, who lived by such pithy maxims as "Things don't just happen; somebody makes them happen," lectured me for about forty minutes on the do's and don'ts of every aspect of behavior that might be required in the world that lay ahead of me.

As Father delivered his catalog of instructions and admonitions, Mother sat quietly and listened. Looking back over my life, I can see many ways in which my father's cogently articulated guidance affected me. But Mother's impact has been just as great, if not greater. Her influence, though, flowed less from lectures than from her behavior. Her liberal social views are a good example. In contrast to my father, who believed in compulsory church attendance, my mother wasn't religious at all. In fact, I would consider her an agnostic. But she was staunch in her conviction that everyone had a right to his or her own beliefs. Once, when she was still a young bride, Algona's first Catholic family moved into town. Anti-Catholic prejudice in Iowa was rampant and the local female social arbiters refused to accept the newcomers. My mother was so infuriated that she gave a big dinner for the Catholic couple and more or less forced the other social leaders in town to accept them.

I remember another incident when one of my nieces became pregnant "out of wedlock," as they used to say. Her mother dreaded breaking this shocking news to Mother and asked me to do it. When I told Mother, she merely threw back her head and laughed and laughed. Her only comment was that she had been wondering for years when this was going to happen in a family as large as ours.

Now, with my father having finished his lecture, my mother's approach to my impending departure was characteristic.

"Mike, you'll get no instructions or rules from me," she said after my father left the room. "I'll ask one favor, though. When you are about to do something you think might be questionable, stop and ask yourself: Would you do it if I were in the room watching you? That's the only obligation I want to put on you."

She was, of course, a much better psychologist than my father. That seemingly simple and innocuous question has often influenced my behavior during my lifetime, and on many occasions it has kept me from doing things of which I knew she would not have approved.

NEWSPAPERING IN DES MOINES

From the time I was a very small boy, I lived for the day when I would be old enough to work on *The Register* and *Tribune*. I could hardly wait. When I was only five, I used to watch the activities in the newspaper's cashier cage. Employees were then paid in metal coins—silver dollars for lower echelon people and five-dollar gold pieces for more senior people. My father, who made up the payroll, put the money in manila envelopes. When I was eight, he paid me 25 cents for every editorial I proofread. When I was at Harvard, I worked summers as a reporter.

Even when I didn't have any work to do there, I used to visit the papers' offices and make a pest of myself asking questions of everyone on the staff. One of my favorite targets was Harvey Ingham, the editor, who became my idol and one of the most important influences in my life. Mr. Ingham was somewhat older than my father and was much more popular in Iowa. A very handsome man with a fine sense of humor, he was a superb public speaker and had a great booming voice. It was he who first provoked what became my consuming interest in foreign affairs.

He also profoundly shaped my sense of an editor's role. In 1955 I told an audience of educators at Simpson College, in Indianola, Iowa, that "The greatest editors I know are just like the greatest educators and are successful for the same reason. They are thoughtful men with scrupulous regard for the truth. They are men who strive to stir the best in the human race, not pander to the worst. They are men who dare to lead, even when the direction is temporarily dangerous and unpopular." I was thinking quite specifically of Harvey Ingham.

Another target of questions during my growing-up years was William Wesley Waymack, managing editor at the time. Bill was an outstanding editor who in 1938 won the Pulitzer Prize for Editorial Writing and later became a member of the Atomic Energy Commission. But what most impressed me was his strong sense of promotion. He had a lot to do with making me realize, as my father had learned, that people generally just don't automatically go out and buy a publication—either a newspaper or a magazine—even if it is a superior product. You have to persuade them to make the purchase. You have to promote—or sooner or later you're likely to find yourself out of business.

When I entered Harvard, my brother John advised, "Mike, do one of three things: Go out for the freshman football managership, try for *The Harvard Crimson*, or get yourself well acquainted and run for class office." He had done one of the three: he had become editor of *The Crimson* (and of *The Lampoon* and *The Advocate* as well). He was also a better student than I was and graduated from Exeter and Harvard with honors. I had always had a secret desire to outdo him at both schools, and so I resolved to do all three of the things he suggested. With a little luck I succeeded, becoming freshman football manager, class treasurer and, by my senior year, editor and president of *The Crimson*.

During that last year, I learned a lesson in publishing that I have never forgotten. A chapter of the Ku Klux Klan had been formed on the campus, and I made it into a very big story. The Boston newspaper picked it up and also played it very big. Along with the story, I had published a box saying that while I obviously couldn't reveal the names of the students involved I had the names and would turn them over to the proper authorities.

The next day, Laurence Lowell, the president of Harvard, summoned me to his office. He was clearly upset. "I guess I'm the appropriate authority, Mr. Cowles," he said. "Now, let me have the names."

I refused to give him the names. But in the course of the conversation I felt myself compelled to acknowledge what had been uncomfortably sitting in the back of my mind almost from the beginning: I had blown the story out of proportion and was clearly guilty of sensationalizing. I only knew four students who were involved and it appeared they had set up the KKK chapter more as a prank than anything else.

President Lowell proceeded to deliver the most severe dressing down that I had ever received. He told me that I either ought to grow up or I shouldn't be running a daily newspaper. The painful but valuable experience made me a more prudent and cautious editor than I might otherwise have become.

I was so anxious to get to work at the Des Moines papers that I took extra courses so that I would be able to graduate from Harvard in three and a half years. My mother tried to talk me into going to Oxford or Cambridge or the London School of Economics for a year. But I wanted to start working, and I've never regretted the decision to forego further schooling. In fact, the only thing I regret about my education is that I never did learn to speak and read French very well.

John had joined the Des Moines papers five years earlier, in 1921, after a then traditional *Wanderyahr* or grand tour of Europe. During the tour, he visited with our eldest brother Russell in Rome. Under Russell's guidance, John furthered his interest in art that led, years later, to his establishing a fine collection of paintings and sculptures in Minneapolis.

Despite much pressure from Father, Russell had little interest in joining the newspapers after his graduation from Dartmouth. He did work briefly in the classified ad department at one point. But "I couldn't take it anymore," as he once said, and he enrolled in a New York art school. This deviation from expectations did not sit well with Father until Russell, who became an accomplished muralist, won the prestigious Prix De Roma, which included a three-year fellowship for study in Rome. "Up to that time," Russell said, "Father hoped that art was something foolish that I would get out of my system and then settle down to the business." But with this distinction, Father's disappointment gradually began turning into pride. Later in life, Russell and Father, who had not been especially close when Russell was growing up, developed a warm relationship. "He had a perfectionist standard which the children all automatically inherited," Russell said. "That was an excellent heritage. I'm a perfectionist too, and that has helped me greatly in art."

SECURE IN HIS OWN IDEOLOGY

At *The Register*, John soon distinguished himself. He became very interested in political reporting and traveled extensively in this country and abroad writing on national and international affairs. In 1923, he managed to get into Russia for a first-hand look at the turbulent post-Revolutionary period. His balanced and perceptive fourteen-part series was not welcomed by some more conservative Iowans, who advocated a "holy war" against the Russians. The president of the Iowa Bar Association denounced him as a "red-bellied Bolshevist." John, though, was never bothered by ideologically motivated attacks. He was quite secure in his own ideology even though it was more liberal and internationalist than that of many of his readers. He later said that the three most important problems confronting the Twentieth Century were attaining an enforceable peace, controlling human fertility, and cultivating better relations between races.

John's reporting achievements were such that few complained of nepotism when, less than three years out of Harvard, he was appointed by Father as vice-president, general manager, and associate publisher of the Register and Tribune Company. John proved that his business acumen was up to his editorial abilities. One of his first and lasting business successes was the launching of the Register and Tribune

Syndicate, a highly profitable move and later one of the key factors that carried the papers through the Depression.

I joined the staff of *The Tribune* as a fulltime reporter in 1925. Subsequently, I switched to *The Register* and advanced through such editorial positions as city editor and executive editor until I was named publisher and finally chairman of the board.

By 1935, John and I decided that the time had come for us to branch out from Des Moines. Father, who knew that the Register and Tribune Company was too small an operation for both of his ambitious sons, heartily concurred. We conducted an elaborate search, looking for an evening paper with strong reader loyalty and a high percentage of home-delivered circulation that served a relatively literate and educated market. That led us to *The Minneapolis Star*, an evening daily, for which we paid $1 million.

The price was reasonable because—just like *The Des Moines Register* when my father acquired it—*The Star* was the weakest newspaper in a hotly competitive three-paper city. Because of Father's quick success, John and I were perhaps a bit overconfident on how quickly we would be able to get *The Star* into the black. That required three long years of aggressive promotion in the face of heavy losses. My father was not always sure we were going to make it and at one point told us we should build up *The Star* so that it could be sold. John and I were not so sure either. *The Star*'s readership was heavily working class, which was not very attractive to big display advertisers. Nor was the business community pleased with the *The Star*'s policy of resisting advertiser pressure. Once a well known business executive was arrested on a charge of violating the hunting laws. He asked the newspapers to ignore the incident. *The Star*'s two competitors agreed. But much to the executive's amazement, *The Star* ran the story. *The Star*'s circulation jumped. But, as John later remarked, "It took many years for the business community to get used to the idea that news would be printed regardless of whose interests might be harmed."

History, though, eventually repeated itself. In 1939, we bought up one of our rivals, *The Journal*. A few years later, we acquired *The Tribune*, which gave us a monopoly position in both Des Moines and Minneapolis.

Monopolies have never been looked upon very fondly in this country—and usually with good reason. In a speech before a journalist group, John—and I would agree—argued that the newspaper business should be regarded as an exception. "The best papers in America," he said, "do not have a paper competing with them in their morning or evening local field. (They are) the most responsibly edited, the fairest, the most complete, the most accurate and objective." Being more secure financially, he said, they are "better able to resist the pressure to sensationalize the news, to play up the cheap sex story, to headline the story that will sell the most copies rather than another story that may be

24

Text continued on page 41

ALBUM PHOTOGRAPHS

It was 1910, and I was proud of that pocket watch with the shiny fob.

I was quite serious in this 1919 photo with Father and brothers Russell (center) and John.

My official graduation photo (opposite page), Phillips Exeter Class of 1921.

With Lois Thornburg, my
wife and mother of my
three oldest children, at
Lake Okoboji.

The family with Father
and Mother on their 50th
Wedding Anniversary,
1934. L. to r.: Sisters Helen
LeCron, Florence
Kruidenier, Bertha
Quarton; Brothers John
and Russell.

THE WHITE HOUSE
WASHINGTON

October 17, 1932.

My dear Mr. Cowles:

Your work in arranging the splendid
and heartening reception at Des Moines is
deeply appreciated, and I wish you to know
how it warms my heart to remember this evidence of your friendliness and faith.

Yours faithfully,

Herbert Hoover

Mr. Gardner Cowles, Jr.,
Register and Tribune Bldg.,
Des Moines, Iowa.

Herbert Hoover sent this note after his '32 campaign reception in Des Moines.

Opposite, top: Hollywood, circa late '40s, with Douglas Fairbanks, Jr., John, Cecil B. deMille, and Ginger Rogers.

Opposite, bottom: John and I look over a copy of *LOOK* in 1937.

THE WHITE HOUSE

WASHINGTON

Dear Cowles

Please do!

Dining with Eleanor
Roosevelt, a great and
gracious lady.

The note (opposite
page) that brought me to
Washington and the
O.W.I. in January, 1942.

With Wendell Willkie and
John in Minneapolis, 1940.

A memento (left) from a
memorable trip around
the world in 1942.

It was 4 a.m. when Joe Barnes (left) and I were summoned to the Kremlin to join Willkie and Stalin. An interpreter is in the rear.

I was dubbed "Chief Northern Star" (right) by the Siowan Rosebud Tribe in 1945 at Yankton, S. Dakota.

35

Eisenhower (upper left) is pleased to read a "Convention Special" edition of the *Minneapolis Tribune* at Chicago's Blackstone Hotel, 1952 GOP convention.

Nixon listens while I talk (lower left) at a White House Press Photographers Association awards dinner.

LOOK's Directors, 1958: At my left, seated, Marv Whatmore, Jack Harding, Shap Shapiro. Standing, l. to r., Vern Myers, Don Perkins, Dan Mich, Les Suhler, Hal Webber.

Jan and I share a light moment with Premier Khrushchev in the Kremlin, 1968.

A 'copter trip (right) in Vietnam, 1965. Ed Swenson (not shown) also was aboard.

President Johnson asked me to get my brother John to back off from his plea for a tax increase in this 1966 White House meeting. It didn't work. Ex NBC chief Bob Kintner, of the Johnson staff, was there.

I greet Adlai Stevenson on his return from his 1954 *LOOK*-sponsored round-the-world trip.

My grandchildren in 1967, l. to r., standing, Gardner Mark Harrison, John Patrick Harrison, Gwen Beatrix Strauss, Elizabeth Lois Strauss, Kent Alfred Harrison, Lois Eleanor Harrison. I'm holding Kate Anne Strauss.

Both lower photos are of my children, l. to r., Kate Cowles Rummel, Gardner (Pat) Cowles III, Lois Cowles Hooks. Their mother was Lois Thornburg Cowles. At right is Virginia Cowles Kurtis. Her mother is Jan Streate Cowles.

of far more importance and significance." Editors and publishers, he maintained, can have "a deeper feeling of their responsibilities and obligations to their communities and readers because of the very absence of competition."

John and I began dividing our responsibilities not long after the purchase of *The Star*. At my father's urging, John moved to Minneapolis to take over as fulltime resident publisher. I remained in Des Moines to look after *The Register* and *Tribune* and to develop my plans for *LOOK* magazine, which was launched in 1937. Yet right through the 1960's, after I had moved to New York, we collaborated in the management of the Register and Tribune Company. This was a less imposing feat than it may seem at first glance. For one thing, we were in continual communication by telephone—two or three half-hour conversations weekly. And, more important, we were pretty much in agreement on most policy matters. John was once quoted as saying: "Our views are 98 percent identical on any major subject."

AN EARLY MARRIAGE

Because of my great admiration for John, I used to run around with him and his friends, preferring them to people of my own age. One member of John's circle was a charming girl named Helen Curtiss, whose father was Dean of Agriculture at what was then called Iowa State College, now Iowa State University. She was a charming woman, a few years older than I, who was fanatical about horseback riding. I never cared much about horseback riding, but I did start dating her.

It did not seem as if anything much would come of the relationship until one day when John said to me, "Mike, stop dating Helen Curtiss. She's too old and sophisticated for you." With typical younger-brother defiance of an older brother's warning, I not only did not stop dating Helen but I married her.

We both soon realized that we had made a foolish mistake, and not much more than a year later, we decided to get a divorce. It was all very amicable: After a three-minute hearing before a local judge, we then threw a late afternoon cocktail party in our small frame house on the outskirts of Des Moines to announce our decision to our friends. I think it came as a surprise to about nine-tenths of those present.

The episode shocked Des Moines, and I know my family was deeply distressed. As a member of the Cowles family, I could have seen to it that the news of the divorce was buried somewhere on *The Register*'s back pages. But, it was front page news, and that is where the story was printed.

My marital status would continue to be a fertile source of news for the Des Moines papers. In 1933, I married Lois Thornburg, who had been a reporter on *The Des Moines Tribune*. She was a graduate of the University of Iowa and her father had been superintendent of schools in Des Moines. My admiration for her character and abilities was boundless, and from my marriage to her we had three wonderful children who have given me much happiness.

Our first child was a daughter named after her mother. Young Lois was graduated from Madeira School in Virginia and Wellesley College. She married John (Jack) Harrison after college and they had three sons—Gardner Mark, Kent Alfred and John Patrick—and a daughter—Lois Eleanor. Kent died as the result of an automobile accident in Florida in June, 1981.

Following in her mother's footsteps, Lois has given much time to the work of Planned Parenthood and is president of the Central Florida unit. She also has worked diligently for passage of the Equal Rights Amendment and has served as president of the Florida League of Women Voters and on the League's National Board. She now is married to Homer Hooks and they live in Lakeland, Florida.

Our second child was a son, Gardner III, nicknamed Pat. After his graduation from Bowdoin College with a degree in engineering he worked for several years on Florida newspapers which I and Cowles Communications owned, and was publisher of our *Suffolk Sun* on Long Island. Following suspension of that newspaper he bought and is publisher of *The Three Village Herald,* a weekly based in Stony Brook. Pat is married to Sharon Whatmore, a daughter of my long-time business associate, Marvin Whatmore.

Our third child was Kate, who also was graduated from Madeira School. She went on to Cornell College in Ithaca, New York, where she met and married Julian Strauss, by whom she had three daughters, Elizabeth Lois, Gwen Beatrix and Kate Anne. Kate once ran unsuccessfully on the Democratic ticket for the Florida Public Service Commission. Later the commission was changed to an appointive body and Gov. Robert Graham appointed her a member and recently she was reappointed to a second term. She is now remarried and lives with her husband, H.E. Rummel, in St. Petersburg and Tallahassee, Florida.

Thinking back now, I regret I did not spend more time with my older children when they were growing up. I was just too involved with my business problems.

After I moved to New York in 1945 to devote myself fulltime to *LOOK,* Lois and I decided to get a divorce. Sometime later, I married Fleur Fenton, a rather glamorous advertising executive who made very substantial contributions to *LOOK.* We remained married for nine years when she went off to England to marry Tom Meyer and became a distinguished author and artist.

Two years later—now 28 years ago—I met and married Jan Hochstraser, who had been divorced before I met her from James Cox, the newspaper owner and publisher. This marriage has proved to be a very happy one. She has made a charming life for me in our homes in New York, on Indian Creek Island just north of Miami, and in Southampton, Long Island. Not only has Jan been a wonderful hostess and mother, but she has devoted many hours of her time to community affairs; notably, helping raise money to support Phoenix House, the New York Botanical Garden, Memorial Hospital-Sloan-Kettering Cancer Center and several others. She recently has been a Trustee and moving spirit in establishing the Miami, Florida, Center for the Fine Arts.

Jan and I have a lovely daughter, Virginia, now 26, a graduate from New York University with a major in art. She is now Mrs. Jon Kurtis living in New York.

By a previous marriage, Jan had a son, Charles, who attended Stanford University, was the publisher of *ARTFORUM* and curator of modern art at the Seattle Art Museum. Charles is now a New York art dealer with his own gallery in Soho. He has greatly assisted his mother and me in collecting art over the past decade.

A LOVE AFFAIR—WITH AVIATION

Sports and aviation were more than just hobbies when I was growing up: They were abiding passions. When I became city editor of *The Register* in 1926, I had a chance to put those passions to use—and to develop a new passion: pictures.

I have never been much of a sportsman myself. The only sport I was ever halfway decent at was squash. But I more than made up for my lack of participation by my zealousness as a spectator. Even today, I find it hard to pass up a football or baseball game on television and I have the profusion of statistics rattling around in my head that characterizes the confirmed sports fan.

I was convinced that *Register* readers shared my vicarious interest and I worked hard to expand our sports coverage and make it more interesting. Our Sunday sports section grew to ten pages, far more than most other papers. To make it stand out, we began printing the daily section on colored paper, first green and then orange.

Our coverage was greatly enhanced by our purchase of a company airplane in 1928. The idea of an airplane was initially conceived by John as a promotional scheme to capitalize on the extraordinary public interest in the transatlantic Lindbergh flight the previous year. After we bought the plane, we launched a contest to name it. Tens of thousands of suggestions were submitted by readers. The winning name was, appropriately, "Good News." Over the next twenty years, the company operated eleven different planes, each faster and more up-to-date than the last. We soon discovered after buying the first one, though, that an airplane can have editorial as well as promotional uses. We began sending photographers and reporters all over the Midwest to produce

43

on-the-scene coverage of sports events, an innovative journalistic technique that was a precursor of more sophisticated strategies I later developed for *LOOK*. Our sports coverage brought us many new subscribers often far from Des Moines—including the great Knute Rockne of Notre Dame, who said we had the best sports section of any paper in the country.

I gradually began to appreciate the tremendous but still unrealized potential in photojournalism. I never owned a camera and I do not especially like to be photographed. But I do love looking at pictures, and I could tell that not only were readers responding to all of our on-the-spot photography but the reaction was especially strong when we would run a series of pictures about, say, a long football pass, with shots showing the passer throwing the ball, the ball in the air, the catch, a key missed block, and so on.

My conviction on the power of pictures was further confirmed when I hired George Gallup, who was then studying for his doctorate at the University of Iowa, to do a survey for me on what stories had the greatest reader appeal. In conducting this survey, incidentally, Gallup discovered that he got pretty much the same results from a small sample of selected readers as he did from a large group. He found sample polling to be such a useful idea that he went on to found the American Institute of Public Opinion, the progenitor of the Gallup poll.

The results of Gallup's survey for us established that the best-read stories in *The Register* contained both words and related pictures. I proceeded to greatly expand picture usage in *The Register* and *The Tribune*. One tabulation in 1937 reported that *The Tribune* carried more photographs in one six-day period than any other leading newspaper in the country including *The New York Daily News* and *The New York Mirror*. The most popular picture stories of all were the ones we ran in our Sunday rotogravure section, where we were able to give several pages to groups of well-displayed photographs on a single subject. Once, on Shirley Temple's sixth birthday, we published two huge pictures of her that, pasted together on cardboard, made a near-life-size poster. It was a smash success. The popularity of the roto section was another major factor in getting the papers through the Depression.

MEMORABLE TRIPS BY AIR

My infatuation with aviation, which has spanned all my adult life, is nearly as intense as my love of publishing. It was sparked by the Lindbergh flight, and three years later, I began taking flying lessons and earned a license as a private pilot. I purchased a single-engine four-place Stinson plane which I flew all over the Middle West for the next three years.

On summer weekends I used to fly up to a resort on Lake Okoboji in northern Iowa. A rough pasture served as a landing strip and, depending on the wind, I frequently came in over a tall stand of trees, barely clipping the tops, then braking sharply for a short landing to prevent crashing into a fence at the far end of the pasture. Occasionally, when I was foolhardy enough to fly into that pasture after dark, I would phone ahead to ask a couple of friends to light a bonfire to guide me in.

One weekend I invited an extraordinarily pretty girl to fly with me to a Notre Dame-Southern California football game in South Bend, Indiana. She had never traveled far from home before, let alone flown in a plane. It was a hazy, gray November day when we landed without mishap at South Bend. The game was not decided until the last minute and we didn't leave until it was over. Because the taxi I had ordered to drive us to the airport never showed up, it was forty minutes before I could get transportation to the airport. By the time we were airborne it was dark. Even worse, we were soon enveloped in a dense soup consisting of fog and smoke from the steel mills in Gary, Indiana, and the area south of Chicago. I was trying to head for Chicago's Midway Airport, but I couldn't see a thing below. For an hour, I foundered, completely blind and directionless. I stayed as low as I dared, hoping to spot some kind of landmark. The poor girl at my side was petrified with fear, and I was not feeling much better. Suddenly she pointed toward some misty lights below and, in desperation, I headed for them. Miraculously, it was the airport. Since there was no radio in the plane, I had no way to contact the ground, so I made a tight circle—about four hundred feet above the ground—and came right in for a landing. Airport officials and police lost no time in giving me a well-deserved bawling out for my reckless act.

Traveling—whether by car, train, boat, plane or whatever the means of transportation—has been a lifelong obsession of mine. I made my first trip to Europe, by boat of course, when I was a sophomore at Harvard with two fellow editors of *The Harvard Crimson*. Since then I've traveled to Europe at least every other year except during World War II. In 1933 I made my first trip to the Soviet Union. Three years later I was off to Russia again. My most memorable trip, which I've saved for a later chapter, was accompanying Wendell Willkie in his trip around the world in 1942. In 1962 I had a three-hour interview with Premier Khrushchev in the very same room in the Kremlin in which Wendell Willkie and I had been received by Stalin in 1942.

Nearly as exciting as the Willkie trip was an excursion in the spring of 1936. I had been married in 1933 to Lois Thornburg. Three years later, we left for Russia on a belated honeymoon. To break the journey we stopped for a few days at the Adlon Hotel in Berlin. The first evening before dinner we had a drink at the bar. The Adlon bar was a famous hangout for journalists from all over the world. I ran into Webb Miller, then vice president in charge of all of the United Press operations in Europe. With him were half a dozen other international correspondents.

The buzz of conversation was unusually animated. It turned out that the Germans were inaugurating transatlantic flights from Germany to the United States on the dirigible Hindenburg and had invited some correspondents along with other international celebrities to go on the inaugural flights. These preliminary flights were to be rehearsals for regular commercial runs to begin the following spring.

Germany was particularly proud of its superiority in construction of dirigibles, and Goebbels, Hitler's chief propagandist, was wasting no time in exploiting it. The German leaders felt that the Hindenburg would be a powerful propaganda instrument in helping reestablish Germany's great-nation status in the world. The Hindenburg had already flown to Brazil and Argentina—with large swastikas painted on the tail fins—to demonstrate Germany's technical skills to Latin America. Its predecessor, the Graf Zeppelin, a smaller dirigible than the Hindenburg, already had been flown around the world.

As soon as I learned of the upcoming junkets on the Hindenburg I excitedly went to work trying to wrangle a ride on it through my newspaper pals. The next day, with Webb Miller's help, I met the chief publicity officer of the airline that owned the Hindenburg and succeeded in persuading him to reserve two berths for my wife and me for one of the flights about two weeks hence. That gave us time to make our visit to Russia.

100 HOURS FOR A 60-HOUR TRIP

The crossing from Friedrichshafen to Lakehurst, New Jersey should have taken about sixty hours. But head winds over the North Atlantic forced the captain to turn south and make the crossing over the South Atlantic. Consequently it took us over one hundred hours to fly from Germany to New Jersey.

The Hindenburg was 800 feet long and a tour of the ship was equivalent to a walk around a New York City block. It carried a maximum of seventy passengers and a crew of thirty and was powered by four diesel engines located well toward the tail. Though it was highly maneuverable despite its size, it was also remarkably stable. Even in strong head winds it did not pitch and roll as a steamer would. The swish of the wind against the isinglass windows was the only indication that we were riding through very rough winds.

My most vivid recollection of the trip was of the extensive precautions that had to be taken to prevent a fire. For military reasons, the United States, practically the only producer of helium, refused to sell the nonflammable material to Germany. Highly flammable hydrogen thus had to be used to give the dirigible its lift. Passengers were prohibited from bringing aboard anything that might produce even a spark.

We were all thoroughly frisked, and matches, cigarette lighters, even flashlights were taken from passengers to be returned upon arrival at Lakehurst. Smoking was permitted, I was somewhat shocked to discover, in a special room, about twenty feet square, lined with asbestos, which could only be entered through a revolving door. A guard stood on duty at the door twenty-four hours a day. Once inside, a passenger could find cigarettes and cigars on a table in the center of the room and a lighter fastened to a wall. That room was better protected than a bank vault.

The airship was designed to save as much weight as possible. The furniture was all upholstered aluminum so that a chair could be lifted by a finger. Although the ship was equipped with fine china and silver they were made of the lightest materials. The floor of the passenger compartment was made of thin laminated wood which sank slightly under each footstep. Though they resembled those on an ocean liner, the cabin walls were made of linen, and it was possible to hear conversations clearly in the next room. If one leaned on the rail of a passenger compartment it would bend a little. Nothing seemed absolutely solid, which created an eerie but almost euphoric sensation of near-weightlessness.

Fortunately, I flew in the right year. Because it was on May 7, 1937, almost exactly at year after my flight, on one of its regularly scheduled flights to America, that the Hindenburg caught fire just as she was being tied up to the mooring mast in Lakehurst. A violent electric storm was raging at the time and a bolt of lightning was said to have ignited the hydrogen. Since then there has been considerable speculation and some evidence that the destruction of that fabulous airship was not entirely an "act of God." At least half a dozen books have been written to disprove the lightning theory, calling the accident an act of sabotage on the part of anti-Nazis. The crash was covered in *The Des Moines Register* one day after the tragedy occurred. A series of wirephotos on the front page vividly illustrated the effectiveness of photojournalism.

My subsequent experience with airplanes was a good deal less thrilling than my blind landing at Midway or my Atlantic crossing by dirigible. But I remained deeply involved with aviation. One of my civic responsibilities in Des Moines was the chairmanship of the Chamber of Commerce's aviation committee, and in 1943 I was asked by the city council to head a committee to make a survey for a new airport, which the rapidly expanding city badly needed. We came to an agreement on a convenient site and took an option on the land for ninety days.

Before the purchase could go through, however, a special election had to be held on a bond issue to provide the financing. We expected easy approval. To many residents, though, flying in airplanes was a luxury only the rich could afford. It was felt that if wealthy businessmen wanted an airport, they could build their own. The bond issue was defeated.

The civic leaders were in quandary over what to do. Rather than see the idea die, I exercised the option myself and purchased the land for

$122,000. I then gave the city an option to buy the land from me within a year at the same price I had paid for it.

A second vote on the bond issue was scheduled in six months, and I began organizing support. Our newspapers, of course, were actively behind it. But our most powerful weapon turned out to be a young executive by the name of W.A. Patterson, head of rapidly growing United Airlines. He made perhaps a dozen speeches during a four-day trip to Des Moines. A dynamic speaker, he talked expansively of aviation's future as a means of quick travel throughout the world for the mass public, not just an elite few. His enthusiasm was contagious. The bond issue passed and the airport was built. It is today one of the most successful small airports in the country.

FRIENDSHIPS THAT LASTED

Pat Patterson's generous support in my campaign led to a close friendship that lasted through the years. A year later, he asked me to join the board of directors of United Airlines. I became an active member of the board and watched the company grow into one of the giants in its field. While on United's board I became close friends with another director, Justin Dart, and his wife Jane. Together, we made many trips to various parts of the world over a thirty-year period. Justin was an extraordinary human being who made a great success in the business world after graduating from Northwestern University, where he played guard on the school's Big Ten title-winning 1926 football team.

In the late 1960's, the board decided that Patterson, among the few industry pioneers still remaining in office, should retire because of his declining health. Pat understandably was reluctant, and I was designated to persuade him. The board felt strongly about it, I said, adding that if he retired now, he would be able to designate his successor as chief executive officer. If he held on, that might not be possible. He finally agreed. Pat's choice was George Keck, an apparently well-qualified 24-year United veteran who had come up through the ranks on the engineering side.

The economy turned downward in 1970 and most of the airlines began running heavily in the red. Keck, it became clear to some of us on the board's executive committee, was not dealing effectively with the situation. Another change in top management was imperative.

Tom Gleed, a Seattle businessman who was chairman of the executive committee, and I called a special meeting of the whole board the night before a regularly scheduled meeting in late 1970. Gleed presented the recommendation of the executive committee to replace Keck. Not eager to become involved in what would have to be an unpleasant and nasty piece of business, most of the other directors stayed silent. Finally Tom forced a vote. It was unanimous in favor of the recommendation. Keck

48

would not be fired but he would be moved upstairs to chairman of the board to make room for a new chief executive officer.

I was given the job of breaking the news to Keck the next morning. It was one of the most difficult experiences in my whole business career. He erupted with anger after I told him of the board's action. When I explained that the vote was unanimous, he accused me of lying. Finally, he accepted the truth.

Our selection to succeed Keck was a big surprise to the rest of the industry. We brought in an outsider: Edward E. Carlson, chairman of Western International Hotels (now Westin Hotels) and an old friend of Gleed's. Carlson had recently joined the United board after Western International had been acquired by United. There was predictable skepticism about whether a hotelman could run an airline. But we knew from his outstanding record at Western International that he was an extremely able manager. During his stewardship at United he proved himself admirably.

When I retired from the United board in 1973, Eddie Carlson insisted on naming a 747 Boeing jet in my honor. The christening took place in April, 1973, at the Boeing plant in Seattle. There is a plaque in the passenger compartment of that plane expressing appreciation for my long service on the United board. And as an even grander gesture, my name is prominently painted on the nose of the airplane. I have never flown in that plane since the christening but periodically I hear from people who have flown the "Gardner Cowles" in this country and to and from Hawaii.

I also maintained a close friendship with another oldtime aviation pioneer: Juan Trippe, the head of Pan Am. Pan Am has since fallen on hard times. But during the more expansive 1940's and 1950's, Pan Am organized frequent promotional junkets to persuade the general public that exotic and faraway places were becoming easily accessible to the ordinary traveller. Trippe often invited me and I accepted the invitations gladly when my schedule permitted.

I remember in particular a round-the-world trip in 1947 aboard a Lockheed Constellation that, among many places, took us through Manila. During the stopover President Roxas gave a fantastic outdoor banquet for us in an almost theatrical moonlit setting. Oveta Culp Hobby, then publisher of *The Houston Post*, was among the VIP's in our group and Roxas took the occasion to present her with the Philippine Military Merit Medal for her service during World War II as head of the Women's Army Corps. Oveta had been tipped off to the presentation and had dressed in a stunning white gown. Probably carried away by the moonlight, the glamorous array of dignitaries, and his flowery speech, Roxas unfortunately pinned the medal right through Oveta's dress into her flesh. She let out a howl. The President was very embarrassed and shocked but he continued to probe with the pin until it broke.

49

Proceedings were delayed for about twenty minutes until an aide could rustle up another medal.

From Manila we headed for a three-day stopover in Tokyo. Each member of our party was granted a private fifteen-minute interview with General Douglas MacArthur who had decided he was going to make a run for the presidency. He had obviously primed himself carefully on the names, backgrounds, and publications we represented. When my turn came I was impressed with his knowledge and questions about Iowa, *The Register* and *Tribune* and *LOOK*.

On the flight back from Tokyo there was naturally a lot of discussion about MacArthur's candidacy. Roy Howard of the Scripps-Howard papers, James Maloney, the publisher of *The Chicago Tribune*, and Paul Patterson of *The Baltimore Sun* had been so impressed by MacArthur they tried to get a written commitment from the rest of the news representatives on board to support MacArthur for the Republican nomination. I refused to sign, and so did Oveta Hobby and Helen Reid of *The New York Herald-Tribune*. For one thing, I saw no reason to commit myself so formally to any candidate. And for another, while I had a high regard for MacArthur as a general, I could not see him as President. I found him quite autocratic.

EVITA PERON—HER SOURCE OF POWER

Three years later, I found myself aboard a luxurious Boeing Stratocruiser named *El Presidente* on Pan Am's inaugural flight to Rio de Janeiro and Buenos Aires. For me and most of the other members of the press on board, it was to be our first encounter with Juan and Evita Peron. In my memory of the trip, Juan remains a shadowy, bland figure.

It was Evita who most intrigued me. I had read very contradictory reports about her. To some observers, she was a devout humanitarian, a benevolent and beloved representative of the *descamisados*, as she called them, the "shirtless" members of the working class. To her critics, she was an egomaniacal demogogue who, for her own material and political gain, cynically exploited those who worshipped her. During the usual cocktail preliminaries after our arrival in Argentina, I managed to maneuver Evita away from the crowd. And after a lavish dinner, I was able to resume my conversation with her.

I had a hard time not being immediately taken in by her glossy exterior, by the charm, glamour, and quick intelligence that she exuded in abundance. None of the actresses who have depicted her recently on Broadway and on television captured the almost overwhelming power of her personality, her incredible dynamism. I asked her some blunt questions about such matters as her widely publicized charitable work which, according to some accounts, was largely a sham. Completely unruffled, she answered my questions deftly, though never permitting

50

herself to be pinned down in any way by specifics.

Perhaps sensing my skepticism, Evita invited me to spend the next day with her visiting the various charitable organizations with which she was involved. I jumped at the chance. I was told to be at the Pink Palace (the equivalent of our White House) the next morning at eight o'clock. The early hour startled me but I made sure to appear on time. I was served some coffee when I arrived. Evita appeared at eight-twenty and off we went. We must have made the rounds of at least a dozen institutions—kindergartens, hospitals, schools. Always there were the little children, probably marshaled for my benefit, waving small Argentine flags, shouting, "Evita, Evita, Evita!" She emanated a hypnotic power that seemed to reach out and embrace her audience. We did not return to the Pink Palace until about six in the evening. Exhausted, I thought the day was over. But it wasn't. Apparently indefatigable, Evita ordered me to return to the palace at nine o'clock for still further conversation.

I was to witness Evita in action later at her weekly evening rally and nationwide radio broadcast at the opera house. She was seated stage center on a thronelike chair. I was seated alongside her in a chair that was smaller and lower than hers. The house was jammed with the *descamisados*. A radio announcer in her early days, Evita knew all of the tricks of grabbing and holding an audience. Sliding back and forth from a childlike whisper to a blaring crescendo, she mesmerized her listeners. Again and again, they roared their approval.

After her speech, and with a nationwide audience still tuned in, she held court as probably pre-screened families approached and told pitiful stories of poverty and distress. Evita turned to an aide and directed that a certain amount of pesetas be given to each of the supplicants in turn.

It seemed clear to me that Evita was a consummate con woman who had taken in an entire nation. But while still repulsed and dismayed I could not help but be impressed by her masterful performance.

A RALLY FOR HOOVER

In the fall of 1932, I received an unexpected call from my father. He was in Washington, having recently been appointed to the Reconstruction Finance Corporation, and he was calling about President Herbert Hoover's reelection campaign against Franklin Roosevelt. My father and Hoover, who was also a native of Iowa, were very good friends, and my father wanted me to take charge of a Hoover political rally that was scheduled for Des Moines. The rally, which would include a speech outlining his second-term farm program, was to be held in the coliseum and would be broadcast on national radio. My father wanted to make sure that Hoover was accorded the proper reception.

That, I knew, would not be a very easy task. The Depression was then at its worst. Over three hundred banks had failed in the state of Iowa alone which, in those days before the Federal Deposit Insurance Corporation, had simply wiped out depositors' savings. I have always felt that Hoover was treated unfairly by history and that the main cause of the world-wide depression was not his mishandling of the national economy but excessive credit and spending by the private sector during the 1920's. Most people, though, blamed the Hoover Administration. Local feelings were so intense that a few weeks before Hoover's visit, a federal judge had been dragged from his bench in a courtroom in northern Iowa by enraged farmers after he had foreclosed on some farm mortgages held by an eastern insurance company. The farmers put a noose around the judge's neck, paraded him down the main street of the town, and threatened to hang him. About three days before the Hoover rally, the FBI arrived in Des Moines and rounded up some of the most vociferous Hoover opponents, who were thrown into jail—without any charges filed against them—until Hoover left town. That didn't make it any easier for me, though, to come up with some people who would even be friendly, let alone enthusiastic, toward Hoover.

I first went to Iowa governor Dan Turner, who was running for reelection on the Republican ticket. Turner wanted no part of the rally. Hoover, he felt, was a political kiss of death. He even refused to invite the President to dinner.

"This is ridiculous, Dan," I told him. "The President of the United States is coming to your state, you are both members of the same party, and you won't even give him the courtesy of having him to dinner. Our newspapers will make a laughing stock out of you."

Eventually Turner agreed to have the President to dinner at the Governor's mansion before the rally—on the condition that no one else was invited other than me, his wife, and Hoover's wife, who was accompanying the President.

I have been to more convivial dinners. At best, Herbert Hoover was not exactly loquacious. Now, with his chances for reelection somewhere between remote and impossible, he was very depressed. Governor Turner made little effort to observe the conversational amenities. Mrs. Turner, who was raised in a small Iowa town and had rarely if ever been out of state, was clearly petrified about having to entertain the President of the United States and his wife. So it was left to Mrs. Hoover and me to keep the dinner party alive. Fortunately, Mrs. Hoover—gracious, charming, well-educated, well-traveled, in a class, really, with Eleanor Roosevelt—was up to the occasion.

The streets were deserted as I drove the Hoovers to the coliseum. Not wanting to have Hoover appear before the crowd prematurely, I steered them through a rear door and into a dressing room where we could wait before it was time to go on. As Mrs. Hoover and I talked quietly, the President slumped in a chair, his hands gripping his bowed head in despair.

52

Suddenly, Mrs. Hoover got up from her chair and walked over to her husband. She looked at him directly. "Herbert," she said sternly, "be a *man!*" Hoover looked up at her. Then he threw back his shoulders and stood up—with what appeared like a fresh infusion of resolve. A few minutes later, the signal came to go on stage.

The speech went much better than the dinner. We had packed the meeting with several thousand American Legionnaires—about the only available constituency whose loyalty to the President we felt remained intact. They had been brought in by bus from all over the state of Iowa. To put them in a good mood, we had provided them with plenty to eat and drink. We even had a kind of cheerleader who had briefed the Legionnaires on when to cheer and applaud and we had seated them in front rows so that their vocal enthusiasm would come over clearly on national radio. The Legionnaires performed well, and any radio listener might have concluded that the state of Iowa was solidly behind the President.

THE RFC—A CREATION OF HOOVER

After the election, I joined my father in Washington as an executive assistant. Roosevelt had asked all of the members of the Reconstruction Finance Corporation to stay on at least temporarily during the transition period. Most people are not aware that the RFC, a very imaginative effort by the government to save failing banks and other essential financial institutions, was a creation of Herbert Hoover, not Franklin Roosevelt.

The RFC, though, had only a limited budget—about $800 million— and was forced to allow many important and worthy institutions to go under. Among those who were in the worst trouble was the huge Bank of America. On Thursday of the week that Roosevelt closed the banks, the RFC board met with A.P. Giannini, the Bank of America's founder and chief executive. The board had decided unanimously that the Bank of America was so insolvent that it would not be allowed to open the following Monday, the end of the bank holiday.

Giannini was furious when he was told about the decision. "We'll see whether or not I open the Bank of America next Monday morning," he snapped. With that, he clamped down his hat on his head and left the room without saying goodbye or shaking hands with anyone.

On Sunday night, Roosevelt held the first of his fireside chats. He talked about the end of the banking holiday scheduled for the following morning and said that the full faith and credit of the United States would stand behind every bank that reopened.

Shortly after noon in Washington—nine o'clock California time—the RFC received a frantic call from its California office reporting that, in direct violation of the RFC's orders, the Bank of America had just

53

opened all of its 410 offices. Jesse Jones, the Texas Democrat who headed the RFC, ordered that federal marshals be dispatched to arrest Giannini.

"Before you do that, Jesse," my father said, "I think you'd better go over to the White House and explain the situation to Roosevelt."

"That's a good idea," Jones replied, "but you have to come with me. I don't trust Roosevelt."

They went to the White House and were admitted to Roosevelt's office immediately. Jones told him what had happened.

"Jesse," the President responded when Jones had finished, "last evening I told everybody in America that the full faith and credit of the federal government stood behind every bank that opened today. It's unfortunate, but now that the Bank of America has opened, it's up to you fellows at the RFC to keep it open."

My father later learned that Giannini had had a private dinner with Roosevelt during the evening of the same day of his meeting with the RFC board. I never knew what the two men talked about, but I could guess. Giannini, almost alone among major bankers, had been a generous contributor to Roosevelt's campaign—reportedly $100,000—and to the Democratic party generally. My suspicion is that FDR simply told Giannini to open on Monday regardless of the RFC and that he, Roosevelt, would handle things in Washington.

"MANY WAYS OF SKINNING A CAT"

One evening some years later, in 1940, I ran into both Hoover and Giannini at the exclusive Bohemian Grove encampment in the redwoods north of San Francisco. A number of well-known political and business figures had assembled to pay their respects to Hoover, who received them on a bench beside a huge campfire. By 10:30, Hoover had gone to bed and just about everyone else had drifted away. I found myself alone with A.P. Giannini. He had just poured himself a new highball, obviously enjoying the relaxed atmosphere created by the campfire among the redwoods. After some casual chit-chat, I ventured a question.

"Mr. Giannini," I asked, "so many years have passed that it doesn't matter anymore. But just to satisfy my curiosity, would you answer something that has puzzled me all these years? When you had dinner with Franklin Roosevelt alone, during the bank holiday week, did the President tell you to open on the Monday following the bank holiday even though you didn't have permission from the RFC? Or was it your own idea?"

Giannini scowled at me for a minute. "Young man," he said finally, "when you are as old as I am, you will learn there are many ways of skinning a cat." Then he bowed, shook my hand, and wandered off into the darkness.

54

THE CARDIFF GIANT

One day in the early 1930's, I noticed a short item in *Variety*, the show business weekly, on the bankruptcy of a small circus in Texas. One of its assets, *Variety* said, was a huge stone figure of a man—10 feet 4 1/2 inches tall, weight 2990 pounds—known as the Cardiff Giant. Working through a local law firm, I bought the Cardiff Giant for $4,500 and paid another $1,500 to ship it from Texas to my home in Des Moines.

The Cardiff Giant had its origins more than 60 years earlier in a stone quarry near Fort Dodge, Iowa, about forty-five miles from where I was born. Since its early days, I had followed the giant's travels with boundless fascination bordering on obsession, and the opportunity now to own it was irresistible.

The giant was the creation of one George Hull, a tobacco farmer and cigar maker from Binghamton, New York. One evening in 1866 while visiting his sister in Iowa, Hull got into a heated argument with a Reverend Turk over a Biblical passage in Genesis: "There were giants in those days." Reverend Turk, a confirmed fundamentalist, interpreted the passage literally, that in some early time there had actually been a race of giant human beings. Hull, a confirmed agnostic, took vehement issue with the Reverend, but Turk would not budge. Infuriated, Hull resolved to perpetrate an elaborate practical joke on Turk and all other religious fundamentalists. He also is said to have felt that there might be a little money in it.

At the Fort Dodge stone quarry, he obtained a block of gypsum twelve feet by four feet by two feet—ostensibly for an exhibition in Washington of building stones. In a trip that exhausted several teams of horses and broke several wagons and bridges, Hull managed to move the block to the nearest railroad station seventy-five miles to the south in Boone, Iowa. It was shipped to Chicago where a team of three stonecutters carved it into the likeness of George Hull. Though the face was serene, the body was somewhat contorted: knees drawn up and one hand over the abdomen, suggestive of a serious stomach ache. A metal hammer was used to simulate skin pores and a bath in sulphuric acid gave the figure's surface an aged, weathered look. Attempts at hair failed, however, and the head was left bald.

The now lifeless giant was packed in a crate labeled "finished marble" and shipped by steamer to Buffalo. From there, it was hauled by two teams of horses to a farm owned by William C. Newell, a relative of Hull's, in the hamlet of Cardiff, just south of Syracuse. By lantern light one dark night in 1868, the giant was secretly buried at the bottom of a twenty-foot hole dug in back of a barn. Seed was planted in the fresh earth. At this point, Hull was out of pocket about $2,200.

A year was permitted to pass. Newell then engaged two men to dig a well in the same spot in back of the barn. A few feet down they struck something hard. Rocks being relatively rare in the area, the men investigated. Soon, amid considerable excitement, the Cardiff Giant was uncovered.

News of the huge petrified man spread rapidly. Professor James Hall, director of the New York State Museum and the most distinguished paleontologist of his day, pronounced it "the most remarkable object yet brought to light in this country." Ralph Waldo Emerson is said to have called it "very wonderful and undoubtedly ancient." Theories of the giant's origin were legion. As Hull had hoped, numerous fundamentalist members of the clergy in sermons pronounced it indisputable proof of the passage from Genesis and of the Bible's literal accuracy generally. As one prominent theologian intoned, "This is not a thing contrived of man, but is the face of one who lived on the earth, the very image and child of God."

Whatever it was thought to be, it became an object of intense curiosity. Thousands of people journeyed to Newell's farm to view the giant. Hull and Newell, of course, charged admission. The giant was moved to Syracuse, where still larger crowds greeted it.

After a time, suspicions began to develop. People who had seen Hull in Fort Dodge and who had witnessed the giant's transport came forward. Hull decided the time had come to confess everything. The fundamentalists, of course, were richly embarrassed. The Dean of Yale Divinity School, who had been among the most outspoken in heralding the giant's discovery, was apparently so grieved that he committed suicide.

Public interest in the Cardiff Giant, though, was only slightly diminished. Now thousands wanted to see what had hoodwinked some of the greatest minds of the day. It was exhibited in numerous fairs, museums, and expositions. After a few years, its drawing power ebbed. Hull having long since taken his profits—at one point he and Newell sold a three-quarters interest to a syndicate of local businessmen for $37,500—it was sold and resold until it ended up with the circus.

When the giant arrived at my home in Des Moines, I placed it in the corner of our "whoopee room"—called a den nowadays—installed some theatrical lighting to give the proper dramatic effect, and covered the walls with posters featuring the giant's more glamorous early life.

One day my seven-year-old son and two of his playmates decided it would be great fun to smash the giant's penis with a hammer. They succeeded in breaking off the tip. I was enraged—perhaps a little more than the occasion warranted—at the mischief. Eventually I found a craftsman who cemented the tip back on.

In 1938, I was surprised to receive a letter from H.L. Mencken, iconoclastic literary and social critic who was editor and publisher of the *American Mercury* and *Smart Set* magazines. He said he was so intrigued with my involvement with the Cardiff Giant that he would welcome an invitation to spend the weekend with me in Des Moines. I had never met

Mencken, and while I was flattered by the request I was also curious about why he wanted to subject himself to what was then a long and tedious trip just for a weekend visit. It required taking an overnight train from Baltimore, where he lived, to Chicago, then laying over in Chicago for a day before catching the night train to Des Moines.

Mencken, who had brought along a friend to keep him company, was one of the most delightful house guests I ever had. He regaled us with endless and often hilariously bawdy stories and, in more serious moments, with his notoriously low opinion of the American public, its stupidity, greed, and gullibility.

Not until late in the visit did Mencken get around to its true purpose. He had a plan involving the World's Fair, which was to open the following year in New York, that he said not only would be a lot of fun for us but would prove once again that Americans would swallow any "bunk," as he put it, that was foisted upon them.

"Mike," he said, "you arrange to buy exhibitor's space for the giant. Then I'll get a sculptor I know in Baltimore to sculpt a female giant the same size, and we'll bury her at a convenient spot off the New Jersey Turnpike. After the fair opens, we'll arrange to have the female discovered, move her in next to the Cardiff Giant, and we'll have the biggest love story known to man! I'll write the publicity, and we'll have a hell of a time!"

The scheme would have been vintage Mencken, but it never came to pass. Not long after returning to Baltimore, he suffered the first of a series of strokes that eventually totally incapacitated him in 1948. He died in 1956.

When I moved to New York City in 1945, I decided to present the giant to the Iowa State Historical Society. But when the president of the New York State Historical Society heard of my plans, he pleaded with me to give the figure to his institution. After all, he argued, only the gypsum block was cut in Iowa. The great hoax was perpetrated in New York.

I yielded to his importuning. The giant that has given me and my friends—and countless thousands of other people—so many laughs over the years now has a permanent resting place in the Farmer's Museum in Cooperstown, New York, which the New York State Historical Society operates. When the acquisition of the giant by the museum was announced, the *Louisville Courier-Journal* commented: "It probably would not be true that you can fool all of the people some of the time if they didn't want it that way. In this vale of tears there is a craving for marvels—the tall tale, the haunted house, the who-dunit, the two-headed calf. A hoax may become an institution of social significance, if in the end we could all laugh and particularly if the laugh is on us, and nobody has been hurt.

"This is why the Cardiff Giant deserves the place in a museum where that colossal humbug after all these years has been ensconced, a monument to fantasy and the human race's addiction to it."

AN IDEA THAT BECAME *LOOK*

If I had to fix a precise moment when the idea that would become *LOOK* magazine was born, it would be in 1933 when I first looked through some advance proofs of a lavishly illustrated book called *The First World War* by Lawrence Stallings. My initial reaction was that the book could be adapted for a terrific feature for *The Register*'s Sunday rotogravure section. I worked with Vernon Pope, editor of the roto section, to lay out what turned into a ten-part series that included about four hundred pictures. The series gave a dramatic push to our circulation and we later syndicated it to fifteen other leading Sunday papers, where it was equally well received.

The enthusiastic reaction from readers did more than confirm again my belief in the popularity of photojournalism. It started me thinking about the possibility of producing a new national Sunday supplement in competition with *The American Weekly*, *This Week*, and *Family Weekly* and devoted exclusively to picture stories. Discussions with my father and John, though, convinced me this was not the proper tack to take. Sunday supplements, I was advised, are not especially profitable: they produce no circulation income and newspapers that carry them are rarely willing to pay you very much more than your costs. The way around this problem was obvious: a separate picture magazine—costing ten cents, I reckoned—to be sold on newsstands. I had had no magazine experience—indeed, had I had any conception of the problems, risks, costs, and crises that would plague us, I would have been much more cautious about plunging ahead. But by the mid-1930's, with bountiful optimism born in large part from ignorance, I was directing nearly all of my energies toward a venture that, while it ended sadly, would provide me with more than thirty-five years of excitement, happiness, and fulfillment.

I have sometimes been credited with originating the idea of a picture magazine in the United States. But while I would love to claim that distinction, I must concede that it was among the classic examples of an idea whose time had come. Picture magazines such as *Vu* and *Pour Vous* in France and *Illustrated London News* and *Weekly Illustrated* in England, were already thriving in Europe and that had not gone unnoticed by American publishing entrepreneurs. By the time I began pasting up dummies for *LOOK* with Vernon Pope in 1936, perhaps half a dozen or more individuals and organizations were proceeding with similar plans.

One that I had heard rumors about was Time Inc., and I arranged an appointment with Harry Luce. Luce and Roy Larsen, general manager of Time Inc. and later *LIFE* magazine's first publisher, were friends of mine. Larsen and my brother John had been classmates at Harvard and had remained close ever since. Before Larsen went to Time Inc., John had tried unsuccessfully to lure him to The Register and Tribune Company.

Luce examined with great interest the crude dummy I had brought along—which had been named *LOOK* after an elaborate culling through candidates assembled from the dictionary and Roget's Thesaurus. Then he pulled out a dummy for *LIFE*, a project Time Inc. had been working on for several years and which at one point had also been tentatively named *LOOK*. We discussed our respective editorial plans and philosophies, which turned out to be quite different. *LIFE* was to be a weekly while we were planning a monthly. *LIFE* planned to cover the news while we saw *LOOK* as feature-oriented. *LIFE* would be a rather "upscale" publication aimed at the relatively affluent, well-educated sort of people who read *The New York Times* while *LOOK* would seek a more downscale audience, the sort of people who read New York's *Daily News*. *LIFE* was to be a slick, high-cost venture that would accept advertising immediately. *LOOK* would be printed on less expensive paper and would not accept advertising until its circulation base had been established.

Because the two publications seemed aimed at quite different markets, Luce decided to make what I recall was a $25,000 investment in *LOOK*, which was to be a separate corporation from the Register and Tribune Company, though my family and the Register and Tribune Company would be the major shareholders. In studying the *LOOK* venture later, Roy Larsen and Charles L. Stillman said that "if our plans for *LIFE* prove to be top-heavy with overhead and bigness, as they might, the modest scale of operations proposed by the Cowles brothers is so much the opposite extreme that they might well succeed where we might fail." Time Inc., in other words, was hedging its bet. Eighteen months after we were on the market, though, it became clear that the two magazines were much more competitive than anyone had thought. We all agreed that it would be best for the Cowleses to reacquire the Time Inc. interest.

While I was in New York seeing Luce, I also talked with Mike Morrissey, a burly but friendly Irishman and tough businessman who was president of the American News Company. His company was the major national distributor of newspapers and magazines and controlled newsstand concessions in practically all of the railroad terminals. He examined the *LOOK* dummy and was enthusiastic. He said the time was exactly right for such a magazine.

While their enthusiasm was not as great as mine, both my father and my brother John also urged me to proceed. But John did convince me not to bring out *LOOK* until *LIFE* was on the newsstands and we had a measure of public reaction to a mass-circulation picture magazine.

The first issue of *LIFE*, dated November 30, 1936, was such an instant success that it came close to bankrupting Time Inc. *LIFE* had sold advertising for the first year that was priced on the basis of a per-issue circulation of 300,000. Yet the magazine was soon printing over a million copies and still not satisfying the demand. One Time Inc. executive remarked, "Having *LIFE* isn't like having a baby. It's like having quintuplets." Advertisers flocked to take advantage of the bargain: several times the circulation they were paying for. *LIFE* was not a cheap magazine to produce—Time Inc. had invested $10.5 million even before it began publishing—and the costs of supplying over a million copies every week were far greater than circulation and artificially low advertising revenue. *LIFE* lost over $5 million before edging into the black in early 1939.

LIFE's soaring circulation, though, convinced us to move ahead with *LOOK*. Our first issue, dated February, 1937 and on sale January 5, featured Hermann Goering on the cover advertising a story entitled "Will Former Dope Fiend Rule Germany?" Our inside stories were a typical potpourri, from "Mishandled Paroles—America's Shame" and "A Psychologist Reveals the Secret of Roosevelt's Popularity" to "Auto Kills Woman Before Your Eyes" and "Trained Goldfish" to profiles of Joan Crawford and Delores Del Rio, and a dramatic head-and-shoulders color picture of Greta Garbo on the back cover.

THAT GARBO PICTURE

Our initial print order was 400,000 and it was apparent almost immediately that it would be a sellout. We began another printing, and sales climbed above 700,000. Within a few days, we discovered one of the main reasons for the reader interest: the Garbo picture. It turned out that when the page was folded in half, the result looked very much like a female crotch. Word of this curiosity spread with amazing speed. It was said, in fact, that the fold-over effect had been discovered by some telegraph operator who had quickly alerted fellow telegraphers throughout the country. Police in Montreal actually seized several hundred copies. John and I decided we had no choice but to recall all of the unsold copies, which cost us over $100,000.

Our embarrassment, though, generated considerable free publicity. Thanks to news reports of our blunder and word of mouth, *LOOK* was instantly known all over America. Circulation soared: 1,203,000 in March, 1,323,800 in April. In April we decided to go bi-weekly, a step, we thought, toward eventually becoming a weekly in full competition with *LIFE*, *Collier's*, and the *Saturday Evening Post*. By October we were selling two million copies per issue.

The time had come to consider advertising. Not going after ads had been part of our essentially shoestring philosophy in getting *LOOK* out—in distinct contrast to Time Inc. and *LIFE*. We knew *LOOK* was a big risk, and the idea was to keep that risk as low as possible. We had a staff of only 18 which was working out of cramped offices on the 11th floor of the

Register and Tribune Building in Des Moines. We were borrowing most of our pictures from the newspaper's morgue. By the same token, we thought it was unwise to go to all the expense of organizing a high-powered advertising department when we might not have a magazine to put ads in a few months down the line. But our circulation now seemed sufficiently solid that we hired Ned Doyle, formerly ad director of *Cosmopolitan*, and began building a staff. The first issue with advertising was November 9 and carried 35 ads. Our circulation guarantee to advertisers was 1,500,000, about 200,000 less than we were actually delivering. Soon, with sales still climbing, we issued a new rate card effective May 10, 1938, guaranteeing 2,000,000.

We never made it. I later recalled a comment from my father during the summer of 1937 that I had disregarded at the time. "Mike thinks the circulation of *LOOK* is just going to keep going up," he had said to an associate. "But I think he's wrong. I think he's going to get a little bump." Though circulation in early 1938 was below the peak of 2,083,964 achieved with the November 23, 1937, issue, it still seemed sufficiently strong that as a respite from my long hours getting *LOOK* launched, I went off to Europe on a two-month holiday. I soon received a cable from John reporting that the "bump" was in fact a veritable crash. I canceled the rest of the vacation and headed home—an agonizingly slow trip by boat.

John, who by now had taken over as publisher of *The Minneapolis Star*, came to meet me in New York and fill me in on what was happening. Circulation was sagging at an alarming pace. By July, it would be only 1,013,471—an incredible drop of a million copies. Returned copies were piled so high around the Register and Tribune building that people were having trouble getting through the doors. Advertisers were beginning to cancel advertising for new space. And because our circulation had fallen below the 1,500,000 guarantee, we were feeling compelled to give rebates on the ads we had run.

What had gone wrong? The U.S. economy, for one thing, had turned down sharply and since *LOOK* was almost exclusively a newsstand magazine, we had immediately begun feeling the pinch in people's pocketbooks. For another thing, the market by this time was flooded with at least a dozen other picture magazines. Many if not most were pallid imitators of *LIFE* and *LOOK*, but they were diverting some of our readers.

But we had to take a big share of the blame ourselves. When we had started *LOOK*, we had taken considerable pride in our amateur status. We even took an ad in *Editor & Publisher* with the headline: TWO NEWSPAPERMEN WHO HAVE HAD NO MAGAZINE EXPERIENCE ANNOUNCE A NEW PUBLISHING VENTURE. We had also been a little cocky about the way we had launched *LOOK* on a shoestring. Magazine publishing, though, is no place for underfinanced neophytes.

Our circulation department, we belatedly realized, was just not up to the demands of distributing nationally over a million copies of a bi-weekly magazine. Because we had failed to hire an experienced art director, the magazine had a very unprofessional look. Though the stories were generally lively, the layout was badly designed, a hodgepodge with little cover-to-cover continuity or flow. We had bragged in the *Editor & Publisher* ad that *"LOOK* is not a magazine designed to impress prospective advertisers, but to interest readers. Don't look for coated paper or fancy printing in *LOOK."* Readers, though, like coated paper and fancy printing just like advertisers. They did not like the cheap paper we had chosen for *LOOK*, which, among other things, took color so poorly that we had to rerun many of our early advertisements.

Frantic with worry about the enormous losses we were suffering, John was in favor of killing *LOOK*. At his insistence, I went over to Time Inc. to talk to Harry Luce and Roy Larsen. They agreed with John. While they obviously would have liked one less competitor for *LIFE*, their arguments had merit. They said *LOOK* had undeniable reader interest. But they doubted whether the magazine would ever be able to overcome the image of vulgarity created by the Garbo picture and the impression of cheapness and crudeness from our low-quality paper, printing, and layout. It was all too much of a stigma. If I really wanted to stay in the magazine field, they said I should discontinue *LOOK* and a year or so later start a new picture magazine under a different name.

After the meeting, I walked aimlessly up to Central Park and sat down on a park bench for a couple of hours. I tried to calm down and clarify my thinking. The situation was obviously grim. John's argument that I should cut my losses before I was totally wiped out had merit. Both John and I had invested in *LOOK* a major share of our liquid assets. But my pride and my unwillingness to admit failure were stronger than my disappointment and my apprehension about the future. True, I had made a disastrous beginning. But I still had a magazine that over a million people were paying money for every two weeks. My idea was sound—even if my execution had been lacking.

I resolved to play the thing out. I returned to Des Moines and began attacking our most crucial problem: circulation. What we needed, it was clear, were some high-powered professionals to take over from the amateurs. The first was Les Suhler, circulation director of Rand McNally's *Child Life*, who was charged with building up our tiny subscriber list. Our almost total dependency on newsstand sales had made our issue-to-issue numbers erratic, and we needed a much larger cushion of subscription circulation. Within a year, Suhler had increased the subscription share of our circulation from four percent to over twenty percent.

Perhaps the greatest credit for our turnaround goes to S.O. "Shap" Shapiro. Vice president for circulation at MacFadden Publications

62

before we hired him and still in his thirties, Shap was aggressive, outspoken, brash, and generally regarded as the most imaginative circulation man in the magazine business. Despite his age, he had an encyclopedic knowledge of the mechanics of magazine distribution throughout the country.

Shap's moves paid off. Circulation began climbing again, from 1,170,000 in the third quarter of 1938 to 1,244,000 in the fourth quarter. Newsstand returns dropped from 37 percent of the total printed (684,000 copies) to only 13 percent (198,286 copies).

Meanwhile, we began bringing in a strong cadre of people on the editorial side to improve the appearance and quality of the magazine. The most notable was Dan Mich, previously the managing editor of the *Wisconsin State Journal*, who eventually became Editor of *LOOK*. I've known many editors, but I regard Dan as the finest.

Within a year after my visit to Central Park, I felt that *LOOK* had turned around. We still had a long way to go before we achieved the kind of results I had anticipated in my pre-publication naivete. But the worst, I was confident, was behind me.

AROUND THE WORLD
WITH WENDELL WILLKIE

3

I will never forget my first look at Wendell Willkie. It was in April 1940, and my brother John and I were in Washington for the annual convention of the American Society of Newspaper Editors. The highlight of the convention was a debate between Harold Ickes, the Secretary of the Interior, and Willkie, an Indiana-born corporate lawyer and president of Commonwealth & Southern Corporation, a large privately owned utility holding company headquartered on Wall Street. The subject of the debate was public versus private power. Since the early 1930s, Willkie had been conducting a vigorous feud with the federal government over the unfair competition he claimed private utilities faced from Roosevelt's public power projects, especially the Tennessee Valley Authority, which served some of the same areas as Commonwealth & Southern.

Speaking without notes, Willkie took virtual control of the debate and thoroughly demolished Icke's arguments in favor of public power. But what impressed me most was not Willkie's position on the issue. It was the overwhelming magnetism of the personality. A great hulk of a man, with attractively shaggy hair, a booming voice, and a genial homespun manner, he exuded charm, vitality, and that all-important, if difficult to define, political asset: charisma.

Originally a Democrat, Willkie relatively recently had turned Republican. Though serving as head of a utility is not generally regarded as a stepping stone to the Presidency, he had been attracting increasing attention, especially from businessmen, with his outspoken criticisms of the New Deal and its restraints on private business. The month I was in Washington, Willkie had published a widely circulated article in *Fortune* called "We, the People." In it, he stressed the advantages of free enterprise over what he called "state socialism," Washington's takeover of more and more services that used to be performed by the private sector. The article was accompanied by an editorial endorsing Willkie, called "Business and Government," written by Russell Davenport, the managing editor of *Fortune*.

Willkie's views on the New Deal were only slightly more liberal than those held by many other Republican politicians, including Tom Dewey, then a racket-busting district attorney in New York City, and Robert Taft, a freshman senator from Ohio, who were the two leading contenders for the Republican nomination for President. Willkie's foreign policy positions, though, were sharply divergent. Dewey and Taft were confirmed isolationists who wanted no part of the war that was brewing in Europe. Willkie, like Roosevelt, was an internationalist who favored aid to America's allies. As Hitler invaded country after country, sentiment in the United States turned away from isolationism toward outrage and support for the victims of Hitler's aggression. Dewey's and Taft's campaign lost momentum while spontaneous grass roots movements for Willkie began springing up all over the country.

Two days after Willkie's debate with Ickes, Russell Davenport of *Fortune* invited my brother John and me to meet Willkie at a private dinner in New York. Davenport, who had co-authored Willkie's *Fortune* article, was actively promoting Willkie's candidacy as was Harry Luce and the Time, Inc. publications. (In May, Davenport temporarily resigned from *Fortune* to become Willkie's unofficial pre-convention campaign manager.) During the dinner, at which only the four of us were present, Davenport and Willkie presented their analysis of Republican Party prospects in the upcoming election. The outlook, they said, was grim. As they saw it, neither Dewey nor Taft stood a chance against Roosevelt. The Republican Party's only hope was Willkie. Davenport argued that, though still a distant dark horse, Willkie, if he received enough help from his friends, had a good chance to capture the nomination as a compromise candidate.

John and I were much less optimistic. Willkie was virtually unknown to most of the delegates. And if he was known at all, it was as a lifelong Democrat. Yet my brother and I nevertheless decided to help. For one thing, we were obviously captivated by the magic of Willkie's personality. For another, John and especially I had inherited from our father and grandfather an enduring fascination with politics and belief that it was our duty as citizens to become involved. Like Father, I was never prominent, but through my association with *The Register* and *Tribune* and later *LOOK* I was usually close enough to the action to gain some interesting insights into how the process worked.

Willkie's only hope, we all agreed, was to gain exposure to as many delegates as possible in the little time remaining before the convention, scheduled for June in Philadelphia. "Come out to Minneapolis and St.

Paul," John said. "I will see to it that you will be the main speaker at a Republican dinner scheduled in St. Paul next week." I promised to deliver the Iowa delegates if he would come down to Des Moines after the St. Paul meeting.

John flew back home and went directly to see Harold Stassen, then the boy-wonder governor of Minnesota. Stassen reluctantly agreed to accept Willkie as the main speaker at the Republican gathering. John then bought time on six radio stations in Minnesota. As with many brilliant extemporaneous speakers, Willkie's delivery of written addresses was flat and unimpressive. Obviously underwhelmed, the delegates responded to Willkie's thirty-minute speech with a little polite applause. But then Willkie the natural showman took over. The night was hot and he removed his coat. He tossed his speech up toward the ceiling and the pages fluttered down over the audience. "Now that we're off the air," he said, "I'm going to tell you how I really feel about the Roosevelt Administration." Twenty minutes later he had those staid Republicans standing on their chairs, applauding, whistling, and yelling their heads off. The Willkie magic had worked, and to insure its staying power John invited the Minnesota delegates to his house for drinks and to talk to Willkie personally.

It was a repeat performance in Des Moines, only this time the speech was extemporaneous from beginning to end and I too had the Iowa delegates to my house to meet Willkie. He was as effective as he had been in Minnesota. Carried away by the enthusiastic reception in the two cities, he wanted to meet every damn delegate in the United States before they gathered in Philadelphia. He insisted that I accompany him on a barnstorming trip through the Midwest and mountain states. I knew most of the newspaper people in those states and was very helpful in setting up meetings and interviews.

By convention time Hitler's inexorable progress across Europe had thrown the rest of the world into panic and fear. More than anything else, it was Hilter's successes that threw the vote of even the most conservative Republicans to Wendell Willkie. He won the nomination on the sixth ballot.

Willkie's charisma was effective on the campaign trail. But he faced too many obstacles. His previous Democratic Party affiliation hurt him with Republicans and he did little to assuage these feelings by courting Republican leaders. His Wall Street affiliation, meanwhile, hurt him with Democrats, whom Willkie had hoped would desert Roosevelt over the third-term issue. Willkie did not have any special advantage on the issues. Though he advocated a better government environment for business investment, he supported most of the New Deal reforms. And he supported FDR's "short of war" stance, to give aid to the Allies but to stay out of the war. He carried only ten states, mainly the isolationist Midwest. But he did receive 45 percent of the popular vote, the largest ever for a losing candidate or for a Republican up to that time.

A CALL FROM THE WHITE HOUSE

My involvement with national politics resumed unexpectedly in January 1942 when I received a call from Harry Hopkins, Roosevelt's close advisor, summoning me to the White House. Japan had bombed Pearl Harbor on December 7, 1941. On the flight to Washington, I kept wondering what the President would want with a Republican who had played a rather important role in trying to get him defeated in 1940.

When I walked into the Oval Office, Roosevelt came right to the point. He wanted to appoint me Domestic Director of the Office of War Information. Roosevelt had created the OWI, actually an amalgamation of four existing federal agencies, to facilitate the flow of information about the war. To run the agency, he had selected Elmer Davis, an experienced and well-known radio commentator. He had designated Robert Sherwood, the playwright, to run the overseas branch and Archibald MacLeish to run the domestic division. All three men were prominent liberals, and Republicans in Congress castigated the OWI as nothing but a propaganda vehicle for the Roosevelt Administration. When MacLeish resigned, Roosevelt and Hopkins decided that the replacement should be someone with solid Republican credentials who supported the Administrations' foreign policy. I fit the bill precisely.

I wanted to help the war effort. Indeed, at the time I was considering joining the Air Force where, with my many years of flying credits, I felt I could obtain a commission as a major, or even a lieutenant colonel. But I was not anxious to get involved with the OWI and the political turmoil surrounding it. When I told Roosevelt I would much rather enlist in the Air Force, he insisted that I could serve the country best by taking the OWI post. He dismissed me with the suggestion that I think about it overnight and return the next morning.

As I left Roosevelt's office, I ran into Hopkins and told him of our conversation. He was sympathetic to my feelings, but later, over dinner, he tried to change my mind. I asked him if there wasn't some other way I could serve the government. He said he would talk to the President and see what could be arranged.

Late that night there was a knock on my door at the Carlton hotel. A federal agent handed me a note from the President. "Dear Cowles," it read, "Please do!" and it was signed "FDR."

"Mike," Roosevelt said the next day with his dazzling smile, "I'll make you a deal. I'll appoint you as Ambassador to Australia if you'll give me your solemn promise not to ask to be relieved so long as the war continues in the Pacific." As Roosevelt probably knew it would, that sounded like banishment to Siberia. And probably for a long time: many people were predicting that the war with Japan would continue for ten years or more. With more than a few qualms, I agreed to join the OWI.

I had four days to return to Des Moines and put my affairs in order. I turned over management and editorial control of *LOOK* and *The Register* and *Tribune* to their respective staffs, with full confidence that they were in the hands of completely loyal and competent people.

Taking immediate advantage of one of my major assets—that I was a Republican—Roosevelt gave me my first assignment: to get the OWI budget through the Republican-controlled Congress. I was to testify at a hearing before the House Ways and Means Committee. Never having seen a budget of a federal department before, I was appalled that the OWI budget was as thick as the New York City telephone directory. I sat up all night studying the huge volume and showed up on the Hill at ten o'clock the next morning.

After my swearing in, a congressman asked me to hold up my hand again and to swear that everything in the budget was devoted to winning the war and to nothing else.

"Mr. Congressman," I said, "I can't swear to that. I will swear that to the best of my knowledge everything in this budget is solely directed to winning the war."

"Well, Mr. Cowles," the Congressman said, "turn to page 388."

Page 388 was an appropriation of about $250,000 which Archie MacLeish had been trying to get through the Congress over several previous budgets to record Southern folk music for the archives of the Library of Congress. The congressman asked me to explain how that would help win the war. I replied that I didn't think it would help and if they were going to cut items out of the budget I would suggest that that item would be the one to start with.

"Mr. Cowles, you're making a good start," the congressman said, smiling.

Despite the auspicious beginning, I don't look back on my two years with the OWI with much fondness. I'm not certain how much of a contribution the OWI made, for Roosevelt made all of the important decisions himself on how the war news was to be handled. Other than handling the budget and keeping the Republicans in Congress happy, my role often seemed to be shooting down silly proposals made by others. Once Robert Patterson, Under Secretary of War, wanted to impose what I regarded as an unnecessarily severe increase in the rationing of paper. His goal was to shock the country into realizing that they had to go onto an austerity-type of living during the war. He proposed that I, as domestic head of the Office of War Information, grade all of the newspapers, magazines and other periodicals into three categories—essentials, semi-essential and non-essential.

This idea was unanimously approved by a committee set up to deal with such proposals—it included a number of Cabinet officers and other top officials—and was given to me more or less as a fait accompli.

I proceeded to make an impassioned speech to the committee pointing out how ridiculous the idea of grading publications was. "How," I asked, "can anyone judge whether the *Christian Century* is more essential than the *Boone* (Iowa) *Republic*, the only newspaper published in that town? Who can say whether the *American Magazine* is more essential than the leading Catholic Church paper? Who can say that the *New York News* is less essential than *The New York Times?*"

The proposal was eventually killed.

As I had feared, there were frequent nasty controversies and intramural fights. At one point, after we drastically slashed the unwieldy volume of pamphlets we were publishing, a small group of employees resigned in a huff and made the ridiculous charge that the agency was "now dominated by high-pressure promoters who prefer slick salesman-ship to honest information . . . They are turning this Office of War Information into an Office of War Ballyhoo." The incident caused such a fervor that, for the first and last time in my life, I was investigated briefly by a Senate committee.

Roosevelt, though, seemed pleased with how I was doing. He began to include me in the small group, three or four people at most, that he met with for thirty or forty minutes before his weekly press conferences. We were supposed to anticipate the questions the press might fire at him and suggest answers. Frequently he would throw back his head and say, "No, I don't agree. That isn't the way to answer the question." These sessions greatly increased my respect for Roosevelt's political acumen. Invariably his answers would be better than the ones we had proposed.

A BRILLIANT PLAN

The late summer of 1942 was perhaps the low point of the war. In North Africa Rommel was pushing Montgomery back into Egypt. Hitler was launching his gigantic offensive against Stalingrad and rampaging through Europe. The Japanese controlled the Pacific and German submarines were roaming the Atlantic freely and sinking Allied ships. Roosevelt felt that some dramatic signal had to be given that domestic politics had been put aside and that all Americans, Republicans and Democrats alike, were firm in their support of the Allied war effort.

He came up with a brilliant plan. With the enthusiastic support of Winston Churchill, Roosevlt decided to send Wendell Willkie on an around-the-world trip to reassure the embattled nations in Europe and elsewhere of the U.S.'s determination to defeat Germany and Japan. Roosevelt knew that Willkie was still a very popular figure on the national scene and he was convinced that Willkie's persuasive powers would work internationally as well.

Probably because of my newspaper background and the fact that Willkie and I had remained good friends after the election, the President released me from my OWI job to accompany Willkie. Joseph Barnes, then Deputy Director of OWI's overseas branch and an experienced foreign correspondent with a good working knowledge of Russian, was added to the official party. Without question the trip was the greatest thing that ever happened to me.

On a Saturday, two days before our departure on August 26, 1942, Roosevelt invited Willkie and me to lunch at Hyde Park, the historic Roosevelt home where neither of us had ever been. We arrived at twelve noon, as requested, in a driving rainstorm. Harry Hopkins let us in and casually informed us that the President was not up yet. Harry then took us on a tour of the house for about three-quarters of an hour.

Suddenly a radiantly cheerful President appeared in his wheelchair. "First, we've all got to have one of my famous old-fashioneds," he announced as he wheeled himself over to the bar and mixed four very strong drinks. Tossing his off rather quickly, he decided we needed another round. I preferred Scotch to bourbon but had no choice.

Instead of talking about the war and the upcoming trip Roosevelt began to exchange jokes with Willkie about the 1940 presidential campaign. Roosevelt recounted a not-so-well-kept secret about the vast individual and corporate donations to their respective campaigns— openly to Willkie and much the same amount to Roosevelt privately. He was particularly amused by the Du Ponts, who had meticulously totalled up what all the members of the Du Pont family had given to Willkie's campaign and then contributed the same amount to Roosevelt's.

I was amazed at the President's relaxed attitude. I had expected to see a worried, tense man, deeply disturbed by the terrible news from all the war fronts. Joking, laughing, and reminiscing, he didn't mention the war until we had finished with luncheon.

We followed Roosevelt out of the dining room to his study. As he wheeled himself up to his desk, he looked up at Willkie, and said, "Wendell, I'm going to give you a personal letter to Stalin. Why don't you and Mike make yourselves comfortable while I write it." He spent about thirty minutes composing that letter while Wendell and I sat by quietly. When he was through, he sealed the letter and handed it to Wendell. "Wendell," he said, "this letter is to be handed by you to Stalin personally, and not to any aide no matter how important in the hierarchy." With repeated assurances by Wendell that he would follow the President's injunction to the letter, we bid the President good-bye. Roosevelt wished us great good luck and we left.

THE JOURNEY BEGINS

The journey, which was to cover 31,000 miles over 49 days, was made in a 4-engine Consolidated bomber converted for transport service. It was appropriately named *The Gulliver*. At that time no plane had the range to

71

cross the North Atlantic non-stop so we did it in short—by today's standards—hops from New York to West Palm Beach, Puerto Rico, Belem and Natal in Brazil, and finally across the South Atlantic to Accra in what is now Ghana, the shortest distance between South America and Africa.

From Accra we flew on to Khartoum, then followed the Nile north to Cairo. Even before we left Washington we had heard rumors that Cairo might fall to General Rommel any day. So it was with some concern that we prepared for our scheduled meeting with General Sir Bernard Montgomery, Commander of the British Eighth Army in North Africa.

With Major General Russell Maxwell, recently appointed commander of the American forces in Egypt, we left Cairo and drove north along a desert road to meet Montgomery at the front in El Alamein on the shores of the Mediterranean. The General met us in his headquarters hidden in the sand dunes. A lean, intense, ascetic-looking man, he was so passionately preoccupied with the war that he almost never left the front. Though General Maxwell had been in Cairo for several weeks, Montgomery had not yet met him. "Who is that officer with you?" he asked as we drove up.

Montgomery was in the final phases of a battle against Rommel, and after being pushed back again and again, Montgomery was convinced he had stopped Rommel at last. Eagerly, he spelled out his battle strategy. In fluid, amorphous desert warfare, complete coordination of tank forces, artillery forces, and air power is essential, and that, at last, he said he had achieved. Of particular help, he added, were the American tanks that had begun to arrive in great numbers at the docks of Alexandria and Port Said. "It is now mathematically certain that I will eventually destroy Rommel," he insisted. "This battle was the critical test."

We spent the night in the desert and at six o'clock in the morning, I went swimming in the blue-green waters with Montgomery. Later, he summoned representatives of the press. No news of the battle had reached Cairo or had been given to the press. Now, Montgomery released a carefully worded statement: "Egypt is saved. Rommel is stopped and a beginning has been made on the task of throwing the Nazis out of Africa."

Used to empty claims from generals, the newspapermen seemed skeptical. Despite Montgomery's almost fanatical dedication and belief in this ultimate victory, even Wendell and I were not completely convinced. Fortunately, our misgiving proved thoroughly unjustified.

From Cairo we went to Beirut, then part of Syria. We were met at the airport by a band and an elaborately bedecked escort and driven to the beautiful residence of General Georges Catroux, High Commissioner for the Levant—in effect, Governor General of the whole French Middle Eastern empire. Catroux, with many years experience in the Middle East, was the top-ranking French official in the area.

Charles de Gaulle, then leader of the Fighting French movement, was staying with General and Madame Catroux. Wendell had requested a meeting with de Gaulle, and we met with him in a small office in the sumptuous Catroux palace. Sparsely furnished with a desk and a couple of chairs, the room had one notable decoration: behind the desk was a bust of Joan of Arc.

De Gaulle strode in, shook hands brusquely, and told Willkie to proceed. Since Willkie spoke no French and understood very little and the same applied to de Gaulle's English, an interpreter was present.

Acting on orders from Roosevelt and Churchill, Willkie was anxious to secure de Gaulle's help for Montgomery's drive against Rommel. The matter, we knew, was sensitive for the French and the British were maneuvering against one another for eventual domination of Syria and the Middle East. Montgomery, though, was in perhaps mortal trouble and the French fleet, under orders from de Gaulle, was sitting idle in the harbor at Alexandria. Wendell pleaded with de Gaulle to activate the ships so that they could assist British convoy supplies going across the Mediterranean to Montgomery and attack German convoys delivering supplies to Rommel.

De Gaulle began his response by making it clear he resented the fact that Roosevelt and Churchill had also had dealings with other French leaders. (During the German occupation, the French government was in disarray, and de Gaulle had several rivals.) He and he alone, de Gaulle said forcefully, spoke for France, and Roosevelt and Churchill had no right to deal with anyone else. And he and he alone, further, gave the orders as to the disposition of the French military and naval forces.

De Gaulle said that he had no interest in becoming involved with Montgomery's campaign. Forty minutes of pleading and arguing by Wendell were to no avail. At one point, in a sincere attempt to soften the General's inflexible attitude, Wendell expressed his admiration for the Fighting French movement. De Gaulle's response was sharp and typical. "The Fighting French are not a movement," he said. "The Fighting French are France itself. We are the legatees of all of France and its possessions."

Abruptly, he turned and put his hand on the head of the bust of Joan of Arc. "She saved France," he said curtly. "I will save France. Good day, gentlemen." He left the room without the courtesy of a handshake.

AN ASTONISHING PROPOSAL

That evening General and Madame Catroux gave a big glittery dinner party which, I learned, the military did with some frequency even in the midst of a horrible war. There were about fifty guests, all ranking French, British, and Americans from miles around. The party was in honor of de Gaulle. Despite my high-sounding title—Domestic Director of War Information—I was outranked by the array of generals, admirals, and ambassadors and seated below the salt.

As we were finishing our dessert and coffee, the *maitre d'hotel* came around and handed me Madame Catroux's place card. Down in one corner was the word "over." On the other side in almost illegible French, it said, "Meet me in the garden immediately after dinner."

When the hosts rose to indicate that dinner was over I sauntered into one of the most magnificent gardens I have ever seen. The house itself was almost like a small Versailles and the manicured lawns and terraced terrain in the moonlight were a superb setting for what turned out to be a bit of intrigue right out of an Eric Ambler novel.

I strolled around deeper into the gardens and finally sat down on a stone bench to wait—and waited and waited. Deciding that I had not understood the message on the card, I was just about ready to rejoin the guests indoors when Madame Catroux emerged from the shadows. Communication was extremely difficult: her English was as poor as my French.

"You are an intimate friend of President Roosevelt's?" she asked.

"I'm not an intimate of the President," I responded, "but I know him well and I can see him whenever I have anything of importance to convey."

"You are an intimate friend of Mr. Churchill?"

"No, I'm not. I've met Mr. Churchill on a number of occasions with Bernard Baruch, who is a friend of Churchill's. I've been to dinner at his home in London and in the country, but I don't regard myself as an intimate friend."

She pressed ahead anxiously. "Well, could you get to see Mr. Churchill if it were something important?"

"Certainly, Madame. If Mr. Roosevelt decided it were important for me to see Mr. Churchill about anything concerning the war, I would certainly carry out his wishes."

The suspense over where our conversation was leading was becoming unbearable. After some further parrying, she apparently concluded she could trust me. She talked about how difficult it had become to cope with de Gaulle's monumental arrogance. Wasn't it true, she asked almost rhetorically, that even Roosevelt and Churchill were having problems with him?

Then she presented her proposal. She would arrange for an "accident" to happen to de Gaulle in Beirut. In return for removing this obstruction to the Allied war effort, she wanted assurance from both Roosevelt and Churchill that her husband, General Catroux, would lead the French troops when Paris was liberated from the Germans. After that triumphant moment, she said, her husband would be assured of playing a major role if not *the* major role in the new French government.

I don't think her husband knew about the proposal, but it seemed quite clear to me she was very serious. I repeated her proposal in English and my broken French over and over again to make absolutely sure that I had understood her shocking message correctly.

The next day during the flight to Ankara, our next stop, I related the episode to Willkie. He listened without saying a word, looked out of the window for about three minutes, then turned to me. "Mike, you never told me that story. If it ever gets out, I'll say I never heard it. When you get back to Washington, if you want to tell it to Roosevelt, you're on your own."

I did exactly that. My first day back in Washington I phoned Harry Hopkins and told him I had an important message for the President. Harry told me to come over to the White House and he'd work me into the President's schedule. The President was at his desk signing a flock of papers when I was ushered in. "Sit down, Mike," he said cordially, and gestured to a chair. "What's on your mind?"

He listened intently as I told him the story. When I finished he dropped his pen, gave me a long, penetrating look and said, "Now start all over again and don't leave anything out." I did, and he heard me out to the end. He remained silent for a few minutes.

"If I asked you to, Mike, would you fly to London and repeat the story to Churchill?"

"Certainly, Mr. President," I said. "You're the Commander-in-Chief, we're at war, and I'm here to carry out your orders.."

He stared at the ceiling, lost in thought for a while.

"Mike, I want you to promise that you will never repeat that story until the war is over. After that, I don't care."

"You have my word, Mr. President," I said.

Though I believe Roosevelt seriously considered taking Madame Catroux up on her offer, he never did send me to London to report the story to Churchill and I never mentioned it to anyone until well after the war. When Paris was liberated, incidentally, the general leading the French forces was Leclerc, head of the 2nd Armored Division. And it was de Gaulle, of course, who became head of the provisional government.

Some years later, I attended a dinner party in Paris. The hostess led me around introducing me to her guests. Suddenly I was face to face with Madame Catroux.

"Madame Catroux," the hostess said, "this is Gardner Cowles, the distinguished publisher and editor from New York."

Madame Catroux looked me straight in the eye. "We have never met, have we, Mr. Cowles?"

I smiled. "No, Madame Catroux, we have never met."

She nodded graciously. "Thank you," she said.

Our official itinerary in the Middle East consisted of meetings and elegant banquets with heads of state, foreign ministers, military leaders, and other dignitaries. We spent most of our time in sumptuous palaces, lavishly furnished guest houses, and ornate hotels. But one didn't have to look hard to see another, more real Middle East beyond this facade, a land of extreme poverty, filth, and disease, of millions of people living in squalor and clinging to ancient ways of life while a wealthy few lived in splendor and enjoyed the conveniences of modern technology. The westernized and western-educated leaders in these countries were attempting to drag their countrymen into the twentieth century, but the task seemed Herculean at best. It was made even more difficult by the behavior of the colonial powers who seemed less interested in improving the welfare of the people than in scrambling for the best cut of the pie when peace came. While nobody could be sure what would happen after the war, it was obvious to me then that the Middle East would be a highly volatile caldron for many years to come.

THE DANCING GIRLS OF BAGHDAD

Ankara, the capital of Turkey, was one of our most important stops on our journey. Since the chaos that followed the collapse of their Ottoman Empire after World War I, the Turks had made tremendous progress, more than any other nation in the Middle East, in modernizing their economic, social, educational, and health institutions. They were determined to protect what they had achieved, and their stance toward the war in Europe was to maintain their neutrality. In fact, we were not permitted to fly *The Gulliver*, a United States Army plane, into Ankara; we had to take a Pan American Airways flight from Cairo.

Roosevelt and other Allied leaders, though, were worried about Turkey. It was a small, rather weak nation with a population then of only sixteen million. Though it had sided with Germany during World War I, its sympathies were toward the Allies. Yet it was being bombarded with Nazi propaganda and the Turkish leaders were watching events in Europe with great anxiety. They were terribly fearful of a German invasion. Their willingness and ability to remain neutral seemed directly related to the extent of their faith in an eventual Allied victory.

Willkie, in my opinion, played a masterful role in convincing the Turks to stay neutral. They were worried that at this point the U.S. presence in Europe was relatively small. Willkie explained we were determined to invest enormous resources in beating Hitler but that it took time for American factories to gear up to produce sufficiently large quantities of airplanes and other war materiel. He tactfully reminded them of their misjudgment during World War I, when the U.S. was also slow in responding but, when American production really got rolling, the Allies had run right over the German armies. Do not, Willkie told the Turkish leaders, make the same mistake again.

From Ankara, after picking up *The Gulliver*, we flew to Baghdad, the capital of Iraq, where we arrived about five in the morning. We were met by a man from the foreign office who drove us to a guest house and then informed us that, in two hours, the foreign minister would arrive to pay his respects. We greeted that piece of news with distress and exasperation. The past few days had been a blur of interminable receptions, banquets, and speeches and long, tedious hours in the air. We were exhausted.

"I'm too tired, Mike," Wendell said. "I've got to get some sleep and I'm going to bed. You've got to take over." When the foreign minister arrived, I explained how tired everyone was. He was very understanding. But he stressed that we were expected to attend a state dinner that evening hosted by Prince Abdul Ilah, the Regent, and another dinner the next night by Nuri as-Said Pasha, the Premier. Ilah had only recently been restored to power by Great Britain, who had landed an army to oust the leaders of an anti-British and pro-Axis military group that had seized power. Though Iraq later formally joined the war against Germany, at the time of our visit it was a non-belligerent ally of Great Britain.

Before the foreign minister had arrived, a member of *The Gulliver's* crew, which was being invited to the Nuri dinner, had suggested I tell him that Mr. Willkie would like to see the famous dancing girls of Baghdad, whom we had often heard about in America. That seemed like a good way of conveying the sleeping Willkie's interest in the foreign minister's country and I passed the request on. His face took on a strangely quizzical expression. "Well," he said, "if that is the wish of Mr. Willkie, it will be arranged."

Prince Ilah's dinner—held outside under a full moon on a vast lawn—was among the best we had in the Middle East. The Regent received guests seated on a throne on a thirty-foot-long oriental carpet. The scene seemed right out of the Arabian Nights.

Premier Nuri's dinner proved to be the most memorable, though. It was also outside. The American Ambassador had told us that liquor for religious reasons was not served in Iraq, but we soon saw, at the far end of a beautiful garden, the largest bar I had ever seen. It was about 100 feet long and only partially concealed by a magnificent carved wooden screen. In front of the bar the Iraquis were lined up three or four deep putting away the booze at a rate more rapid than I'd ever seen in the United States or in Europe.

The "cocktail hour" was followed by a sit-down dinner. I was next to the only female present, the wife of the British Ambassador, a very interesting woman of about sixty renowned for her archeological discoveries in that part of the world. After dinner and the usual toasts and speeches Premier Nuri announced, "Mr. Cowles, Mr. Willkie's aide, has requested that the dancing girls of Baghdad perform. They will now do so."

The audience burst out with applause, whistling, and considerable laughter. I was almost as bewildered as Wendell, who was hearing about my request for the first time. Soon we understood the audience's reaction. As I suspected, the *Gulliver* crew member who came up with the idea already knew that the dancing girls of Baghdad were the city's whores. At least eight of the best whorehouses in town were represented. The madam of each house introduced her girls one by one, who did a little dance, waved to the customers they recognized, and trotted off.

The British Ambassador's wife was shocked. "Why, Mr. Cowles," she said turning to me, "I'm disgusted with you. I thought you were a fine young man." She assured me that I wouldn't be the least interested in the spectacle, and while the girls danced, she talked on relentlessly about archeology.

THE SHAH OF IRAN AND SORAYA

Teheran, the capital of Iran, was our next port of call. The city itself was almost unbelieveably dirty, even by Middle East standards. The city's water supply ran along open gutters on the sides of the streets, and people used it for washing, cooking and even drinking. Disease was rampant, and only one out of every five children lived to the age of six.

Joe Barnes and I were given a small taste of what it's like to live in the Middle East when one is not a Presidential envoy. The American Ambassador gave his guest room to Willkie. Joe and I, we were told, had been booked into the "best" hotel in town. It turned out to be extraordinarily filthy. There were no private bathrooms, only one big communal toilet for men (and another, presumably, for women) where one simply squatted. We were scheduled for three nights in Teheran, and I decided I just couldn't take it. I asked the American Ambassador to let me use the couch in his living room and he agreed. Joe Barnes gamely stuck it out in the hotel.

We met briefly with Mohammed Reza Shah Pahlevi. Only twenty, he had taken over the government the previous year from his father. His father had been the father of modern Iran and had served as a dictator for many years. Yet, after he arranged a rapprochement with Germany, British and Russian forces invaded Iran in 1941 and forced him to abdicate in favor of his son. The young Shah had never been up in an airplane. Wendell took him for a ride in *The Gulliver* and flew him around for about an hour over the city and countryside. He was ecstatic.

Many years later the Shah and his beautiful wife, Soraya, visited the United States. After the usual official receptions in Washington, where President Eisenhower gave them a state dinner, they expressed a wish to see something of America. They decided on a visit to Disneyland in California, and then they unexpectedly changed their minds and decided to fly to New York for a week. The State Department was thrown into a dither. Secretary of State John Foster Dulles phoned me, very embarrassed. State would provide the official suite in the Waldorf Towers but he asked if my wife and I would be their hosts during their stay? I said we'd be glad to.

The beautiful Soraya, I discovered, did not speak English. And their sole interest turned out to be nightclubbing. For the following five evenings I entertained them in every well-known nightclub in New York. I have never been to so many nightclubs before or since. They liked staying up most of the night and then sleeping until noon the next day. The Shah also liked dirty stories—the simple, schoolboy kind, because if there was any subtlety involved he'd miss the point. I tried to remember some of the off-color stories I had heard during my Exeter days and would tell them when we were in "men-only" gatherings for after-dinner drinks or coffee. He would laugh delightedly and then run into the room where the ladies would be chatting and tell the story to Soraya, who apparently shared his taste in humor.

When the time came for the Shah and Soraya to leave, my wife and I drove them to Idlewild (now Kennedy) airport. There an aide to the Shah took me aside.

"You and Mrs. Cowles have been so kind and hospitable all this week," he said. "I'm sure the Shah will want to send you a gift from Iran. And it might as well be something that you'd really like to have."

"That's very kind of you," I said. "If you're really serious about it, please do not send me an Oriental rug. Perhaps it's a flaw in my taste but I just don't care for Oriental rugs. However, I would love to have some Iranian caviar; it's the best in the world. Perhaps you could send me a small bucket of it through your embassy so that it would get to me while it's still fresh. That would be the nicest present the Shah could send me."

"That's no problem," the aide said. "It will be done."

Three weeks later we received our gift from the Shah—an eight by twelve foot Oriental rug.

In 1968, when I was on the university's Board of Overseers, Harvard decided to award the Shah an honorary Doctor of Laws degree. The reason was that the Shah had given about one million acres of crown land to the peasants in Iran. Some members of the faculty, though, were sharply critical, for while Iran was a steadfast American ally, the Shah had turned out to be as much of a dictator as his father.

Before the ceremony, I went up to the Shah and reminded him of our earlier encounters. He said he remembered and expressed his gratitude for all I had done for him. During the ceremony, as is Harvard custom during commencements, senior faculty members were seated on the dais along with the President and the members of the Harvard Corporation and the Board of Overseers. When the Shah's award was announced, everyone rose and applauded—except John Kenneth Galbraith. The world-famous economist and former Ambassador to India remained seated as a gesture of disapproval.

When the world later began learning more about the Shah's corrupt and repressive regime, I found myself often thinking about Galbraith's silent protest.

RUSSIA—1942

As we flew from Teheran toward Russia in September, that nation was going through the worst agonizing days of the German invasion. Five million Russians had already been killed, wounded, or reported missing. Most of the rich farmlands of the Ukraine were in Nazi hands. Transportation and factory production were in a state of chaos. Food supplies were alarmingly low.

The German army was so close to Moscow that flashes of their artillery fire could be seen from the parapets of the Kremlin. Most of the government and diplomatic corps had moved eastward to Kuibishev, which was where our plane was headed.

We were met by Andrei Vishinsky, who had been chief state prosecutor in the notorious treason trials of the late 1930s. It was difficult to believe that this white-haired, scholarly-looking man was the same person responsible for the purge of some of the most beloved and honored heroes of the Russian Revolution. Deputy Commissar for Foreign Affairs at the time of our visit, Vishinsky later became foreign minister and the permanent Soviet delegate to the United Nations.

After a brief stay in Kuibishev we were permitted to fly to Moscow. Stalin remained in his Kremlin office throughout the war. His nightly radio broadcasts from the Kremlin to the Russian people did a great deal to bolster their morale and give them the courage to fight on despite unbelievable odds.

Stalin was not immediately able to fit us into his crushing schedule. We were turned over to some top brass and, at Willkie's request, we were taken on a trip to the front at Rzhev, about 150 miles northwest of Moscow. In addition to our own group there were the U.S. military attache in Russia and two other ranking American officers. We started out in comfortable cars, riding all night. But at dawn we had to switch to jeeps—American jeeps—and that was a fourteen-hour trip that I shall never forget: in a steady rain, through marshlands and forests and endless miles over pitted corduroy roads. It was ten days before I could sit down again with any degree of comfort.

When we reached Rzhev, the day's fighting had quieted down. In one trench I saw four soldiers cooking their supper. Two of them were women. On that particular front, I learned, at least twenty-five percent of the soldiers were women. Suddenly I noticed a severed arm just lying on the ground and jumped back with an exclamation of horror, to the amusement of the four war-weary Russian soldiers.

We were invited to have supper with the commanding general and

80

some of his officers and soldiers. The cold driving rain was persisting, and about forty of us had to squeeze into one tent. Supper consisted of cold boiled bacon, black bread, potatoes, and cabbage. The inevitable toasts in vodka went on all through the meal. At one point Wendell asked the general, a powerfully built Cossack who was only 38 years old, how large a section of the two-thousand-mile front he was defending. Translating the general's words slowly, the interpreter said, "Sir, I am not defending. I am attacking."

After our return from the front an appointment was finally set up for Willkie's meeting with Stalin. One night at about eleven o'clock the phone rang in our very elegant guest house just outside the Kremlin walls. The caller, who spoke excellent English, said that a limousine would pick up Mr. Willkie in about fifteen minutes to take him over to the Kremlin to see Stalin.

"Wendell," I reminded him, "don't forget the letter."

"What letter?" he asked.

"The letter Roosevelt gave you when we left Hyde Park to deliver *in person* to Stalin."

"Oh my God! I haven't thought about it since we left Hyde Park!"

Knowing how absent-minded and forgetful Wendell could be, Joe Barnes and I started a frantic search. We went through his briefcase in which he carried all his important documents and then through all the pockets of his suits. No letter. In desperation, Joe and I took all Willkie's belongings, dumped them on his bedroom floor, and went through them piece by piece. Crumpled up on the bottom of Wendell's dirty-laundry bag, I finally found the letter. No one knew how it got there. Unperturbed, Wendell smoothed the wrinkled envelope and put it in his pocket.

When the car arrived for him Barnes and I told Wendell not to forget that we, too, wanted to meet Stalin after his private talk. "Get him to send the car back for us when the private visit is over," we urged. "Okay," Wendell said. "Don't go to bed and I'll do the best I can."

At four in the morning we got our call. The timing was not unusual because Stalin preferred to work from midnight until six a.m. That was his regular schedule, and not only during the war years. The car picked us up and drove us to the Kremlin. We were taken to Stalin's office, where we met him and Molotov, his foreign minister. The office was a good-sized room, its walls covered with pictures of Marx, Lenin and Engels. A huge globe stood in a small adjoining room. Stalin was shorter (about five feet four or five) and stockier than I expected him to be. His face was hard and tough-looking and, not surprisingly, he looked very tired.

Years later, when I went back to the Kremlin to interview Khrushchev for *LOOK*, I was able to make a comparison between the two Russian leaders. They were total opposites in personality and temperament.

81

Khruschev reminded me of General David Sarnoff, the longtime head of RCA. In fact, I think if Khushchev had been brought to the United States as a child—as Sarnoff had been—he might also have ended up running a large corporation. He was ebullient, talkative, outgoing, and candid. Stalin seemed to me a completely different breed of cat. I found him aloof, suspicious, and cunning, I never would have trusted him.

Stalin was not a man given to small talk, and after fifteen minutes we knew it was time to leave. We had our pictures taken with him and Molotov, and left to be driven back to the guest house. Willkie, though, saw Stalin at least four times, twice for two long, private talks. Those talks, I think, had considerable influence on Stalin. Stalin was certain that Roosevelt and Churchill had secretly decided between them to delay establishing a second front against the Germans. Their hope, Stalin apparently thought, was that the Germans would destroy the Communist regime in Russia. Great Britain and the United States would then have a free hand, after defeating the Germans, to set the terms of the peace. Willkie tried to convince Stalin that the Allied delay in establishing the second front derived from the time lag in gearing up America's war production apparatus. As Willkie had told the Turks, once we were operating at full speed, we would throw everything we had at Hitler and defeat him. I think Willkie went a long way toward assuaging Stalin's doubts abut American and British intentions

AN UNAMUSED STALIN

During the days while we were in Moscow, we often toured around the city. One scene remains particularly fresh in my mind. For the first time in my life, I saw men and women standing in block-long queues to buy newspapers. The Russian people have always been voracious readers, and the daily newspapers, all with huge circulations, could not meet the demand. For a newspaper publisher, it was a truly heart-warming sight. Later, when we landed in Tashkent, our first stop after Moscow, we were surprised that though we were the first Americans to visit the Central Asian city in many years, we were practically ignored even by our official hosts. The reason was that they had discovered our plane had brought the latest Moscow papers.

Our evenings in Moscow were spent attending several state banquets with vast quantities of superb food and wines. We were amazed at the amount of official entertaining the Russians were able to manage even during the darkest days of the war.

The dinner Stalin gave for Willkie and our party was especially sumptuous. I was seated between two Soviet generals. Through an interpreter—one was behind every third chair or so—they promptly announced they were going to drink me under the table. I laughed, but warily. The Russians are confirmed drinkers: during a toast, it is considered proper to completely drain one's glass of vodka. But I was able to hold my liquor very well in those days, and miraculously, at the conclusion of the dinner the generals were sound asleep on either side of me, their heads resting on the table.

When Stalin and Willkie left the table to take their coffee in an adjoining room, I followed them. I took Stalin by the arm and pointed back into the dining room. With a broad smile I told him of the generals' challenge to me and that I had survived while the generals had passed out. I was instantly sorry I had mentioned it because Stalin was clearly not amused. He barked instructions to a couple of aides and four waiters soon carried the generals out of the dining room.

To assuage his anger, I switched the subject to his generosity as a host. Our guest house had been provided with several large bowls of caviar. I thanked him and told him that I adored Russian caviar. Through the interpreter came the response: "Mr. Cowles, you insult me! I wouldn't think of serving Russian caviar. What you have eaten is Iranian caviar. It's the only decent caviar in the world!"

Another victim of Stalin's wrath that night was Sir Clarke-Kerr, the British Ambassador to Russia and one of the guests at the banquet. Stalin let loose a blast at Winston Churchill and Roosevelt for postponing the opening of the second front. But, to Stalin, Churchill was the particular villain. During a long speech Stalin quoted facts and figures to prove his point that the British were withholding—stealing, he said—war materiel earmarked for the Russians and as a consequence causing the needless deaths of thousands of Russians. A pale and shaken Sir Clarke-Kerr rose to defend the British position. The British had been taking enormous losses getting the convoys through attacks by German bombers, he said. Churchill was loath to continue shipping large quantities of supplies when he desperately needed these things to protect London. Nothing the British Ambassador said seemed to make any difference to Stalin, who just sat there grinning.

The climax of the remarkable evening was a thirty-minute screening of the most brutal propaganda film I have ever seen. Very shortly after that long and lavish banquet, we found ourselves watching a seemingly endless succession of German atrocities including such scenes as German soldiers cutting off a baby's head and blood spurting out of the stump of the neck. It was a struggle not to throw up in the screening room.

It was not until we were headed back to the United States that I remembered to ask Wendell how Stalin had reacted to Roosevelt's letter. "My God," he exclaimed, "I forgot to give it to him!" I heard later that Wendell had given the letter to his very good friend Irita Van Doren, editor of the book section of *The New York Herald Tribune*. Irita died in 1966 and I have no idea what happened to it after that. What did Roosevelt have to say to Stalin that was so important it had to be handed over personally by Willkie? We will probably never know.

A STOP AT YAKUTSK

From Moscow we flew to Yakutsk, the capital of the Siberian republic of Yakutsk. We could see the subtle changes in the character of the landscape which soon became mile after mile of dense, snow-covered forests. We had expected to stop only briefly there before flying on to our first stop in China: Tihwa, called Urumchi by the Russians. However, when we landed we were informed that bad flying weather was going to delay us for at least a day, if not longer. A man who introduced himself as Muratov, President of Yakutsk Soviet Socialist Republic, seemed cheered by the bad weather report because it was going to give him an opportunity to show the Americans the great achievements of socialism in this Siberian outpost.

"What would you like to see, Mr. Willkie?" he asked as we drove toward the town.

Willkie mentioned the first thing that came to his mind. "Have you a library?"

Muratov bridled. "Certainly we have a library," he said sternly. He gave some rapid instructions to the driver and we were driven directly to the library. It was an old, well-lighted and well-staffed building. In a town of fifty thousand people the library housed 550,000 books!

Before 1917, Muratov told us later, only two percent of all the people of Yakutsk were literate; ninety-eight percent could not read or write. Now the figures were exactly reversed.

"Moreover," he went on smiling, "I have now received an order from Moscow to liquidate the two percent illiteracy before the end of next year." He obviously intended to accomplish that order. A tough-looking if pleasant son of a peasant farmer and at only 37 running a republic twice the size of Alaska, Muratov did not seem a man whose intentions one casually doubted.

We were taken to the only hotel in town, a new building made of logs, with a Russian stove in each room. However, there were no private toilet facilities or running water. Just as in any old-fashioned back-country farm or inn, a big basin and a pitcher of water was set out for washing. At the end of a corridor was the public toilet for the floor. In the large room a throne-like chair had been placed on a platform and a large hole had been cut in the chair's seat. Underneath, sat an enormous chamber pot. At either end of the platform motherly peasant women squatted day and night. After you completed your efforts on the throne the ladies would nod and smile approvingly.

With the usual Russian hospitality, Muratov laid on an enormous dinner for our party. Siberia being a cold country, every meal, even breakfast, included vodka so potent that the Russians themselves had to water it. Whether this was their daily fare we had no way of knowing, but we were served a whole roast pig at breakfast, plus sausages, eggs,

84

cheeses, soup, chicken, veal, and the inevitable potatoes and cabbage—all of which was washed down with hot tea and vodka.

At dinner Muratov seemed like he would never let up singing the praises of socialist accomplishment, with statistical accompaniment. He sounded like a first-rate American Chamber of Commerce promoter. I tried a ploy to divert the increasingly tedious monologue. "Is there a theater in Yakutsk?" I asked. Indeed, there was, and he promised to take us to a performance after dinner. By eleven o'clock Muratov's words were still flowing endlessly, on a river of vodka. A bit impatient, I pressed with a further question. "What time did you say the show started?" He poured himself another drink and answered, "The show starts when I get there."

A half hour later we entered our box and the curtain went up. A Leningrad touring company gave an excellent performance of a gypsy opera.

No matter where we went in our quick sweep across the country, big cities or hamlets, collective farms or factories, I sensed one fundamental, centuries-old Russian quality common to all the people—a deep love and appreciation of music, dancing, and literature. Sadly, the fiats issued by their Communist rulers on what was and what was not "socialist realism" have suppressed though not destroyed the great artistic, creative force of these people.

THE BACK WAY TO CHINA

We came into China through the back way and not through the "treaty ports" on the Pacific—Shanghai, Hong Kong, Canton—which were all under the control of the Japanese at the time. They had displaced, temporarily at least, earlier generations of Western powers who had dominated and plundered the fabulously rich coastline of China.

Tihwa was tucked into the northwest corner of Sinkiang and was the capital of that huge province. It was the point at which Russia and China met and thus of great political and strategic importance to both countries. The street signs were in Russian, the government was Chinese, and the people a mixture of both. We dined with the Chinese governor of the province and the Soviet consul general. The town seemed pervaded by an atmosphere of intrigue and suspicion, probably based on the uneasy alliance between the two countries during the war. But there was no question about the sincere good will and admiration for America here and everywhere in China.

As a formal welcome to China, Generalissimo Chiang Kai-shek, head of the Nationalist government, had sent two of his closest personal friends to accompany us on the remainder of our trip through the country—Dr. Hollington K. Tong, Vice-Minister of Information, and General Chu Shao-Liang.

85

The flight from Tihwa to Chunkging, the wartime capital of China, took us over some of the most breaktakingly beautiful landscapes I have ever seen. Snow-covered mountain ranges, miles of desert, red loam hills, cultivated green fields unfolded beneath us like a slowly opening fan.

We arrived in Chungking late in the afternoon at an airport about ten miles from the city. We were unprepared for the friendly mass demonstration that awaited us. Our motorcade drove slowly into the city along a road lined with thousands upon thousands of men, women, and children, all waving little paper Chinese and American flags. As far as the eye could see, on all the hills of this very hilly city, people stood and cheered and waved their flags. Even if they didn't know who Wendell Willkie was—they may have mistaken him for the President of the United States—we were the first Americans most of them had even seen and the show of friendship was a deeply moving experience for us.

The magnificent modern home of T.V. Soong, Madame Chiang Kai-shek's brother, was our headquarters for our six-day stay. It was equipped with all sorts of luxurious trappings, as well as dozens of perfect servants to attend to our needs.

The six days were filled with long daily talks between Willkie and the Generalissimo, visits with many officials, and nightly banquets given by the Generalissimo and Madame. One evening the mayor of Chungking was the official host. I had had an upset stomach from something I had eaten the day before and was picking my way carefully through the numerous courses. The mayor rose to make the usual speech, and through the interpreter we learned there was a special treat in store for us. As the American guests probably did not know, came the translation, an outbreak of cholera in the area had forced the authorities to pass an ordinance making it a criminal offense to use dairy products. But in honor of Mr. Willkie and his party, the mayor said he was pleased to announce that he had repealed the ordinance for just this day so that "we could serve you ice cream tonight." We ducked the ice cream as best we could and prayed that our anti-cholera inoculations were in good working order.

Among our many unforgettable experiences was a trip to the front where China was defending itself against the Japanese army. Our guide was Dr. "Holly" Tong, a graduate of the Columbia School of Journalism. Holly had been an important newspaper publisher before becoming Minister of Information. He was also the Generalissimo's translator, secretary, and close personal adviser. Willkie was very keen on seeing the front and had to press "Holly" to get permission from Chiang. The Generalissimo's reluctance was apparently due to his concern for our safety.

We flew to Sian, one of the old capitals of China, not far from the Yellow River. We drove some miles out of the city and then climbed, by the light of lanterns strung out along a mountain path, to one of the military academies where many of the famous Chinese revolutionary leaders had received their training in the early 1930's. That night while we slept in sleeping cars, we traveled on one of the few remaining railroads left intact in China. Before daybreak we were taken by handcars along track laid on the Great Wall of China. We sat on the equivalent of a park bench which had been bolted to the front of the handcar. It was very cold and we were given a heavy chinchilla robe to wrap around us. Four men pumped the handcar along for about fifteen miles. We finally reached the Yellow River, the no man's land between the Chinese and the Japanese forces.

I wanted to know why the Chinese had been able to endure five years of bitter fighting with the Japanese and still hold them at a standstill at the borders. The Chinese arsenal was made up of an astonishing assortment of the most primitive and the most modern fighting material. The army was led by West Point-trained professionals who, in turn, trained disciplined, dedicated men ranging from crack units, graduates of the national military academies, to eight-year-old Boy Scouts. We were impressed by the determination and the will of the Chinese to rid themselves of the foreign invaders.

In some respects, however, there seemed to be an unreal quality to the war that one would never find on the battlefields of Western Europe. For example, we learned that there was some very active commercial trading going on between the Japanese and the Chinese across the Yellow River. Also, we suspected that some of the shooting we heard as we left an area and then approached another had been staged to show us that vigorous fighting had been going on all along that front. In fact, the front may have been relatively dormant.

The Japanese never were able to penetrate past the Yellow River in northern China, though they did occupy large portions of the country. Yet despite massive aid from the United States, the Nationalist government was badly weakened by the eight long years of warfare with the Japanese and proved unable to resist a more potent internal challenge from the Communists under Mao Tse-tung.

MADAME CHIANG AND WILLKIE

Before the Communist takeover, family dynasties ruled China for many centuries. Few, though, have left a greater mark on recent Chinese history—for better or for worse, depending on which history book you read—than the Soong family. T.V. Soong and his three sisters, all educated in America, literally shaped the future of China until their downfall with the collapse of the Nationalist government. T.V. was China's Foreign Minister. Mei-ling was Chiang Kai-shek's wife—and was said to be the sister who loved power. Ai-ling was the wife of Finance

Minister Hsiang-hsi K'ung—and the sister who loved money. Ch'ing-ling was the wife of Sun Yat-sen, founder of the Chinese Republic. She was active in the Nationalist government after his death and was said to be the sister who loved China. I met all three sisters during our visit, but it was Madame Chiang who most fascinated me—and Wendell.

One evening back in Chungking, the Generalissimo gave an enormous reception for us. It took place in a vast hall and it seemed as though thousands of people had been invited. The Generalissimo and the Madame made a dramatic entrance, walked to a platform at the far end of the hall and to applause seated themselves on two throne-like chairs. After a few welcoming remarks, the Generalissimo, the Madame, and Willkie formed a receiving line. About an hour later, as I was mingling in the crowd, a Chinese aide appeared beside me with a summons from Wendell. As unobtrusively as I could I appeared behind Willkie. He whispered that he and the Madame were disappearing in a few minutes and that I was to take his place and cover up for them as best I could. Sure enough, ten minutes later they were gone.

I stationed myself alongside the Generalissimo and unleashed a flurry of questions about China every time I felt his attention wandering. He stayed at the reception for another hour and then suddenly clapped his hands to summon his aide. He was leaving, and I decided to do the same. My aide took me back to the Soong house where we were staying. Finding myself quite alone, I poured myself a Scotch, a rarity in wartime China which was selling at the American PX in Chungking at $100 a quart. The Madame had generously sent it over when I told her that I could not drink the Chinese rice wine. It tasted and smelled of ether, and reminded me of hospitals.

I wondered where Wendell and the Madame had gone. By nine o'clock, I began to worry. I told the servants to go ahead with dinner for one. Shortly after dinner there was a great clatter in the courtyard. The Generalissimo stormed in, visibly furious. He was accompanied by three bodyguards, each carrying a little Tommy gun. Trying to restrain his rage, the Generalissimo bowed coldly and I returned the bow.

"Where's Willkie?" he asked when the amenities were over.

"I have absolutely no idea. He's not there in the house." I followed this with a quick invitation to have tea with me. I had been in China just long enough to know that to refuse an invitation to tea was an offense.

Impatiently, he shouted to the servants to bring tea. We drank quickly and in silence. As soon as he gulped his tea, we repeated the bowing routine.

"Where's Willkie?" he again demanded to know.

"I assure you, Generalissimo, he is not here and I do not know where he could be," I told him firmly and, as it happened, honestly.

With me and the bodyguards in his wake, the Generalissimo stormed through the house. He searched every room, looking under beds and opening closets. Satisfied at last that the two were not in the house, he took his leave without a parting word.

Now I was really scared. I had visions of Wendell in front of a firing squad. Unable to sleep, I just sat up, drinking by myself, expecting the worst. At four o'clock in the morning, a very bouyant Willkie appeared, cocky as a young college student after a successful night with a girl. After giving me a play by play account of what had happened between him and the Madame, he concluded blithely that he had invited the Madame to return to Washington with us. I exploded. "Wendell, you're just a goddam fool!" I exclaimed angrily.

I enumerated all the arguments against this mad idea. I agreed with him wholeheartedly that Madame Chiang was one of the most beautiful, intelligent, and sexy women either one of us had ever met. I could understand the tremendous attraction between these two charismatic people. But there was already considerable gossip about them among the press corps in Chungking. Then I said, "You represent the President of the United States here. You want to be nominated again in '44 and you want to be elected the next President." His wife and son would probably meet him at the airport in Washington, I added, and the presence of the Madame would be a considerable embarrassment. Willkie angrily stomped off to bed. I was pretty exhausted by then, and I retired too.

I was up at about eight and found Willkie already having breakfast. We ate in silence. He had a speech to make at nine o'clock, and as he got up to leave, he turned to me and said, "Mike, you're going to see the Madame and tell her that she cannot fly back to Washington with us."

"Where will I find her?" I asked.

Sheepishly, he gave me the information. "She has an apartment on the top floor of the Women's and Children's Hospital here in town. It's her pet charity." I subsequently learned that the Madame had her private secret service to protect her, quite apart from the Generalissimo's, and that with this protection Willkie and the Madame had gone to her apartment at the hospital the night before.

I went to the hospital about eleven and asked to see the Madame. When I was ushered into her sitting room I told her bluntly she could not fly back to Washington with Mr. Willkie.

"Who says I can't?" she asked.

"I do," I said. "I told Wendell that he could not take you along because it would be unwise politically for Mr. Willkie to do so."

Before I knew what was happening she reached up and scratched her long fingernails down both my cheeks so deeply that I had marks for about a week.

About four months later, Madame Chiang came to the United States alone on an official visit, bringing her own linen and a large contingent of servants. In New York she engaged an entire floor at the Waldorf Towers.

89

A BLACK-TIE INVITATION

One morning I received a call at my OWI office in Washington from the Chinese ambassador. The Madame wanted me to come to a black-tie dinner that evening in her Waldorf Towers apartment. I was expected at eight-thirty. It was most inconvenient for me to dash up to New York and, besides, I had to get an appropriate permit during the war to fly on a commercial airline. But I did make it to New York, decked myself out in black tie, and showed up at the Waldorf on time.

I was met in the lobby by the Madame's major domo, who escorted me to her floor. The door to her suite was opened by the same butler who had taken care of Willkie and me in the T.V. Soong house in Chungking. "Madame begs your pardon, Mr. Cowles," he said. "She's going to be a few minutes late. I recall that you prefer Scotch and water." A Chinese waiter appeared with a Scotch and water on a silver tray. I accepted the drink, sat down and wondered what would come next. Madame appeared in an exquisite gown, greeted me warmly, and said, "Shall we go to dinner?" I realized it was to be a private tete-a-tete.

Four servants were stationed in the dining room, one at each corner. "Don't be nervous about the servants, Mike," she smiled. "None of them understands English. We can speak freely." But not until we had finished eating did she get around to the reasons for the invitation.

Her marriage to the Generalissimo, she began, was one of convenience that had been arranged by her mother. As in many such marriages, the bride and groom scarcely knew one another. On their wedding night the Generalissimo told her that he did not believe in sexual relations except for the purpose of producing a child. And since he already had a son by a previous marriage and was not interested in having any more children, there would be no sex between them. I wasn't sure whether I believed all of this, but I kept listening.

That revelation was only a warmup. It was time now for serious business. She was convinced that Willkie could be nominated again for the presidency in 1944. It was my duty, she told me, to give up whatever I was doing and devote myself exclusively to getting him the 1944 Republican nomination. I was to spend whatever amount of money I thought was necessary. She would reimburse me for all expenditures. With the intuitive sense of timing of the born pitchman she wound up her sales talk with a remark I shall never forget: "You know, Mike, if Wendell could be elected, then he and I would rule the world. I would rule the Orient and Wendell would rule the Western world." And she stressed the word *rule*.

It was a totally mad proposal, of course. But I was so mesmerized by clearly one of the most formidable women of the time that this evening I would not have dismissed anything she said.

As it turned out, Willkie decided to make a run for the presidency in

1944 without Madame Chiang. He was buoyed by the great success of *One World*, a book he wrote with Joe Barnes' help about our trip. It also expressed Wendell's longstanding belief that narrow nationalism had become obsolete in an increasingly small world, that barriers between nations and races had to be broken down, and that the United States should lead the way in creating a new society of free and independent nations. Though these were not widely popular views at the time, the book became a best-seller and sold a million copies.

In the spring of 1944, Wendell, against my advice, ran in the Wisconsin primary and suffered a terrible defeat. He withdrew, and Tom Dewey, the leading Republican contender, got the nomination. Some months later, Wendell arranged a meeting with me in New York at which he gave me some startling news: he had just met with Harold Ickes, who relayed a request from Roosevelt that he join the Democratic ticket as the Vice Presidential candidate. Willkie was seriously considering the offer. I told him it would be an insult to the millions of Republicans who had supported him so ardently in 1940. He bought my advice.

Shortly before the election, he suffered a heart attack, and at the age of 52 he died. It was a terrible loss for me and his many friends—and for the country.

It was with a sense of sadness, and of pride, that I accepted an invitation to speak, on February 18, 1950, at ceremonies in which a plaque in memory of Wendell was dedicated at the State House in Indianapolis. Here is what I said in full on that occasion:

"If Wendell Willkie is watching us here today, he is very happy. For Wendell loved Indiana. He loved his home town of Elwood. He loved his county Madison. He loved his farms at Rushville. He loved the State University he attended.

"The greater he became as a national leader and a world figure, the more he was impelled to think back over his early life here in the Midwest, and the life of his parents and his friends and neighbors. And the more he pondered on the *reasons* why America had earned the most freedom, the most liberty, and the highest standard of living, the more convinced he became that people everywhere should have a chance to progress toward this same freedom and abundant living.

"Wendell Willkie wanted all the world to have the good life the people of Indiana have. He had the faith that that miracle could be accomplished.

"I know these things because they are the things Wendell talked about, for hours on end, in the autumn of 1942, when I had the unforgettable privilege of being his companion on his flight around the world. I know them because he talked about them many times thereafter, in many places and on many occasions, before his sudden death.

"That the people of his home county, Madison, and particularly the

91

school children, should want to present this bronze plaque to the State of Indiana in his memory, would, I know, make him proud. For it would reaffirm to him that his ideas, his principles, his impassioned faith, are growing in the hearts and minds of America.

"Wendell Willkie died nearly five and a half years ago. That seems hard to believe. For those who knew him can still feel the strength and the conviction of his personality. And yet, enough time has passed for us to gain some sense of that historical perspective, that measure of time, which appraises the stature of men. History judges a man by how well he comprehended the central issues of his time, by how much he influenced the crucial decisions of his day, by how significantly he shaped the destiny of his age. By these standards Wendell Willkie's place in history is surely secure.

"He was a national figure for less than five years, a world figure for less than four. That is a short time in which to leave an imprint on the world. Yet when he died, men everywhere on the face of the globe—men of white skins and dark, men of many different tongues, men whose lands and customs and faiths were alien to us—sensed that they had suffered a personal loss. They grieved for a friend. They mourned for a champion who had fought for what they know, or for what they vaguely sensed, was right and just and sound. Could any man hope for a greater memorial?

"Many people forget how right Wendell Willkie was on the great issues of our times. Let's take a minute and call the roll:

"He first achieved national fame as the most articulate spokesman of private enterprise when bureaucracy from Washington threatened to change the United States. He foresaw the danger which unhampered federal power represented to a nation built on the idea of individual freedom. His own life had taught him that it was freedom of opportunity, *individual freedom*, which had made America great. He awoke the country in a great crusade which stopped Washington from smothering the initiative and stifling the dynamics of private business.

"He understood what many still forget, that only by producing more and more can we improve our standard of living. He wanted a better life for all with freedom. History will long remember the rallying cry: 'Only the productive can be strong, only the strong can be free.' Now the whole world is beginning to realize the truth of those words: 'Only the strong can be free.'

"When Hitler started his mad war of conquest, Willkie understood instantly that if Western Europe and England lost their freedom, our freedom too would be in jeopardy. This thought is so commonplace today, we forget how unpopular it was in 1939. Yet Willkie cried out about the danger of Hitler, with passion and eloquence, when he was warned from every side that it would mean his political death.

"I shall never forget the pressures on Willkie in the midst of the 1940 campaign when he was running for the presidency of the United States.

Remember that was long before Pearl Harbor. Strong elements of the Republican Party wanted him to preach isolationism. They wanted him to charge that Franklin Roosevelt was deliberately and unnecessarily leading us into war. The temptation on Willkie was enormous. The temper of the country was such at the time that a campaign of that sort might have given Willkie the election.

"But he refused to be a hypocrite. He refused to compromise. He refused to say what he did not believe. He knew the United States might have to get into the war to save freedom. It is to Willkie's eternal credit that *he* was not the candidate in the 1940 campaign who promised the American public that American boys would never be sent into a war in a foreign land.

"Wendell Willkie fought for the minority groups in the United States because he knew it was the just thing to do, but also with statesmanlike vision he realized that the United States could not have moral leadership in fighting for justice 'round the world if she did not practice it at home.

AN END TO IMPERIALISM

"Early in the war and almost alone among leaders of the Western world he called for an end to imperialism. He denounced exploitation of the weaker nations by the stronger. He lamented the fact that the Atlantic Pact by its very name seemed to ignore the half of the world's population living between the Red Sea and the Yellow River.

"He pleaded for greater and greater international trade so the living standards of all could be raised. Paul Hoffman today, sweating to make the European recovery program succeed, is repeating Willkie's prophecies of ten years ago—that we cannot achieve a prosperous and stable Europe unless the trade barriers are torn down and that continent becomes one economic unit.

"Willkie with uncanny insight foresaw our present troubles with Russia. He urged time and time again that we settle on the terms of the peace *during the war* when our bargaining power was at its height. He recalled that through all history allies always quarrel after a war's end unless the peace terms have been firmly spelled out before the enemy collapses. How tragic that his advice went unheeded!

"After his visit to Russia in the fall of 1942, he sensed that the Soviet government would attempt to overrun her neighbors after Germany was destroyed. I recall a long conversation we had in the plane while flying over the ancient route of the silk caravans from Southern Russia into China.

" 'We must get through to the Russian people,' Willkie kept saying. 'They're pretty much just like the folks back home. They want peace and a good living and a chance for their children. We can get along with them if they just *understand* America.'

93

"But then he kept worrying about the Russian leaders. When he was talking with Stalin, Molotov, Vishinsky, and other members of the Politburo, he had detected in them a rebirth of the brutality and imperialism of the old Czarist governments. He kept exploring in his mind during the long flight from Moscow to Chungking how Russia could be bound *during the war* to participate after the war in a real league of nations which would be strong enough to preserve the peace, a union of nations strong enough to promote more equality between the 'have' nations and the 'have-not' nations, and strong enough to break down trade barriers so all people might have a chance at a rising standard of living.

"Wendell Willkie believed so passionately in true democracy and in the dignity of the individual, he never feared that men, given a choice, would turn voluntarily to communism. He felt only men who had lost hope of ever gaining a better way of life would be attracted to communism. Thus he reasoned, that the way to kill the spread of communism was to construct a peace which would give all mankind both hope and an active chance to improve their lot. 'The best answer to communism,' he wrote, 'is a living, vibrant, fearless democracy—economic, social, and political. All we need to do is stand up and perform according to our professed ideals. Then those ideals will be safe.'

"A few cynics and critics like to call Wendell Willkie naive because he talked of 'One World.' I say he was wise before his time. We are living in fear today and spending one-fourth of our income preparing for war just because it actually is 'one world,' but man has not learned how to achieve and maintian 'one world' law and order.

"Willkie spoke to the heart of the great issues of our times—and he spoke with wisdom and faith and hope. The world is better because of what he did and said. History will recall that he lost an election. But history will also say that he won greatness.

"I am proud to join with you in honoring his memory."

THE POST-WAR YEARS

After spending 49 days circling the globe with Wendell Willkie, my OWI job in Washington seemed even more unsatisfying than before. I became restless and anxious to return to publishing. When I mentioned the idea to Roosevelt, he reluctantly agreed to let me go—so long as I found an appropriate successor, in other words a Republican who supported his foreign policy. After something of a selling job, I recruited E. Palmer Hoyt, then editor of the *Portland Oregonian* and later editor of the *Denver Post*.

In 1940, I had moved most of the *LOOK* staff, except for the subscription department, from Des Moines to New York City where most large magazine publishers have their offices. When I left Washington in 1943, nevertheless, I decided to return to Des Moines instead of working out of New York. For one thing, my father was now in his eighties and not well. With my brother John spending most of his time in Minneapolis, I figured I should take as much pressure off Father as I could.

For another, *LOOK* was thriving. It was in what seemed to be the very capable hands of Harlan Logan, whom I had named general manager in 1940. Hiring Logan had been a key part of my effort to professionalize *LOOK*, to inject greater maturity into the amateurish management that characterized *LOOK*'s early years and very nearly did us in. Logan's credentials were impressive indeed: a Phi Beta Kappa graduate of Indiana University and brilliant intellectual, he had spent two years as a Rhodes Scholar before returning to the U.S. to teach journalism at New York University. In one of his NYU courses, he developed a project whereby he and his students would analyze a large number of magazines and criticize their contents. Seeing that the exercise might have commercial as well as pedagogical value, he began offering the service to

97

magazines for a fee. Soon he became acclaimed as a kind of magazine doctor with an impressive record of restoring ailing small circulation magazines to health. In my initial discussions with him, he had impressed me with numerous ideas for improving *LOOK*. As general manager, Logan had jurisdiction over all departments and the central responsibility to build the magazine into the respected and successful publication I wanted it to become.

The fact that *LOOK* had been doing so well in my absence cannot be credited completely to Logan. Due to the rapid flow of news during the war, people were eager buyers of newspapers and magazines. And due to the booming wartime economy, advertisers were eager to buy space. Rationing of paper, though, made it impossible for any of the major magazines to print enough pages and copies to meet the circulation and advertising demand. Basically, you could sell whatever you could put on the newsstand.

Looking back on the Logan era, though, I'm convinced his contributions were substantial. Not only did he inject sorely needed professionalism, but he encouraged me to think in "big league" terms, as it were, instead of in the manner of a provincial Iowa publisher. During the early years, I was excessively cost-conscious and frightened about the amount of money it took to publish a national magazine, and my attitude unwittingly influenced the staff to think small. Logan, who always thought big, helped me to get used to regarding annual expenditures in the millions, rather than thousands, of dollars. During 1937, *LOOK*'s first year, our total cost—including editorial, production, circulation, and everything else—amounted to $889,000. By 1947, the figure had jumped to $4,785,000.

It was largely through Logan's encouragement that in 1942 we began transforming our annual Movie Awards—*LOOK*'s version of the Academy Awards—from brief radio announcements into gigantic Hollywood extravaganzas, and one of the most effective promotional schemes we ever had. Jean Herrick, who ran our Hollywood office, obtained the cooperation of the studios that had the winning stars and pictures, arranged to have the winners broadcast during the Bob Hope Show, then the number-one rated radio show, and secured as the site of the broadcast the Cathay Theater, where many of the great Hollywood pictures had premiered.

My brother John and I arrived at the theater late in the afternoon preceding one of these presentations, and I vividly remember the vast panoply of trucks, searchlights, and bleachers, and the block-long red carpet lined by flowers. With no small amount of disquiet, I wondered how much all of this was going to cost. And that was just the beginning. After the broadcast, we hosted a big party at Ciro's, a posh nightclub, for about 400 guests and 100 gate crashers. Duke Ellington's band performed, as did many impromptu acts, and the festivities didn't wind up until after 3 a.m. Some people there said it was the greatest show of its kind that Hollywood had ever seen.

"Jean, how much did that cost last night?" my brother John asked Herrick the next morning.

"I haven't got all the bills in yet," Jean replied, "but I think it's probably in the vicinity of $15,000."

While Jean with evident nervousness waited for the reaction, John leaned over and said, "If anybody asks you, say $25,000."

John was making an effort to think big, and so was I, but I have to admit I had a hard time at first believing that we would ever be able to recoup all that money with the sale of additional copies of *LOOK*.

For all of his positive influence on the magazine, though, Harlan Logan was gradually precipitating a series of personality and policy clashes that badly impeded our progress and forced me to abandon my absentee management role and take over direct control of the magazine.

Logan's first clash was with Vernon Pope, one-time editor of the *Des Moines Tribune*'s picture page, whom I had brought in to help me launch *LOOK* and who was still editing the magazine from Des Moines. It is difficult to imagine two more disparate individuals. Partly because of his academic background, Logan took a highly structured approach to the editorial process. He held a lot of meetings with extensive agendas, formed task forces to make studies, conducted elaborate surveys to ascertain readers' reactions. In his hiring he not surprisingly tended to avoid established editorial professionals in favor of individuals with impressive academic achievements, including numerous former teachers and scholars with M.A.'s and Ph.D.'s.

Pope, by contrast, was relatively unschooled and cared little about academic credentials. A native of Delmont, South Dakota, he attended Yankton College for a short time and then Drake University in Des Moines. He came to *The Register and Tribune* offering to work for next to nothing just to get the experience. We started him as an office boy at $10 a week, but he didn't stay in the job for long for we soon found he possessed an innate talent as a picture editor, and he was without question among the best I have ever known.

Pope's approach to organizational structures at *LOOK* was unstructured and casual, and that horrified Logan who, being the senior man in 1942, summarily fired Pope because, he said, he couldn't make *LOOK* into the kind of magazine he thought it should be as long as Pope occupied the top editorial spot.

Retaining the title of general manager, Logan named himself editor, and the magazine's fundamental editorial philosophy began to shift. Before Logan's arrival, Pope and Dan Mich, our senior New York editor who worked directly under Pope, had greatly upgraded our editorial quality. Our printing, art direction and paper were still markedly substandard, which was certainly the major reason we weren't taken as seriously in the field as we should have been, but I would match the caliber of our stories against any of our competitors.

Logan felt the magazine's job was not so much to excite or fascinate the reader as instruct him, to perform a service by showing the reader how to lead a better life. After the U.S. entered the war he felt *LOOK* should help people cope with wartime problems and should promote national patriotism, and series after series were devoted to accomplish these ends. They were certainly patriotic and probably helped build *LOOK*'s image as a prestige magazine. But in my opinion—and I'm sure in the opinion of millions of our readers—they were often dull and boring. They were particularly lackluster in contrast to *LIFE*. With its weekly periodicity and orientation toward spot news, *LIFE* was doing a magnificent job covering the war. It wasn't trying to teach anyone anything; it was simply reporting what was happening—and in often unforgettably vivid and dramatic detail. Practically every issue seemed to be more exciting than the one before. To my mind, *LIFE* during World War II was without question the most interesting magazine ever published.

LOOK'S prosaicness vis-a-vis *LIFE* didn't matter very much during the war, when we could sell every copy we could produce. But I worried what might happen after the war, when magazines would no longer necessarily enjoy the built-in profits of a seller's market. Logan seemed to feel that the wartime gravy train would continue forever. But I was sure *LOOK* would face stiff competition for advertising and circulation.

NO ROOM FOR SURPRISES

My concerns intensified as Logan's post-war editorial thrust began taking shape in 1946. Continuing to try to be more of an educator than an editor, he filled the magazine with how-to service features and the how-to approach soon became *LOOK*'s trademark, and I'm sure it achieved a very loyal following among readers. In fact, Logan was anticipating the format of many service magazines of the 1980s. In the 1940s, though, Logan was too far ahead of his time. Magazine readers were caught up with current events and national issues, and *LOOK*'s how-to articles struck me as too timeless, too removed from the news. Further, while *LOOK*'s competitors, especially *LIFE*, were always provocative and full of surprises—you never knew what to expect when you opened an issue of *LIFE* except that you would be intrigued—*LOOK*'s editorial format seemed too confining, too predictable. There was no room for editorial surprises.

Instructing readers in the pages of *LOOK* wasn't all that concerned Logan. Again perhaps prematurely anticipating the future, he resolved to create a huge new communications complex covering the whole field of visual arts, of which *LOOK* would be only a part. To coordinate these activities, he set up a separate department, formally titled Editorial Art

Research, which was popularly known to the staff as EAR. Actually it became a tail that wagged the entire *LOOK* dog. Under his direction, EAR launched a substantial book-publishing operation, produced a series of newsreels for distribution in movie houses, prepared extensive studies for "Project X," a photographic version of the *Reader's Digest*, and even dabbled in television, mainly some shows in conjunction with General Electric and built around *LOOK* features such as "Photocrime" and "Photoquiz."

Many if not most of these activities never got very far, and they consumed a great deal of money and manpower. At the peak of its activity, EAR had more employees than *LOOK*. And much more important, it received more managerial attention from Logan.

All of this gradually brought Logan into a clash with Dan Mich, whom he had promoted from managing editor to executive editor when Vernon Pope was discharged. *LOOK* was blessed with many talented editors during its history, but I rank Dan at the top of the list. I had discovered Mich almost by accident. While I had a high opinion of the editorial quality of the *Wisconsin State Journal*, of which Mich had been managing editor, I had not been interested in recruiting him until I was introduced to him during a Washington, D.C., meeting of the American Society of Newspaper Editors in 1937. We hit it off immediately, and after a day of discussions a few weeks later in Des Moines, I persuaded him to join *LOOK* as an associate editor. He soon became a jack-of-all-trades—writing sports stories, handling letters to the editor, editing text stories, going out on picture-story assignments—and whatever he undertook he performed with distinction.

Mich's editorial philosophy was much closer to that of Vernon Pope than Harlan Logan. Like Pope, he was anxious to surprise, enthrall, delight, and inform the reader. And he felt the magazine should be a personal dialogue between the writer, photographer and editor on a particular story. Though Logan tended to see the magazine as a lecturer addressing a group of students, Mich and Logan initially were good friends.

Yet as time went on, their relationship deteriorated. Completely caught up with *LOOK*'s performance, Mich came to resent Logan's preoccupation with and diversion of scarce financial resources to what he called "extracurricular" activities that didn't concern *LOOK*. Mich felt these pursuits could jeopardize *LOOK*'s future. And he chafed under Logan's increasingly dense organizational structure, with its tangle of committees and task forces and its seemingly unending succession of meetings, which he felt took up an inordinate amount of staff time.

I also was becoming more and more concerned about the way things were going in New York. It had always been my intention, after getting *LOOK* launched and on its feet, to play only a broad supervisory and policy role and delegate day-to-day authority to the senior editors and business-side executives. By 1946, though, both John and I found ourselves becoming progressively more involved with *LOOK* and injecting our own ideas into the decision-making. If Logan had had his way, I suspect, we would have kept all of our energies focused on the Des Moines and Minneapolis newspapers. But it was becoming clear that I would have to move my headquarters to New York and devote the major portion of my time to *LOOK*.

Matters began coming to a head one weekend in mid-1946 when Mich wrote a memo to Logan in which, as Mich later put it, "I protested that all this activity was curtailing production, holding down content for the magazine, and that I thought we should do something about it."

As a result of the Mich memo, and a later confrontation between the two at one of Logan's all-day editorial meetings, Logan and his top lieutenants presented me with a "manifesto" protesting against too much management by the absentee owners—meaning primarily John and me—and not enough management by the managers—meaning primarily him—who were on the scene.

If anything, the manifesto solidified my resolve to take personal on-the-scene charge of the situation. It was, however, a difficult decision for me to make. I felt a family responsibility to manage the Des Moines newspapers which, at that time, were the major assets of the Cowles family. As it turned out, my worries over the move were needless, because Kenneth MacDonald was the editor of the papers. I retained the title of publisher and Ken and I communicated regularly by phone and through my visits to Des Moines, which occurred about every six weeks. Later, my brother John and I decided to name Luther Hill publisher, and he served with great distinction in that capacity until his retirement in 1960, at which time Ken took over, both as editor and publisher, retiring in 1971.

Ken was an attractive and popular editor, with unusual ability and superb judgment. As an indication of his talents as a highly-respected and dedicated journalist he was elected president of the American Society of Newspaper Editors, a director of The Associated Press, and a member of the board making final decisions on the Pulitzer prizes.

Luther Hill (we called him "Hilly"), was a brother of Senator Lister Hill of Alabama. A 1919 graduate of West Point, he was in World War II from 1942 to 1946, ending his service as a Brigadier General and director of the War Department's Bureau of Public Relations.

I shall always be grateful to Ken and Hilly for easing my transition from Des Moines to New York, and for the assistance they gave me as I moved around in the newspaper, magazine, and broadcasting fields.

When I informed Logan I was moving to New York and would assume day-to-day command at *LOOK*, he refused to accept my decision. He said the continuation of his role at *LOOK* was essential to the magazine's future success, but I reaffirmed my intentions. It was inescapable that

Logan and I would have to part company. As part of our severance agreement, I turned over to him the rights to the extensive line of *LOOK* books that he had developed, and he went on to make quite a success of them. His talents, I think, were much better suited to book publishing than magazine publishing.

In addition to dropping book publishing, I abolished all other EAR activities.

Mich, who was now in firm editorial control directly under me, called a meeting of the staff—now numbering 103—and announced, "We are going to stick as close to what's going on as possible. We are going to have more reporting and less lecturing."

In retrospect, I may have been too quick to abolish all the projects Logan started, especially the book department. Acting too quickly, I must admit, has always been one of my faults. Years later, when we decided to get back into book publishing, just as many other magazine publishers had, we had to start from scratch. But at the time, I thought it was essential that we devote all of our time, talent, energy, and resources to improving *LOOK*. Our wartime growth—as Logan of course had repeatedly pointed out to me—had been impressive. Circulation had zoomed from 1,700,000 to 2,410,000. Ad revenue had zoomed even more from $750,000 in 1940 to $6 million in 1945 and an estimated $6,250,000 in 1946. But I remained very concerned about *LOOK*'s ability to survive, let alone prosper, in the much more competitive and problematical post-war environment. Even in retrospect, I'm convinced that if we had not focused solely on *LOOK* during this period, it might well have become just one more of the countless numbers of magazines consigned to the post-war publishing graveyard.

A NEW TEAM

It might have been somewhat difficult to convince them of it, considering the traumatic effect of all the operational shifts, but those who stayed were soon to enjoy the beginnings of *LOOK*'s heyday of prominence and prosperity.

As Logan was leaving, a number of individuals were joining or about to join *LOOK* who would play pivotal roles in creating its future success. Donald Perkins, whom I had moved to *LOOK* from *The Register* and *Tribune* and who had returned to *LOOK* after war leave, rose to become advertising manager. His colleague at *The Register* and *Tribune* Vernon Myers, who began at *LOOK* on the Cleveland advertising sales staff, later became *LOOK*'s publisher, president of the *LOOK* division of Cowles Communications, and a corporate officer.

Among Vern's many achievements, and certainly his most unusual one, was his pioneering work at *The Register* and *Tribune* and later at *LOOK* photographing and studying readers' eye movements and adapting his results for use by advertisers. From his research, we were able to show advertisers how to arrange headlines and other copy and how to place their ads to achieve maximum readership. For example, while advertisers traditionally requested right-hand pages, we found that the reader's eye, when he turns the page, invariably goes immediately to the left-hand page. One of our other studies examined people's behavior when they read Photocrime, a text and pictorial depiction of a crime containing key clues that was among the best-read of *LOOK*'s features. The reader typically would read Photocrime, turn to the back of the magazine to check the solution, and then go to the Photocrime page to see what clues he might have missed. Any ad positioned on the page opposite Photocrime thus had a good chance of a double exposure to the reader.

Perhaps Myers' most important finding concerned the claim by such text-oriented magazines as *Collier's* and *Saturday Evening Post* that since readers spent more time reading text magazines than picture magazines, ads in the text publications were better read and therefore more effective as well. Vern's research showed, however, that while readers did indeed take longer to read text magazines, they were often so interested in what they were reading, especially in the run-over pages in the back of the book where most of the accompanying ads typically appeared, that they barely glanced at the ads. In fact, the more compelling the story, the more difficult it was for advertising to compete against the text. Readers of picture magazines, on the other hand, were much more likely to notice ads while they were leafing through the photographs.

The importance of Vern's work to us went beyond specific research findings. It proved to be an extremely effective promotional tool. It was a terrific door-opener, gaining us access to advertisers and agencies at a time when *LOOK* was still not yet taken as seriously as we wanted it to be in the advertising community.

Vern Myer's replacement on the Cleveland ad sales staff was Thomas B. Shepard, Jr., who went on to have an equally illustrious career and become *LOOK*'s last publisher. My judgment on Tom, I should add, is not colored by the fact that he happened to be married to my niece, Nancy Kruidenier.

Among others who were added to the *LOOK* staff during the Logan regime were John F. Harding, who handled litigation for *LOOK* while in the trial department of Cravath, Swaine and Moore and who later became general counsel of Cowles Communications and one of its principle architects. He was among the most brilliant legal experts I have ever known.

After having served as chief of the press branch of the War Department's Bureau of Public Relations during the war, William B. Arthur joined *LOOK* as its only full-time Washington correspondent. Transferred later to New York, he served for 12 years as managing editor under Mich and became the editor following Dan's death in 1965.

Also rising rapidly through the ranks during this period was Marvin C. Whatmore. A native of Albia, Iowa and graduate of Drake University, Marvin first came to my attention in 1936 when I asked the business manager of *The Register* and *Tribune* to find me a young accountant. Marvin at the time was assistant auditor of the Iowa-Des Moines National Bank & Trust Company, making $27 a week. When we offered him a job, he refused to leave without a raise. We added another 50 cents and he came aboard. I still regard the day Marvin arrived as one of the luckier days in my life. He displayed a tremendous capacity to take on more and more responsibilities especially in areas such as advertising, circulation, and printing, and execute them superlatively—with dispatch, enthusiasm, and imagination. Switching to *LOOK* in 1937, he successively became office manager, assistant treasurer, treasurer, business manager, vice president and general manager, and finally chairman and chief executive of Cowles Communications. During *LOOK*'s last fifteen years, Marvin, more than I, deserves the credit for *LOOK*'s success. I doubt that I would ever have succeeded in the business without his extraordinary help and good judgment. But, again, I should add the disclaimer that my assessment of Marvin is not influenced by the fact that his daughter Sharon later became the wife of my son Gardner "Pat" Cowles III.

A FIRING THAT WAS A MISTAKE

Unfortunately, we didn't keep all the talent that was available to us during this period. Shortly after Harlan Logan became general manager, I made the mistake—for reasons I don't remember—of firing Ned Doyle as advertising manager of *LOOK*. Soon thereafter, the man who replaced Doyle fired another member of the ad sales staff by the name of Maxwell Dane. Ned Doyle and Maxwell Dane recovered from this setback to their careers. Together with a fellow named William Bernbach, they formed Doyle Dane Bernbach, which became one of the largest and most successful advertising agencies in the country.

Two new members of *LOOK*'s staff during this period deserve special attention: James Milloy and Fleur Fenton.

Jim Milloy first came to my attention shortly after John and I had purchased the *Minneapolis Star*. At the time, the *Star* had the smallest circulation and was the weakest of the three Minneapolis newspapers, and we were finding it almost impossible to get any national advertising. We had been struggling with the paper for about 18 months or so when Clarence Francis, the head of General Foods who had always been friendly to me, came to me and said, "Mike, I'm here as a spokesman for quite a few friends that you and John have among important national advertisers. It's obviously a mystery to you why you haven't been able to get any significant amount of national advertising in the *Minneapolis Star*, and I want to tell you the reason. There is a man in Washington named Jimmy Milloy who has been tremendously helpful to so many of us—and this is particularly true in the food field—who have had troubles with various government departments, such as the Department of Agriculture, and Jimmy absolutely refuses to take any compensation for the help he gives us. He won't even take any presents from us. He just says, 'All I ask is that when you advertise in Minneapolis, you put your advertising in the *Minneapolis Tribune*.' It's embarrassing to some of us who would like to help you and John with the *Minneapolis Star*. It would make life a great deal easier for all of us if you and John were to hire Milloy."

I flew down to Washington to see Milloy, learn about his arrangement with the *Tribune*, and try to get him to switch to Cowles. Milloy refused to consider moving. He explained he owed too much of a debt to Fred Murphy, publisher and dominant stockholder in the *Tribune*, who had promoted him from stringer to the chief statehouse reporter in charge of writing Murphy's own features for the *Tribune*. After Roosevelt's election in 1932, Milloy approached Murphy and said, "This New Deal is going to cause all kinds of troubles for national advertisers, and I think the *Tribune* could benefit if we were able to help them avoid the pitfalls that are bound to arise. I want to move to Washington. All I want you to do is pay me my present salary, rent a small office and give me a secretary, and then give me 18 months in Washington to see if I can't prove my thesis to you."

Milloy went to Washington in 1933, and by the time I met him a few years later he had proved his thesis and I'm sure beyond the wildest expectations of Murphy or anyone else in the *Tribune*. He assembled an extraordinary network of contacts both within government and among the most important national advertisers. He became intimately knowledgeable about the legislative process. For instance, he would immediately learn about a piece of legislation affecting General Foods and would then be able to arrange to introduce General Foods executives to those Congressmen with the most influence over the legislation. Perhaps most amazingly, he managed to operate without even a hint of anything shady. After he helped General Motors settle a tax case with the Internal Revenue Service one December, G.M. presented him with a Cadillac on Christmas morning. He sent it back the next day.

MILLOY JOINS THE ORGANIZATION

Though Milloy had turned my offer down, he did leave the door open for future discussions. About six months later, Fred Murphy died, which in effect put the *Tribune* on the market and John was able to work out a deal to acquire it. By the time the sale was arranged, Milloy was exploring several offers, and apparently he was under a good deal of pressure from some of his friends in the automotive industry to accept a job representing one of the Detroit newspapers. But after some fast talking on my part, he agreed to join the Cowles organization. He said he would be glad to do whatever he could to help our newspapers, but he made it clear he wanted to spend most of his time working for *LOOK*.

Milloy began bringing in key accounts virtually from the day he started working for us around 1941. Some of them—perhaps all of them—might have come in eventually, but I'm certain Milloy accelerated the process. One aspect of his method of operation, I was told, cost us some business too. He liked to deal directly with chief executive officers and other senior officials, which didn't win him many friends among the lower echelons at advertisers and agencies. But he more than compensated for that. He was especially effective in gaining *LOOK*'s acceptance by the large auto companies such as General Motors and Chrysler and by the major food concerns, such as General Foods, General Mills, Quaker Oats, and Standard Brands. Milloy was also effective during the war in getting us a favorable allotment of paper. While paper rationing forced other magazines to turn away advertising, we were able to run almost all the ads we received, which turned out to be a great windfall and kept *LOOK* solidly in the black.

Jean Herrick of our Hollywood office once told me a story that illustrated Milloy's influence. Shortly after the beginning of the war, Herrick was assigned to try to sign up some West Coast advertisers. Among his targets was California Packing Co., then a major California food products concern. He called on the account executive at McCann-Erickson, Calpac's agency, but was told, albeit politely, that it would probably be a long time before *LOOK* would be an acceptable medium for Calpac. Herrick nevertheless arranged to see Calpac's advertising manager, a man named Wilmot Rogers.

"How's my friend Jim Milloy?" Rogers asked Herrick when he walked into Rogers' office. Herrick had never met Milloy, but did what he could to give Rogers a run-down. Rogers was very cordial but seemed noncommittal and Herrick went back to his office and wrote a report saying that it would be several years before *LOOK* could expect any Calpac business. "At ten o'clock the next morning," Herrick told me later, "I had a call asking me about availabilities for space for the California Packing Co. and we went into an immediate schedule."

Milloy did well by us during his years at *LOOK*. When he joined us in 1941, he received a base salary of only $18,000. But at his request, we agreed to give him half of one percent of *LOOK*'s gross advertising revenue in excess of $2,000,000 up to $11,500,00 and a quarter of one percent over $11,500,000. At the time, our ad revenue was only $1,355,000, and I felt the contract represented something of a pipe dream on his part. Twenty-five years later, though, *LOOK*'s ad revenue went above $80 million, and Jimmy ended up making more money than anyone else in the company, including me. Yet as well as he did by us, we did even better by him. I can't begin even to estimate how many million dollars worth of advertising he brought to *LOOK*.

I first met Fleur Fenton in 1946 when she was executive vice president of Dorland, International-Pettinghill & Fenton advertising agency, which had been commissioned to do an ad campaign for *LOOK*. Fleur personally handled the account. I had recently been divorced from Lois Thornburg, and Fleur and I began going out together socially. She also had a reputation—which I think she deliberately fostered—of being ruthless. Not long after word got around that we were seeing each other, speculation grew about her influence on me. Fleur did not exactly help to put any of this speculation to rest. One day she had lunch with Olive Clapper, a member of *LOOK*'s editorial staff and widow of Raymond Clapper, one of our best-known writers. At one point in the conversation, Fleur announced, "I'm going to marry your boss."

"But you can't," Mrs. Clapper replied, "Dan Mich is already married."

"Oh, I mean your real boss," Fleur said. "I mean Mike Cowles."

Mrs. Clapper duly reported the remark to the staff, which immediately began engaging in what seemed like full-time speculation about what would happen once Fleur "took over." Most of the operational changes that took place in late 1946 were wrongly attributed to her. In fact, I'm fairly certain that Logan blamed Fleur for his departure. "She's taken over and I'm out," he said to a friend before he left.

Fleur and I were married in December 1946 and the following year she joined *LOOK* as an associate editor and a member of the Editorial Board. Over the next few years, she did have a lot of influence on me and on *LOOK* and for the most part it was positive. Her initial responsibility was for the so-called "special departments"—food, fashion, and home living. She persuaded me to include a food and fashion feature in every issue which attracted a growing number of female readers. The food feature, especially, brought in a great deal of advertising.

Fleur's major influence, though, was on *LOOK*'s appearance. Her advertising agency had originally solicited the *LOOK* account on the notion that the magazine's rather crude design was its chief drawback in attracting advertisers. She needled me constantly to do something about it, and in 1947 I finally got rid of our current art director and brought in a very talented, colorful, and gregarious fellow named Merle Armitage.

Merle was one of the most versatile people I have ever known. He was 54 when I met him, but he had already had about six different careers. He had been an engineer, stage director, book designer, author (including a cookbook titled "Fit for a King"), tour manager for opera and ballet, and impresario for such concert stars as John McCormack, Galli-Curci, and Mary Garden. He also founded—and for six years ran—the Los Angeles Grand Opera Association.

Armitage immediately overhauled our graphics. The result occasioned a two-column story headlined "The New Look" in the Press section of *Time:* "A new art director, Merle Armitage, has restyled the covers (with a white background), cleaned up the cramped typography, and given the magazine a fresh, well-ventilated air. *LOOK* has never looked so healthy, or been so prosperous."

AN INFURIATING SPEECH

One evening when *LOOK* was about a year old, I was with an audience of senior publishing and advertising executives listening to a speech by Thomas H. Beck, then head of Crowell-Collier Publishing Co. Crowell-Collier, publishers of *Collier's*, and Curtis Publishing Co., which put out the *Saturday Evening Post*, were at the time the giants of the magazine publishing industry. In discussing the recent appearance on the scene of *LIFE* and *LOOK*, which he clearly regarded as lackluster upstarts, Beck predicted flatly that *LOOK* would be dead in two years while *LIFE* would survive just three years.

I was infuriated, so much so that I resolved, then and there, that someday, by God, I'd buy *Collier's*. With *LOOK*'s impressive advertising and circulation gains during the 1940's, my anger at Beck's prediction cooled. But I continued to view *Collier's* and, to a lesser extent, the *Post* as the magazines I was most anxious to displace.

During the period I was in Washington and before I moved to New York, *LOOK*, as a biweekly, was categorized by agencies and advertisers as a monthly along with such publications as *Ladies' Home Journal* and *Cosmopolitan*. And, in fact, *LOOK*'s advertising staff was promoting it as a monthly. When I moved to New York, though, I resolved to put *LOOK* into the weekly field. It was more than just a matter of going head-to-head with *Collier's*. I was convinced that weeklies, which were gathering an increasing portion of advertiser's dollars, were the wave of the future, and I wanted to be part of that wave. A number of my associates at *LOOK* felt I was crazy and asking for trouble, for we would be taking on the biggest publishers in the industry. The selling job would not be easy. But I was determined to go for broke. As I saw it, either I was going to build *LOOK* into a major force against the toughest competition in the field or I ought to get out of the business entirely.

Quite unexpectedly, a remarkable opportunity presented itself in 1947 when *LIFE* decided to drop its sponsorship of audience studies of the weekly field conducted by the Magazine Audience Group. The MAG studies, conducted under the direction of several leading research firms, report not circulation but total audience, the total number of people who read an average issue. Seizing the opportunity, we were able to assume the sponsorship and get *LOOK* included for the first time in the group of weeklies to be analyzed.

I felt confident we would do well. Thanks to the efforts of Dan Mich,

Merle Armitage, and Fleur, the magazine was looking better than ever. That confidence was not misplaced. The first *LOOK*-sponsored MAG report in the weekly field, which came out in mid-1948, showed LIFE first, of course, with an average total per-issue audience of 27,572,000. But *LOOK* was second, with an audience of 17,439,000, a gain of 1,789,000 over *LOOK*'s total when it was last studied by MAG in 1947 as a monthly. The *Post* was third, with an audience of 15,702,000 and a gain of 1,952,000. *Collier's* had a total of only 10,341,000, a drop of 759,000.

Some of the breakdowns in the figures were even more impressive. *LOOK* showed the greatest increase, both numerically and percentage-wise, in the highly important 20-44 age group. And in the top economic groups, *LOOK* registered a gain of 417,000 while LIFE, *Collier's*, and the *Post* all showed losses.

Tide, the now defunct advertising trade publication, called the figures the strongest sales ammunition I had ever had since starting *LOOK*. Needless to say, we played them for everything they were worth.

The result was dramatic. The year 1947 was a good advertising year for all of the major magazines. LIFE, *LOOK*, *Collier's*, and the *Post* all achieved record ad pages. But 1948 was different. LIFE dropped 90 pages, the *Post* was down by 100, and *Collier's* lost almost 400. *LOOK*, though, was up 150 pages. In 1949, LIFE was off 200 pages, the *Post* about 200, and *Collier's* more than 400 pages. But *LOOK gained* 160 pages.

Crowell-Collier and Curtis did everything they could to discredit us. As they had ever since the first MAG studies, they pooh-poohed the "total audience" concept, claiming the numbers were inflated and meaningless and that audited circulation was the only valid readership barometer.

Much more effective was their claim that *LOOK* basically was a magazine for lower-class, blue-collar readers. Trying to eradicate the image of *LOOK* that that claim evoked—the perception that it was second-class, that it lacked the prestige and respectability of its competitors—was among the most perplexing and frustrating conundrums I ever faced. This image had its roots, of course, in our early days, in the crude art direction, the cheap paper, the shoddy printing and all of the other unfortunate attributes of the shoe-string, amateurish operation that brought *LOOK* into the world. But as they used to say about "loose women," magazines have a tough time trying to live down a checkered past. Even well into the 1950's and 1960's, when *LOOK*'s "quality," by anyone's standards, was in fact in a league with the best, the stigma of being a little second-rate endured and continued to plague us.

In countering the Crowell-Collier and Curtis claims, we had to concede that *LOOK* reached a disproportionate number of people in lower income brackets. But we argued, in effect, that "They're young, just starting out. How do you expect them to have high incomes?" And don't forget, it's the young people who have children and who represent the biggest market for most consumer products." We tried to depict *LOOK* and LIFE as modern magazines for modern people, for the young, active, acquisitive members of the population. We implied that *Collier's* and the *Post* were unexciting, old-fashioned magazines for the middle-aged and elderly. And we attacked the fiction that comprised a large portion of *Collier's* and the *Post's* editorial content as less interesting and compelling than real-life articles, picture stories, and the fresh contemporary journalism featured in *LOOK* and LIFE.

Our arguments would have seemed a bit hollow, though, if *LOOK's* circulation had not been steadily on the rise. Crowell and Curtis were not alone in their professed skepticism of total audience numbers; many advertising executives also put stock only in audited circulation numbers. Fortunately, *LOOK's* circulation was growing by leaps and bounds, quarter after quarter, without interruption—clear proof, we said, of the fact that *LOOK* was one of the most vigorous, appealing and exciting magazines ever published.

A SERIOUS WEAKNESS

I took particular satisfaction in the fact that for the first half of 1948, *LOOK's* circulation, for the first time in history, surpassed *Collier's*, 2,913,000 vs. 2,899,000. During that period, *LOOK* had gained 612,000 as against only 90,000 for *Collier's*.

Behind those gains, though, I spotted a serious weakness. Our post-war newsstand circulation, after peaking at 1,568,000 for the first half of 1946, had begun a steady decline: 1,483,683 for the first half of 1947 and 1,374,048 for the first half of 1948. During the second half of 1948, *LOOK's* newsstand average fell another 172,000. *Collier's*, whose newsstand sales dropped by only 78,000 in the last part of 1948, jumped back up into the overall circulation lead over *LOOK*.

There were some very good reasons for the decline in newsstand sales. During this period, many thousands of people were buying new homes and *LOOK* and other magazines were busily trying to sign them on as subscribers. Newsstand experts claimed that for every two subscriptions you put on, you lost one sale at the newsstand. Most magazines were thus losing newsstand sales. Yet *LOOK* and *Collier's* were declining at a faster rate than LIFE and the *Post*. I felt our newsstand sales, which after all still accounted for a third of our circulation, ought to be a lot better than they were—especially if we wanted to get back ahead of *Collier's*.

In searching around for a top professional to solve the problem, I came up with the same name I had in *LOOK's* early days: S.O. "Shap" Shapiro, who had left *LOOK* to rejoin Macfadden. I enticed him to leave Macfadden once again and rejoin *LOOK*. In November 1948, he became vice president and assistant to the president, with responsibility for all

111

aspects of *LOOK*'s circulation. Shap proceeded to promote Abner Sideman, who had been handling circulation promotion, to the post of newsstand circulation manager, and Ab and Shap worked together as a highly efficient team for the next 19 years.

In newsstand promotion, as in everything else in those days, *LOOK* had a far smaller budget than its competitors. Shap, though, was able to make up in ingenuity for what we lacked in dollars. His basic strategy was to obtain maximum publicity for *LOOK*'s editorial content. Using an extensive network of friends and acquaintances in the media, he was able to make a *LOOK* cover story seem almost like a major news event. He was very close to Walter Winchell, who would frequently refer to an interesting article he had just read in *LOOK*. Even an offhand remark by Winchell could stimulate thousands of copies of newsstands sales. As a result, we tended to put attention-getting stories on our cover, particularly show business personality profiles. Millions of people who did not read *LOOK*, who we were anxious to get reading the magazine, but who knew us only by our covers and the publicity they received, had no conception of the much more serious, substantial, and significant features carried on the inside pages. Our striving for more newsstand sales was damaging our efforts to upgrade our image.

We came up with some strategies to deal with the image problem. At the suggestion of Jim Milloy in 1955, we began holding an annual black-tie staff dinner in New York in honor of a top politician. We kept the dinners small and restricted invitations to only the most senior executives at the largest corporations and ad agencies. Over the years, we were successful in attracting such names as Vice Presidents Nixon and Humphrey and other top politicians, and I'm sure the idea got through to our guests that if *LOOK* had sufficient prestige to get people of that calibre we warranted more consideration as an advertising medium than we were often being given.

One of the major reasons *LOOK* was not taken as seriously as we wanted it to be, especially in the intellectual community, was that virtually no school or public libraries subscribed to the magazine. The problem was that few librarians regularly read *LOOK*. Most accepted the image of *LOOK* as being without any lasting significance. As a result, *LOOK* was not indexed in *The Reader's Guide to Periodical Literature*, for inclusion in *The Reader's Guide* is determined by regular voting by subscribing librarians. Even librarians who might be inclined to subscribe to *LOOK* did not do so because, without a *Reader's Guide* listing, *LOOK* had no reference value.

To combat this, we organized a broad direct mail campaign to librarians advising them of the sort of important articles *LOOK* was carrying and sending them sample copies so they could assess it for themselves. When the next vote was held on the magazines librarians wanted included in *The Reader's Guide*, *LOOK* was high on the list.

112

Despite these victories, a complete solution to the image problem remained elusive. I was especially frustrated by the fact that while both LIFE and *LOOK* often injected a little sex and cheesecake into their stories, only *LOOK* seemed to get hurt by it. As anxious as we were to build circulation, we tried to be restrained. But sometimes we failed to anticipate the degree of reader's sensitivity to the subject of sex — especially readers who happened to work at advertising agencies and large corporations. After a lengthy sales effort, for instance, we convinced Campbell Soup to become a *LOOK* advertiser. But just before its schedule of insertions was due to start, we published an issue containing a black and white photograph of artist Peter Arno in his studio sketching a nude model—not a frontal view, as later became common in *Playboy*, but a discreet, semi-back view. That was the end of the Campbell Soup business for some time to come.

LIFE's SUCCESS WITH NUDES

In reflecting on it, I have to admit that LIFE was much more adept than we were in injecting sex into its issues. When they published a nude, it always seemed to be part of an anthropological study, or an illustration of "great art," or in pursuit of some other high-minded purpose. LIFE's nudes were seen as educational. Our always seemed to be regarded as sensational.

For all of the unfortunate side effects of our campaign to build circulation, though, it certainly achieved its primary goal. We arrested the newsstand circulation decline and kept it above the 1,000,000 level for many years. Our overall circulation grew steadily, each year being greater than the previous year, from 1,897,000 in 1944 to 7,984,000 in 1967.

These gains were matched on the advertising side. Starting in 1946, our total number of advertising pages went up for eleven consecutive years. We were the only magazine in the field to achieve such a record. Advertising revenue, which totaled $6,428,900 in 1946, more than doubled within three years, totaling $15,064,200 in 1949. By 1952, gross advertising revenue was near $21,000,000; by 1955 it exceeded $30,000,000; and by 1957 we topped the $40,000,000 level for the first time, with a total of $43,461,430.

Of even more significance was the dramatic advance in *LOOK*'s share of advertising revenue as compared to all other consumer magazines. In 1946, the first postwar year, *LOOK* ranked thirteenth among all magazines in gross advertising revenue. By 1950, we had achieved sixth place, ahead of *Collier's* for the first time. *Collier's*, a once-proud giant, had dropped from third to seventh place.

Much of the credit for our advertising success must go to the crusading zeal of our ad staff. Not only did they work enormously hard, but they

113

seemed to have so much mutual respect for one another that they avoided the destructive intramural competitiveness that afflicts so many groups of advertising salesmen. Vern Myers put it this way: "You could look sideways and see a group of seven or eight guys who were putting in such long hours and doing their jobs so damn well that you had to respect them. Therefore, all the thrust was outward, with no wasted time on internal back-biting and in-fighting."

The ad staff at LIFE was also very effective. But esprit was not much in evidence at the *Post* and *Collier's*. Many of the senior people at the two magazines had grown old or tired and, in reaction to a lack of leadership and direction at the top, the lower echelon executives became complacent and demoralized, and focused their energies on sometimes bitter jockeying for position.

In 1950, though, we suffered a severe internal setback of our own. For years, Otis L. Wiese, the top editor at *McCall's*, had been trying to hire Dan Mich away from us. While I was abroad, Mich accepted an offer to become McCall's editorial director. Many factors played a role in Dan's decision. High on the list, though, was the fact that Look, Inc. had become Cowles Magazines, Inc., and we had begun publishing two other magazines, *Quick* and *Flair*. Just as he had become disturbed by Harlan Logan's desire to build a large communications empire, Mich resented the high amounts of time and money we were investing in the new publications, time and money he felt could more productively be utilized at *LOOK*. And he continued to resent Fleur Fenton's influence—*Flair* was Fleur's brainchild.

The three and half years that Mich was gone from us would be the most trying period we had endured since the 1930's.

A GO-AHEAD FOR *FLAIR*

I doubt I ever would have launched *Flair* if Fleur hadn't been such a persuasive saleswoman. But almost from the time we were married, she was determined to start a highly original fashion, art, and culture magazine that would appeal to a class instead of a mass audience. I argued that neither of us had ever had any experience putting out a class magazine. But it was true that she had handled some high fashion accounts at her advertising agency and was artistically talented and knowledgeable about the arts. With great reluctance, I gave my go-ahead. The first issue appeared in January 1950.

There is no question that *Flair* was perhaps the most original and certainly one of the most talked about magazines ever published. Utilizing innovative graphic arts techniques that did not become widely accepted for another two decades, it was an art director's dream. Even today, many magazine art directors cherish their old issues of *Flair* and speak of it with reverence and awe. Among other distinctions, issues typically featured an actual hole built into the design of the cover and a profusion of accordion pull-outs on the inside pages. Cartoonists had a heyday. One in *The New Yorker* showed a house detective sitting in a hotel lobby keeping an eye on things through the hole in *Flair*'s cover. Another New Yorker cartoon showed a man on a subway reading the magazine while the man sitting next to him read one of the accordion pull-outs.

These design flourishes were achieved with no small amount of cost. Fleur never had any real concept of costs, and the magazine was extraordinarily expensive to produce, far, far more than she had originally budgeted. It did manage to achieve a circulation of more than 200,000. But by the end of the first year, losses before taxes were roughly $2,485,000—for an actual cash loss after taxes of $1,250,000. That was almost twice *LOOK*'s profits during the war. We were losing about 75 cents on every copy we sold. *Flair* was eating us up alive.

I felt I had been very tolerant until this point but that it was time to put my foot down. I told Fleur that we couldn't go on any longer losing money at this rate and that I had to fold the magazine. I told her she could save face by attributing the failure to increased production costs and the possibility of paper shortages due to the Korean War.

She was incensed and refused to accept my decision. She claimed, with nothing to back the claim up, that the magazine would eventually turn around. Finally, I just quit arguing with her and put out a press release announcing *Flair*'s suspension as of the January 1951 issue. The release cited production costs, which had risen more than 35 percent since publication was first planned, and stated that "the very critical foreign situation, the certainty of further increases in costs and the likelihood of limitations on paper availability in 1951 make unwise at this time the continued publication of *Flair*." I don't think Fleur ever forgave me.

While I'm sure I should never have started publishing *Flair*, I often wonder if I should have stopped publishing *Quick*.

A NEWS MAGAZINE—*QUICK*

For many years, I had been convinced of the need for a weekly newsmagazine that could be read quickly, in fifteen minutes or so. As *Time* and *Newsweek*, fat with advertising, kept carrying more and more words, I became even more convinced. Yet I couldn't figure out how to make such a magazine profitable, and I did nothing with the idea until one day in 1949 when I had a visit from a Baltimore advertising agent named S. J. Lichtman. Lichtman tried to interest me in the idea of a pocket-sized feature magazine, perhaps with a page size only a quarter of the size of a *Time* page. The feature magazine notion didn't interest me. But I was very intrigued by the notion of a small-size newsmagazine, which would be extremely inexpensive to produce, and decided to go ahead. Since nobody can copyright a magazine size, technically I didn't owe Lichtman anything. But I paid him for giving me the idea nevertheless, and assigned some top *LOOK* people to work on the project. Dan Mich worked many weekends as did Woodrow Wirsig, an assistant managing editor at *LOOK* who became *Quick's* first editor.

The first issue of *Quick* appeared in May 1949 with a cover price of 10 cents. It was designed solely for newsstand sale and carried no advertising. We were convinced that production costs could be kept sufficiently low that we could make money on circulation revenue alone. It turned out, though, that we lost money at 10 cents a copy. We had two options: raise the cover price, which we felt could cost us a lot of circulation, or accept advertising. We opted for the latter.

In retrospect, I think we should either have raised the price to 15 cents or increased the page size, for *Quick's* dimensions were just a notch too small to attract very many advertisers. If we had enlarged *Quick* to the size of the *Reader's Digest*, which today produces a huge volume of advertising revenue, *Quick's* future might have been quite different.

Quick's early results, nevertheless, were remarkable. The first issue sold 320,000 copies. Within six months, circulation was up to 500,000 copies a week and by the next year we were over a million. Rather slow at first, advertising began picking up.

Quick became the talk of the magazine business. No less an authority than Henry Luce of Time, Inc. was "fascinated" with the magazine, according to *The World of Time, Inc.*, the official history of the publishing empire by Robert T. Elson. Elson said that "Contrary to the view held by most of his editors, Luce believed that *Quick* had the makings of a successful publication." Imitators started popping up like mushrooms. Publishers in various parts of the world approached us to acquire foreign language rights. One gag had it that we were about to start a Spanish edition called *Pronto*.

By the first quarter of 1953, *Quick's* average net paid circulation stood at 1,368,000 and advertising volume was running 41 percent ahead of the same period in 1952. *Quick* was still losing money, but far less than a new magazine in its position could logically be expected to lose. Within a relatively short time, *Quick* very likely would have moved into the black. It was thus a great surprise to virtually everyone both inside and outside Cowles Magazines when I announced on April 13, 1953 that we were discontinuing *Quick* as a separate magazine after the issue of June 1. *Quick* would be merged with *LOOK* and *Quick* subscribers would have the remainder of their subscriptions filled with issues of *LOOK*.

In my memo to the Cowles staff, I said:

"The decision to discontinue *Quick* was not an easy one to make. It is unusually popular with its readers as proved by its steady circulation growth to more than 1,300,000 (more than half newsstand sale). But its abnormally small page size, while proven effective for some advertisers who use it ingeniously, has proved also to be too great a hurdle for many advertisers. With steadily rising costs, we concluded we could not produce a quality newsweekly without a husky advertising volume."

Quick readers, who had developed an exceedingly proprietary feeling for the magazine, started phoning, wiring, or writing us by the thousands to protest and beg us to reconsider. Many of them even offered to contribute money to help keep the magazine going. Many publishing executives were startled we had given up so easily and felt our decision was premature and unwise.

Very few people, though, realized the reason I killed *Quick*. The problem was not *Quick* but *Collier's*. Passing *Collier's* in circulation in 1950 had been one of the great milestones in *LOOK*'s history. For the first time, it had caused many people in the advertising business to regard *LOOK* as important, as a worthy ad medium. But now, in 1953, it was beginning to look as if *Collier's* was going to take the lead again. For the first half of 1953, *LOOK*'s circulation had been ahead of *Collier's* by 233,000, 3,405,345 to 3,171,910. But we knew *Collier's* circulation was gaining rapidly and that unless we did something soon, *Collier's* would pass us in the first half of 1954. If we had lost that lead, it might have fatally wrecked our forward momentum.

The reason for *Collier's* sudden spurt was that, effective with the August 7, 1953 issue, *Collier's* had switched from weekly to biweekly publication. The tactic was clever and effective: it automatically extended subscriptions that otherwise would not have been renewed. And it gave the magazine two weeks of selling time on the newsstands instead of one.

As it turned out, *Collier's* was able to announce a circulation for the first half of 1954 of 3,800,116, a huge gain of 628,206 that probably would have been ahead of *LOOK* by a few hundred thousand. But in killing *Quick*, we added several hundred thousand *Quick* subscribers to *LOOK*'s circulation. With this boost of our own, we were able to report a circulation for the first half of 1954 of 3,868,394—just 68,278 ahead of *Collier's*.

We were plagued for a few years by allegations from competitive advertising salesmen that *LOOK*'s circulation numbers were inflated by cannibalization of the *Flair* and *Quick* subscription lists. But these allegations hurt us comparatively little, while our continuation of our circulation supremacy over *Collier's* helped us a great deal. As much as I wish I could have avoided killing *Quick*, it died for a very worthy cause.

The setback turned out to be the beginning of the end for *Collier's*. Its fortunes continued to decline and, in 1956, eighteen years after the Thomas Beck speech predicting *LOOK*'s imminent demise, *Collier's* folded. The pieces, including its subscriber list, were acquired by *LOOK*. I am never happy when any publication fails, but I could not help but enjoy the irony.

THE WORST STRAIN

Flair, *Quick*, and the circulation war with *Collier's* put considerable strain on our organization during the early 1950's. But the worst strain, particularly on me personally, developed from Dan Mich's unexpected resignation in July, 1950. As hard as I tried, I could not come up with an acceptable replacement. And while we floundered, *LOOK* deteriorated badly.

When Dan left, my first move was to transfer Woodrow Wirsig from the top editorial post at *Quick* to *LOOK's* executive editor, the senior editorial position below me. Woody had been on the *LOOK* staff for some years and had made some outstanding contributions. But as an editor, his approach turned out to be somewhat pedestrian. Soon a bitter rivalry developed between Woody and the managing editor, William Lowe.

I had met Lowe in Paris in 1949 when he was economics editor of the international edition of the *Herald-Tribune*. Though he was only 29 I was so impressed I offered him a job either writing a syndicated newspaper column from Europe about economic developments or moving to New York as my assistant. He chose the latter, primarily because at the time I was toying with the idea of launching a U.S. magazine modeled after the London *Economist*, on which he would have played a major role. When I abandoned those plans because of our losses on *Flair*, I made him managing editor of *LOOK*.

Lowe's editorial philosophy was quite different from Wirsig's. Lowe wanted more controversy, more features with a current events angle. Each man attracted a group of followers, and soon the two factions were enmeshed in virtual warfare. There was almost total lack of direction and confusion reigned. One of the two men had to go.

I decided it should be Woody. In early 1952, I made Lowe executive editor and promoted Leslie Midgley, who had been foreign editor, to the managing editorship. But that didn't work either. Lowe, at 31, proved to be too unseasoned for the top editorial post. I had to make another change.

A number of people suggested Dana Tasker, an assistant managing editor of *Time* who had been at Time, Inc. for fifteen years and edited in virtually every department. I had always had a great respect and envy— perhaps too much—of the Time, Inc. organization, and I assumed that anyone who had spent that much time in ranking positions could not help but be an excellent choice. In March, 1953, I hired Tasker as editorial director, which put him over Lowe.

That turned out to be my worst choice of all. For one thing, my reasoning that his experience at *Time* had prepared him for *LOOK* was completely faulty. At *Time*, his job had been largely one of selecting from, condensing, and rewriting the huge mass of material, much of it related to breaking news events, produced by the magazine's worldwide network of correspondents. *LOOK*, though, did not cover breaking news and had no such network. Instead of sifting through material which poured in almost automatically, it was the responsibility of *LOOK* editors to initiate. stories, choose the best writers and photographers to do them, and then oversee them during the often several weeks that it might take to produce them. Tasker turned out to be a poor initiator of the sort of feature stories in which *LOOK* specialized.

Tasker, further, had the habit of writing sharp and abusive memos to staff members about their stories—and almost always after the finished pages had been shipped to the printer. Not only did this alienate the staff but it produced a horrendous increase in remake costs.

Tasker's dealings with the art department were especially acrimonious. At *Time*, his responsibilities had included graphics, covers, and other illustrations, and he regarded himself as especially accomplished in this area. News magazine graphics, though, are much different functions than larger-size feature magazine graphics, and Tasker fell into almost immediate conflict with Merle Armitage, our art director. One day, Merle sent him a layout with a great deal of white space around the photographs and text. Tasker sent it back with a note saying, "Why not put a picture of one of the geniuses of the art department in this unused space?"

As appalled as I was by Tasker's performance, I continued to allow myself to be influenced by his record at Time, Inc. When the rift between Tasker and Armitage got so bad that the two men simply could not work together, I decided I would have to let Merle go. In August, 1953, I called Merle into my office and explained the situation to him, that I had to eliminate the rancor between Tasker and the art department. Merle was extremely gracious and understanding. Because he was so decent, I raised his salary by one-third and gave him a year's severance pay. To replace Merle, I brought in Allen Hurlburt, who headed the *LOOK* promotion art department. But Al couldn't work with Tasker either.

By the latter part of 1953, I could no longer talk myself into believing that I hadn't made a tremendous error in hiring Tasker. The evidence was overwhelming. Our editorial content had became the worst it had been in years. There was no longer any advance planning to speak of, and the flow of story ideas submitted and accepted had diminished alarmingly. I found myself having to purchase stories from outside writers and photographers at the last minute, not because the stories were especially good but simply because I had a lot of empty pages to fill in a hurry. Morale among the editorial staff was almost non-existent.

As the situation continued to deteriorate, I held several dinner meetings with staff members to explore possible solutions. Someone suggested we try to get Dan Mich back. The idea stirred almost instant enthusiasm among everyone I tried it on.

I phoned Dan and arranged to meet with him. I told him frankly how bad things were and asked if he would be willing to return. I don't think he was too happy at *McCall's* and he was intrigued with the offer. But several things, he said, bothered him, one of which was Fleur, whom he had never gotten along well with. I had Fleur call Dan later and urge him to accept my offer. Several other editors and practically all of the board of directors of Cowles Magazines also called Dan. Finally, he agreed.

In January 1954, Dana Tasker and Bill Lowe departed. (So did managing editor Les Midgley, regrettably. Les had done very well at *LOOK*, and would later have a distinguished career at CBS, but I wanted to give Mich a totally free hand to select his own senior staff.) Dan Mich was named editorial director, and later he would become vice president and a member of the board of directors, and, finally, would replace me as editor. As Dan's chief assistant, we promoted Bill Arthur to managing editor.

Dan always said that the three and a half years he spent at *McCall's* had been good for him and made him a better all-around editor. I think he was right. I also think his absence was good for those of us at *LOOK* who now knew what it was like without him and who appreciated him all the more when he came back. His return marked the beginning of what I like to think of as *LOOK*'s golden years, when the original dream I had for the magazine reached its fullest realization.

PHOTOGRAPHS FROM LOOK

It has been estimated that 180,000 photographs appeared in *LOOK* during its almost 35 years of existence. What follows is but a minute portion of "The exciting story of people," told through the eyes of gifted photographers who traveled the world in search of what people do, what they feel, what they want and what they think.

Countless writers joined to tell this ever-changing story, with warmth, understanding, and wonder.

"America Beyond the Cities" brought this stark schoolhouse in the West to the camera-eye of *LOOK*'s Photographer-poet John Vachon.

Photo: John Vachon

Drought, swirling dust
drove the Oakies
westward. In this
memorable scene, Arthur
Rothstein captured history
in 1937.
Photo: Arthur Rothstein

Marilyn Monroe and Judy
Garland, enduring legends
whose lives enamored
millions. Their untimely
deaths saddened a world.

Photos: Douglas Kirkland

Reader interest never waned in Princess Grace, the girl from Philadelphia, shown in her Monaco palace.
Photo: Douglas Jones

Liz Taylor (on 19 *LOOK* covers) and Richard Burton joined, parted, rejoined and parted again in a headline romance.
Photo: Douglas Kirkland

The Big Three—
Stalin, Roosevelt,
Churchill—meet in
Teheran, now off-limits to
Americans.
Photo: UPI

Hitler harangues, and sets
the world afire.
Photo: UPI

©Arnold Newman

The Chicago Tribune errs, and President Truman glories. Would "exit polls" have prevented this monumental blunder?
Photo: UPI

Israel's founder and first leader, David Ben-Gurion, holds the Declaration of Independence announcing establishment of the Jewish state.
Photo: Arnold Newman

Ernest Hemingway
returned to Africa on
safari. A scene such as this
would invoke wrath among
today's conservation-
conscious readers.
Photo: Earl Theisen

The enduring strength of New England came to *LOOK*'s pages through "A Visit With Robert Frost."

Photo: Robert Lerner

Carl Sandburg— He'd drop in to chat with *LOOK*'s editors on visits to New York.

Photo: John Vachon

A genius of artistic
expression, Pablo Picasso
was one of nineteen greats
of art featured in a *LOOK*
series by Leo Rosten titled
"The Story Behind the
Painting."
Photo: Michael Vaccaro

Alexander Calder adjusts a
delicate mobile, a fantasy
that whirls in silence.
Photo: Michael Vaccaro

Poland's tragedy
continues, albeit somewhat
different than this family's
flight from a raging fire.
Photo: John Vachon

Bob, the sailor, comes
home to Carol, and joy
abounds as the Korean war
is momentarily forgotten.
Photo: James Hansen

Vietnam—
The price of war.
Photo: James H. Karales

LOOK reporter Sam
Castan, slogs through
Vietnam's mud and
buffalo grass to get the
story. He was killed there
in 1966.

Photo: James H. Karales

This photograph of JFK
and his son John, almost 3,
appeared unpredictably in
LOOK during that fateful
week in Dallas.
Photo: Stanley Tretick

A National Day of
Mourning: November 25,
1963, and a bereaved
family grieves.
Photo: Marvin Newman

"Joined by love:" Society called these children "unadoptable," but Julie and Kurt Lerke, of Whitehouse NJ, adopted nine—seven born in Korea—as their own.
Photo: Robert Lerner

Both were 11, but the girl towered above the boy at Mrs. Potts' dancing class. It was 1967 and twelve lessons cost $20.00.
Photo: Charlotte Brooks

142

Dionis Lindsay was too feverish to drink her tea in this scene from a *LOOK* series on a little girl growing up.
Photo: James Hansen

"I've got it! I know! I know!" A triumph for education, and a prize-winning photo for *LOOK*.
Photo: Charlotte Brooks

Eyes to eyes: Sick dog, heartsick master, at the vets. Reader interest in animal photographs always was high.
Photo: Robert Sandberg

"That's one small step for a
man . . ." It was July 20,
1969, and the moon no
longer was just a subject
for songs and speculation.
Photos: NASA

Mayhem on Sunday: The action merges into a rush for precious yardage.
Photo: Marvin Newman

Jackie Robinson, backed by Walter Alston and Gil Hodges, confronts the ump. Years later, *LOOK* scooped everyone on Jackie's retirement.
Photo: James Hansen

Stanley Kubrick, a
filmdom great, in his teens
was a *LOOK* photographer.
Here he caught Rocky
Graziano in pre-bout
tension.
Photo: Stanley Kubrick

Whoever saw a gown by Rappi displayed so ingeniously and elegantly as this?
Photo: Michael Vaccaro

Afghanistan is hardly the same now as when *LOOK* saw it in this fashion photograph at the Grand Mosque of Herat.
Photo: Fred Maroon

Fire hoses drove the
protestors back. But not
for long.
Photo: Bob Adelman

Social work was the way
Tommy Jacquette, 22,
sought to cool the wrath
that tore apart Watts in Los
Angeles in 1965.
Photo: Douglas Jones

Human dignity was the issue, and the march from Selma to Montgomery in Alabama in 1965 epitomized the struggle.
Photo: James H. Karales

The last Cocopah chieftain Joe San Diego, faced cold winter nights in a mud and scrap shack. Have the years since 1970 made a difference?
Photo: Paul Fusco

151

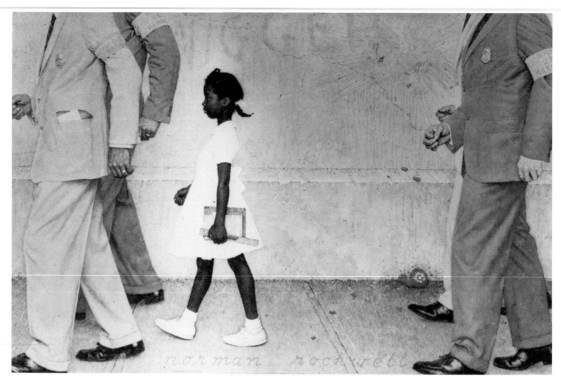

A little girl goes to school,
and Norman Rockwell
etched the scene of her
triumph.

*Photo: Courtesy of the Norman
Rockwell Museum at the Old Corner
House, Stockbridge, MA.*

SOME BRIEF
ENCOUNTERS WITH
NOTABLE NEWSMAKERS

5

LOOK magazine, for me, offered a plethora of rewards, pleasures, and satisfactions. High on the list, I would have to rank the access it gave me to some of the most important, influential, and well-known personalities of the day. As a magazine editor and outsider, I was not in a position to get to know very many of them intimately—with the notable exception of Wendell Willkie. But I was fortunate enough to obtain some close-in, behind-the-scenes glimpses that while usually brief were often quite revealing.

Some of my most fascinating encounters were in Hollywood. In my initial planning to make *LOOK* a magazine that would interest the whole family, I had included entertainment and from the beginning we gave much attention to the movies. In our early issues, we devoted almost half the contents of each issue to Hollywood personalities. *LOOK* was perhaps the first general interest magazine to establish a full-time editorial office in Hollywood. To run it, I assigned Jean Herrick, who had been at *The Register* and *Tribune* and most recently in *LOOK*'s New York Office. Herrick knew almost nothing about the movie industry. But he did have well-developed instincts about photographs and, as a skilled newspaperman, he knew a good story when he saw one. During his twenty years in Hollywood, Herrick became extremely knowledgeable about how the place worked and who made it work, and he did a very able job for us.

At the time we began doing Hollywood stories most movie coverage was by fan magazines and was almost uniformly worshipful, little different from a press release. But both Jean and I wanted to apply the same sorts of journalistic standards to our Hollywood reporting that we applied to any of the other subjects we covered. Jean later recalled the early problems this caused: "Right from the start we offended a good many people because of what they considered a too candid or too frank approach to the motion picture industry. We were perhaps among the first publishers to use candid photos, not the staged, highly stylized and retouched stills put out by the studio publicity departments. Also, we weren't always flattering in what we printed about the stars, whereas they wanted us to say that they were all good to their mothers, had no bad habits, etc. The result was that in many quarters they were not happy to see me when I came in, and it took quite a long period of public relations and cajolery, before I could even get to see people."

The studios' attitude gradually changed. The early non-public relations-type stories we did were extremely popular with readers and got a lot of attention in Hollywood. As our ability to influence the success of movies and stars grew, studios decided it was better to cooperate with us on our terms than not at all. After a time we were able to get to just about anybody we wanted to. We spent quite a lot of our time turning down requests from studios that we do elaborate layouts on their assertedly soon-to-be major motion pictures and stars.

"A LITTLE GIRL. . .WITH SEX APPEAL"

About four times a year, I used to fly to Hollywood to visit with the publicity heads of the major studios and other important figures in the industry. On one of these visits during the late 1930's, I had lunch with Daryl Zanuck, head of Twentieth Century Fox, and then dropped in on Harry Brandt, the highly regarded director of publicity for the studio. After a brief chat, Harry mentioned—quite casually, I thought—that they had a "little girl on the lot who has a good deal of sex appeal. I want you to meet her."

"There's one thing about her which is quite unusual," he continued. "Her tits don't point straight out. They point up quite a bit."

Harry asked his secretary to phone and have the girl sent to his office. About ten minutes later I was introduced to Marilyn Monroe. She was wearing a V-neck sweater. Harry walked around his desk, took hold of one side of the sweater and abruptly pulled it to the side so that her left breast popped out. Sure enough, Harry was right.

The maneuver didn't embarrass Marilyn in the slightest. She stood there, straight and proud and smiling.

At this point, Harry's secretary poked her head through the doorway and said, "Mr. Brandt, your New York call is ready."

"I'll take it in the next room," Harry responded. As he left he turned back and said to Marilyn: "If Mike Cowles would put you on the cover of *LOOK* it will give you a big start toward stardom."

Marilyn walked across the room and went not just up to me, but up against me.

"Mr. Cowles," she said in that high, lilting, flirtatious voice, "*We* should

154

get better acquainted." And we did over the years, though not necessarily in the manner that her remark suggested. *LOOK* did several stories on her and I often saw her when I visited Hollywood.

Her lack of inhibition about her body, as the sweater incident illustrated, always amazed me. We used her in several fashion features, and during the shooting in Hollywood, she would change dresses in full view of the photographer, the lighting man, and everyone else who happened to be around. Not surprisingly, the sessions attracted a fair number of such visitors as advertising salesmen. Sometimes during a break Marilyn, dressed in nothing but bikini panties and shoes, would stroll over to where her audience was sitting and chat casually until it was time for the next photograph.

Some years later, during the mid-1950's, Marilyn and I figured in a little bit of intrigue that never made it into the gossip columns. The intrigue also involved a man named George Schlee, a rather mysterious international society figure. Schlee was married to Valentina, one of the world's foremost dress designers. While Valentina attended to business in New York and Paris, Schlee usually spent the summer sailing on Aristotle Onassis' yacht with Greta Garbo.

Schlee did high-level public relations counseling for an elite group of clients, including Onassis, and one weekend after a holiday cruise on the yacht, he visited me in my summer home in Weston, Connecticut, to discuss a problem Onassis was having. Onassis held the majority ownership in the Monte Carlo Casino as well as a number of other properties in the Principality of Monaco. Tourism in Monaco and all across the south of France, though, was in a serious slump, and Onassis was anxious to generate some publicity about Monaco and attract more visitors, especially glamorous and affluent Americans.

Knowing relatively little about Monaco, I started asking some questions: "What about that Prince who rules Monaco?"

"He doesn't have the greatest personality in the world," Schlee replied. "But as royalty goes, he's really quite attractive."

"What about marrying him off to an American movie star?" I inquired, more on impulse than anything else.

Schlee took me quite seriously. "Whom do you have in mind?" he asked.

"If you like the idea," I said. "I'd start right at the top. I'd start with Marilyn Monroe." At the time, Marilyn was clearly the ranking movie star in the United States.

"My God, Mike, do you think she'd go for it?" Schlee said with a barely suppressed tone of delight.

"I don't know, George, but we can give it a try."

As it happened, Marilyn was spending a month with Milton and Amy Greene just a few miles from my house. Milton was a very well-known fashion photographer who had often done stories with Marilyn. I

155

suggested to Schlee that the quickest way to find out was just to ask the Greenes and Marilyn over to the house. "I know Marilyn so well I don't mind putting it up to her," I said.

I phoned Greene. Would they mind coming about ten o'clock, and bringing Marilyn? Milton was delighted to accept.

After they arrived and the amenities were over, George and I took Marilyn out to the pool house, explaining on the way that we wanted to discuss something privately with her. I presented the idea in a very straightforward manner, almost like a business deal. We would arrange for her to meet Ranier if she would agree to stay married to him for at least three or four years. I told her the glamour of such a marriage would have world-wide appeal, would help her career, and would undoubtedly boost the economy of Monte Carlo.

Quite unruffled, Marilyn thought about the proposition for a few minutes in silence. Then she turned to me and said, "Mike, you've always given me straight advice. Do you really think this would be good for my career?"

I told her that not only would it be great for her career but, as Princess Marilyn, she would be legitimate royalty and not just a Hollywood star.

"I'd really like to think about it a little longer," Marilyn said. "But if you assure me, Mike, that in your opinion it would help my career, I think I might go for it."

Until this point, I had been regarding the episode as a kind of lark. But suddenly everything was beginning to seem very real, and I realized there was a big potential flaw in our scheme.

"Just a minute, Marilyn," I said. "Neither George nor I know if the Prince will go for it. We don't know if he would ask you to marry him even for the sake of Monaco."

I shall never forget Marilyn's reply. "Mike," she said, "if you will arrange for me to spend two nights with him, he'll ask me."

The next morning, however, *The New York Times* carried a front-page story that arrangements were underway with the Kelly family of Philadelphia for the nuptials of their daughter Grace and Prince Ranier. We never found out whether Marilyn could have lived up to her promise, of course, but the Prince at least did marry a beautiful American movie star—to the distinct benefit of the economy of Monaco.

THE UNKNOWN STARLET

One Christmas in the early 1940's my wife Lois, who was chairman of a Junior League charity ball in Des Moines, asked me to get a big star to help promote the affair. I picked up the phone and called Jean Herrick in Hollywood. It was a tough assignment. Even under ideal circumstances an appearance in Des Moines, Iowa, during the height of the holiday season was not the most attractive invitation to a movie star. The best Jean could come up with was a young, almost unknown starlet by the name of Rita Hayworth. Most reluctantly I settled for her. Rita and her husband, Eddie Judson, came by train via Kansas City where they had to take the sleeper to Des Moines. They arrived on the morning of the ball and we put them up in our house.

At first, the Junior Leaguers were disappointed that I could not produce someone better than Rita Hayworth. But at the ball she was absolutely smashing. In the meantime, a storm had left about two feet of snow on the ground, and the following morning none of the trains were running. Rita and her husband remained my house guests for the next twenty-four hours. I could not even get to my office so I had no choice but to stay home and listen to Eddie Judson's life story. Rita Hayworth just sat there, not uttering a word. He had been a Rolls Royce salesman in New York and had made it his business to know which rich men were keeping which beautiful women. Judson would persuade a woman to con her lover into buying her a Rolls Royce. Then he, Judson, would make a deal with her, offering in writing to buy back the car within three years at three-quarters of its cost. After a time, this ploy began to bore him and he decided there must be a better way to make a living. Hollywood seemed a natural for a man of his talents. Once there he assembled a list of promising starlets from the various studios. After looking them over he decided that Rita Hayworth showed the most promise.

"So I decided to marry her," Judson said as Rita listened. "Then I sent her to a voice coach, an acting school, and a dancing school. Mike, you can't believe how awkward she was when I first met her."

Judson turned to Rita. "Get up and go out of the room and come back walking the way you did before I taught you how to walk."

Without hesitation, Rita got up, went out of the room, and came back with a rather awkward, uncertain walk.

"Go out again and come back in the way I taught you to walk," he commanded again. Rita went out and came back walking like a model in a fashion show.

Rita Hayworth, as the world knows, went on to stardom and eventual marriage to Aly Khan. I wasn't surprised when I heard that Judson got a very substantial cash payment from Rita when he agreed to give her a divorce.

L.B.'s LIBRARY

In the early years of *LOOK*, Hollywood was the undisputed film capital of the world. The industry was controlled by five major studios who held tight contracts with the major stars and could build them up or destroy them. Studio heads were powerful and ruthless, and the most ruthless and powerful of all was Louis B. Mayer, of Metro-Goldwyn-Mayer.

I always liked L.B., as he was called by his friends, and I think the feeling was reciprocated. When *LOOK* published something that was critical of Hollywood or, God forbid, MGM, he would deliver a stern lecture to me, but always with a tone of affection. I suspected the affection derived from my background: he knew my father and both men were die-hard Republicans and close friends of Herbert Hoover.

During one of my Hollywood visits, Mayer invited me to a luncheon he was giving at his mansion in Beverly Hills for Cardinal Spellman. I accepted, but misunderstanding the appointed hour, I arrived an hour ahead of time. A haughty butler hesitated to admit me until I assured him that I'd sit quietly in the library and make my appearance at the correct time.

The butler led me into an elaborate library and left me to browse. The walls were lined with well-stocked bookshelves. I made a slow tour of the room, looking for something to help me pass the time. Among all those fine leather-bound volumes there was not a single book in English. There was nothing but French books, from wall to wall, ceiling to floor.

At lunch, Cardinal Spellman sat at L.B.'s right. I was two seats away. During a lull in the conversation, I leaned across the Cardinal and said, "L.B., I didn't know you were such a great student of French."

"I'm not," he answered.

"Then why do you have such an extensive French library?"

"I don't," he said.

"But your entire library consists of French books."

"It doesn't," came the answer.

I let the matter drop—after suddenly realizing that in the twelve years he had lived in the house he had probably never once reached for a book on his library shelves. The books, most probably, had been selected by his decorator because their bindings fit in with the color scheme.

HEDY LAMARR SUES *LOOK*

During the late 1940's, *LOOK* published a ten-part series called "Hollywood Uncensored" that revealed intimate and sometimes embarrassing details about such stars as Joan Crawford, Norma Shearer, and Hedy Lamarr. Among the disclosures was that Hedy Lamarr had had plastic surgery on her nose. Lamarr promptly sued us for $10,000,000, or some such outlandish figure. That she had had plastic surgery was common knowledge, but in preparing for the suit, our lawyers could not find anyone in Hollywood willing to testify to the fact.

As we were trying to figure what to do next, I made one of my periodic trips to Hollywood and was invited to a dinner that Frances and Sam Goldwyn, who were good friends of mine, were giving for me. *LOOK* having long since ceased being regarded in Hollywood as a pariah, Goldwyn had no trouble mustering as other guests the cream of the movie world—about thirty or so top producers, directors, and stars. The day of the party, Goldwyn phoned and asked me to come to his house an hour or so before hand so that he could discuss a private matter.

When we were closeted in the library, he came right to the point. Cecil B. DeMille had just finished shooting "Samson and Delilah" with Hedy Lamarr in the lead. Just about everyone who had seen early versions had pronounced it a terrible turkey, and DeMille was deeply worried. Goldwyn, meanwhile, knew that *LOOK* was deeply worried about the Lamarr lawsuit. And so, acting as an intermediary for DeMille, a longtime friend, he proposed a deal: If I would promise to give "Samson and Delilah" a *LOOK* cover and a big inside layout, DeMille would exercise his considerable influence on Lamarr to get her to drop her suit.

Well, I said to Sam, I hear it's a turkey. No response. I saw an opening for a little negotiation. I won't give it a cover, I said, but I'll give the picture four color pages inside—and no critical judgment. We'll just call it a typical DeMille epic.

Sam picked up the phone, called DeMille, and conveyed my terms. Then he put me on the phone, DeMille and I argued back and forth but I held my ground, and finally he acquiesced. He arranged to have the suit dismissed and *LOOK* gave the picture four pages in full color, called it a typical DeMille epic, and made no adverse comment.

Two months later, I received a bill from Jerry Geisler, the famous Hollywood lawyer who had been representing Hedy Lamarr in the *LOOK* suit. It was for thirty thousand dollars for services rendered. I mailed the bill to Sam Goldwyn with a note saying that I didn't know why the bill had been sent to me. There was no answer from Goldwyn. Three weeks later I got another bill from Geisler, this time for twenty thousand dollars. I sent this bill to DeMille with a carbon to Goldwyn repeating that I didn't know why the bill was being sent to me. I said maybe it should go to DeMille, or to Paramount, who had produced the picture, or to Hedy Lamarr, but certainly not to me. A month later I got a third bill from Geisler, this time for ten thousand dollars. I decided to ignore it.

Two weeks later I had a phone call from a weeping Hedy Lamarr. She said Geisler's office was threatening to garnishee all of her possessions. She didn't know what to do and was appealing to me for help. Hedy's career, by this time, was slipping badly. I gathered that Geisler had been billing me for his work on her suit because Hedy was out of money and I might be a softer touch than Sam Goldwyn and Cecil B. DeMille.

In a way I was, for I felt very sorry for her. "I'll tell you what I'll do, Hedy," I said. "If you can get Geisler's office to issue a new bill for $5,000 and have it marked: 'Payment in full for services rendered to Hedy Lamarr, Cecil B. DeMille, Paramount Pictures, and all parties connected with the film 'Samson and Delilah,' I'll pay the bill."

Two weeks later, I got such a bill from Geisler's office, *LOOK* sent off a check, and that was the end of that rather bizarre matter.

SELZNICK VS. CHAPLIN

I made many trips to Hollywood during the 1950's, which was a time of immense turmoil and trauma in the movie industry. Nowhere was the pernicious and destructive impact of the Joe McCarthy era felt more profoundly. Much has been written, of course, about the blacklist, about wrecked careers and talented individuals who could not find employment unless they worked under pseudonyms.

The deep political polarization that McCarthyism fostered manifested itself as well in many small ways in Hollywood during this period, even on such seemingly innocuous occasions as informal social gatherings. One evening I attended a small dinner party given by Douglas Fairbanks, Jr. Among the guests were Charlie Chaplin and producer David Selznick. Chaplin had been publicly branded a Communist by McCarthy. Selznick, in contrast, was if anything to the right of McCarthy.

No doubt sensitive to this, Fairbanks had prudently seated the two men at opposite ends of the table. But that didn't prevent them from becoming embroiled in a hot political argument. As Chaplin tried to explain his views on Communism, Selznick turned more and more livid with rage, lept from his chair and dashed around the long table toward Chaplin, knocking everything—china, silver, glasses—out of his way. Just seconds before the start of what most certainly would have been a nasty fist fight, the rest of us managed to keep the two men apart.

For years to come, Chaplin's great artistry continued to take second place to his politics in the view of many in Hollywood, and he remained a virtual outcast. Not until 1972, when he was given a special Academy Award for his contributions to the film industry, did he achieve the full rehabilitation that he had so long deserved.

KAY SUMMERSBY AND IKE

One day not long after the end of the war, a woman walked into Dan Mich's office and identified herself as Kay Summersby. She said she had written a story and had some photographs about her relationship with General Dwight D. Eisenhower, who was now president of Columbia University. During the period Ike had commanded the Allied Expeditionary Forces in Europe, Summersby, a member of the British Women's Army Corps, had been his driver. There had already been gossip about Summersby and Ike, and even rumors that at one time Eisenhower had considered divorcing Mamie to marry her.

Dan looked over the story and the pictures. They seemed generally innocuous. The thrust of the story was basically how much admiration she had for the general. But some of the photographs did seem to suggest more than just a simple working relationship. Two or three showed Ike and Kay picnicking on a beach with both clad in rather

160

abbreviated (for those days) swim suits.

Dan, anxious to make a deal, called and asked if I could come to his office and meet Kay and see what she had brought with her. After doing so, I said that I didn't think *LOOK* would want to publish the article and photographs unless it had the general's approval.

"That's no problem," Kay said, much to my surprise. "I'll need a note from Eisenhower saying that he has no objection," I said.

Kay left, and a few hours later reappeared with a note addressed to me on the stationary of the President, Columbia University.

"Dear Mr. Cowles," the note said. "I have no objection at all if *LOOK* magazine buys and publishes the article Miss Summersby is submitting and uses any of the photographs she is submitting. Very truly yours, Dwight D. Eisenhower."

I don't know why Ike was so quick to give his assent, except that perhaps he was afraid there might be more of a scandal if he tried to stop her. I did hear that some wealthy Republicans who were anxious to see Eisenhower elected President in 1952 and worried about Kay Summersby paid her a rather substantial amount of money to go to South America and stay there for six months until the election campaign was over. Evidence that has come out recently, however, tends to suggest that their relationship was close but completely platonic.

I never heard anything from Ike after our story was published. But I did have a brief encounter with Mamie. It was during a victory celebration at the Biltmore Hotel in New York after Eisenhower's 1952 election. Some party official was taking Mamie around the room and introducing her to the many celebrities in attendance. They got to me and the official made the introduction.

"You're the man who published those Kay Summersby photographs," she said curtly. Then she looked away and hurried on to the next person.

AN INTERVIEW WITH STALIN

LOOK, like many major magazines, occasionally commissioned stories from various luminaries whose lack of professional journalistic experience was more than compensated for, we thought, by the recognition value of their byline. Our editors were very adept at transforming even the most tedious and pedestrian results into lively and engaging prose.

Not long after the end of the war, I thought it might be a good idea to send Elliot Roosevelt, the youngest of FDR's four children, and his wife Fay Emerson to Russia to get an interview with Stalin. Elliot not long before had been in Russia on some minor assignment from his father, and I had heard he had established a pleasant friendship with the hard-to-get-to Russian leader.

Elliot was happy to take the assignment. We agreed to pay him a $25,000 fee plus expenses. He agreed that neither he nor his wife would talk to the press, appear on TV, or write any other stories about their trip until after the *LOOK* story had been published.

But after they got back, they were immediately besieged with big-money requests for interviews from all the media. Elliot couldn't resist. He agreed to a $10,000 offer to do a radio show on NBC. The network announced its coup and said the program would be broadcast within a day or two.

I was furious. *LOOK* had already gone to press with the Stalin interview. I got nowhere with appeals to Elliot. In desperation, I called his mother Eleanor. She knew, of course, of her son's contract with us. After I explained the urgency of the situation, she said, "Mike, could you possibly drive up to Hyde Park tomorrow evening? I'll see to it that Elliot and Fay will be here."

When I walked into her comfortable sitting room Mrs. Roosevelt, her son and daughter-in-law were waiting for me. "Mike," Mrs. Roosevelt said after I had seated myself, "I want you to repeat the facts exactly as you told them to me." I did so, and when I finished I offered the contract to Mrs. Roosevelt to read. "That won't be necessary, Mike," she said. Thanking me, she turned to her son. "Do you want to dispute anything Mr. Cowles has said?" From both Elliot and Fay the answer was a very sheepish "No."

"Very well," Eleanor said. "Now, Elliot, you get right on the phone to NBC and tell them you are not going on any radio program, not until after the story appears in *LOOK*. I want you to do that in Mr. Cowles' presence. And I want you to remember that you had given your word."

Elliot did just as he was told.

EARL WARREN AND FOREIGN AFFAIRS

Through the years, I became well acquainted with Earl Warren, former Governor of California and later Chief Justice of the United States Supreme Court. It is my belief that he was one of our greatest Chief Justices, primarily because of the unanimous decision he got out of the Supreme Court in 1954 in the landmark *Brown vs. Board of Education* desegregation case.

I saw another side of Warren in 1948, when he still was occupying the Governor's seat in Sacramento. At the time he was making a serious attempt to win the Republican Presidential nomination. He called me one day and asked if I had any plans to be in his state in the near future. It happened that I was going to be in San Francisco in about two weeks from then, and he asked if I would join him alone for dinner in San Francisco.

In the course of the evening the Governor confessed to me that he had never paid much attention to foreign affairs. He said he had done very little traveling, and that he never read anything on foreign affairs. He

162

even skipped foreign news when he read newspapers.

"Mike," he asked toward the end of the evening, "could you send me two books, not more than two, that I could read carefully that could make me an expert on foreign affairs?"

I didn't know how to respond. I couldn't imagine how reading two books could make anyone even close to an expert on foreign affairs. As politely as I could, I said that the subject was extremely complicated and that probably the best thing he could do was to get into the habit of reading the foreign news coverage in *The New York Times.*

Warren, of course, lost his bid for the presidential nomination and ended up as the vice-presidential candidate on Thomas E. Dewey's losing ticket. Whatever Earl Warren's lack of understanding of foreign affairs, few men have made more of a contribution to the United States in the field of domestic affairs.

A DRESSING DOWN

Early one Sunday morning in the 1950's, I received a call from an aide to Konrad Adenauer, West Germany's Chancellor, whom I had met several times and knew quite well. The Chancellor was visiting New York, the aide said, and would like to see me in his suite at the Waldorf Towers.

We met about noon after he had attended a service at Saint Patrick's Cathedral. He barely paused to greet me before pulling out a copy of *LOOK* published about two months previously. He turned to an article describing how vestiges of Nazism were still alive in some small West German villages.

For the next twenty minutes, West Germany's Chancellor scolded me like a school master. "I have done everything possible to stamp out what remains of Nazism," he said, "and an article like this makes my task more difficult."

Adenauer said he was not denying the possible accuracy of the article but he contended, "It deals with more or less isolated cases, not typical of West Germany as a whole. Germany will have to live down the horrible period of Hitler, but magazines like *LOOK* should help, not hinder, that effort."

"Nazism," he stated firmly, "must never be allowed to raise its ugly head again in Germany."

A LUNCH AT "21"

Not long after the United States entered World War II, I had the pleasure of meeting Albert Lasker for the first time. He wanted to interest me in a manuscript called *Victory Through Air Power* by Alexander P. de Seversky. The book's thesis was that a large build-up in U.S. long-range air power could help win the war quicker with a smaller number of casualties than other strategies. Lasker was engaged in a personal crusade to promote the idea. I found the argument so convincing that I serialized the book in *LOOK*. Over the next few years, Lasker and I developed a close friendship that lasted until his death in 1952.

Air power was just one of Lasker's crusades and crusades were just a part of his extraordinarily rich life. He is best known as a philanthropist, but in fact he was a true Renaissance man, an overused term but appropriate for his diverse talents and interests.

Lasker is considered by many the father of modern advertising, where he made his fortune. Beginning as a ten-dollar-a-week clerk in the Lord & Thomas advertising agency in Chicago, he left 44 years later as president after having made it among the largest and most successful advertising agencies in the world. He then dedicated his money and the rest of his life to public service.

Perhaps his most passionate pursuit was medical research. With the eager assistance of Mary, his third wife, he spent years trying to convince the government to devote more funds to find the cures of cancer, heart disease, and other ills. He opened an office in Washington, hired public relations counsel, and offered large campaign contributions to Congressmen who would agree to support medical research legislation. It is not an exaggeration to say that the many billions that the federal government has spent in this area over the past several decades were largely due to Albert and Mary Lasker's initial prodding.

One day in the late 1940's, Lasker phoned me and said it was a matter of great importance that I join him the next day for lunch at "21," the well-known New York restaurant. I was to be there at noon and agreed to stay until 2:30. Ten of his closest friends were in the private upstairs dining room when I arrived, among them General David Sarnoff and Wild Bill Donovan. When the elaborate meal was finished, Albert ordered the waiters out of the room. He took his watch out of his pocket and placed it on the table in front of him.

I'm sure all of us around the table expected an announcement of another dramatic philanthropic project. Instead, we were to hear the true story of his second marriage. All of us knew that before meeting Mary he had been married rather briefly to a beautiful and intelligent actress named Doris Kenyon. But that was just about all we knew. Before this moment, he had almost never mentioned his second wife.

"I invited you here," Lasker began, "because my analyst insists that I open a festering sore to you, my very close friends. He wants me to tell you a painful story and not to omit a single detail." The story that unfolded was, to say the least, shocking.

After Lasker's first wife died, he had gone into a deep depression, and some of his close friends felt that another marriage to the right woman would restore his spirits. They arranged dates with some very attractive women, but none interested him until he was introduced to Doris

Kenyon by Will Hayes, one-time Hollywood movie czar. Lasker was enraptured—much more so, it seemed, than Kenyon. Kenyon agreed to marry him—but only, she said, if he would give her a million dollars before the ceremony.

On the morning of the wedding, Albert called for his bride-to-be at her hotel in Beverly Hills. He took her to a bank where they were ushered into a private room. The chief officer of the bank brought in one million dollars in government bonds, in ten-thousand dollar denominations, all neatly tied up in a bundle. Doris Kenyon untied the ribbon, opened the packet and carefully counted the bonds. She retied the ribbon, turned to the bank officer and announced, "I want to rent a safety deposit box." Clutching the packet of bonds she excused herself from Albert and followed the bank officer to the safety deposit vault. When she came back to the room where Albert was waiting, she kissed him and said she was now ready to go through with the wedding ceremony. A judge who was a friend of Albert's performed the ceremony at the courthouse. Afterwards L.B. Mayer gave a large wedding luncheon for the bride and groom.

For the honeymoon, Albert had booked about half the top luxury deck of an ocean liner that was bound on a world cruise. Accompanying the newlyweds were a secretary and valet for Albert, and a hairdresser, lady's maid, and secretary for Doris.

They reached Honolulu, the first port of call, early one morning. Albert was on deck to watch the ship dock. Suddenly he heard a slight commotion behind him. Turning, he saw Doris, dressed in travel attire, and accompanied by her maid, hairdresser, and secretary, who were also fully dressed for departure. Dozens of pieces of luggage stood nearby ready to be sent ashore.

Doris came over to Albert, kissed him, and said, "Albert, it's been nice knowing you." With that she and her entourage debarked. She proceeded immediately to the Royal Hawaiian Hotel, took a suite, phoned United Air Lines, and booked a flight to Reno that same day. Sixty days later she had her divorce from Albert.

This experience cost Albert Lasker many tortured hours with his analyst. Finally he accepted the analyst's advice to stop concealing it and to relate it to a few trusted friends. In this bare account of the episode I have omitted, for obvious reasons, some of the more intimate details.

When Lasker concluded his story, there was dead silence for a few moments. David Sarnoff was the first to sense what he needed from us. Sarnoff got up, walked around the table, and flung both arms around him. "Albert," Sarnoff said, "we all love you." That feeling was shared by us all.

My recollection of this very sad and disturbing episode in the life of an obviously tormented man has remained private with me until now.

A FASCINATING WOMAN

In many ways, Margaret Thompson Biddle was as fascinating an individual as Albert Lasker. Her life, at least some of which I had the opportunity to observe at close range, was even more fascinating.

Margaret was the only child of William Boyce Thompson, a mining engineer from Montana. He became very successful as a prospector in the Rocky Mountain area and in 1921 organized the Newmont Mining Company, one of the largest mining concerns in the country with revenues of over $1 billion. Disappointed he had not produced a male heir, Thompson brought up his daughter as if she were a boy. Even during her teens, she was invited to sit in on conferences in her father's offices. She quickly became familiar with the intricacies of Newmont's financial dealings and developed a thorough understanding of the mining business.

Thompson frequently made equity investments in mineral exploration ventures, and one of his dealings was with a British mining engineer named Ernest Oppenheimer, who claimed to have some promising leads on gold and diamond deposits in South Africa. The principal investor in Oppenheimer was Morgan Grenfell & Co., then the London branch of the Morgan bank in the U.S., which put up $250,000 and recommended that the Morgan office in New York match that sum. The New York partners were reluctant but went along with $125,000. William Thompson, who conducted most of his financial affairs through the Morgan bank and was close to senior partner Thomas Lamont, put up the other $125,000.

Oppenheimer drilled and prospected for several years and found veins indicating the presence of gold and diamonds. But the big strike he was hoping for eluded him. When his money ran out, Oppenheimer returned to London in hopes of raising additional capital. Thoroughly disenchanted, the Morgan Grenfell partners turned him down flat. And they suggested to the New York partners that they do likewise if Oppenheimer should turn to them.

Which is what Oppenheimer decided to do. But while he was in mid-passage across the Atlantic, William Thompson, who was on another sea journey, fell ill and died. Margaret Thompson was sole heir to his vast estate, the executor of which was the Morgan Bank. When Oppenheimer reached New York, he obtained an appointment with J.P. Morgan and some of the other partners. As a courtesy, J.P. invited Margaret, not yet twenty years old, to be present.

It was clear from the start of the meeting that J.P. was according Oppenheimer nothing more than a courtesy as well. As the partners gathered in the boardroom Morgan pointed to the foot of the table, indicating to Oppenheimer to take his place there. Then Morgan ostentatiously took out a fat gold watch and told Oppenheimer that he was limited to forty-five minutes to say what he had to say. Oppenheimer pleaded his case with passion and conviction, but to very deaf ears. When the forty-five minutes were up, Morgan snapped his watch shut and, without consulting his partners, announced that his bank would not put any more money into the venture. He added that he was confident that he spoke for the William Boyce Thompson estate as well.

Margaret suddenly stood up. "Mr. Morgan," she said, "I am sorry but you do not speak for the Thompson estate." Turning to Oppenheimer, she declared, with the authority of someone who had been making business deals for years, "Mr. Oppenheimer, the Thompson estate will put up $250,000." Ernest Oppenheimer came around the table, bent and kissed the young woman's hand. Then he bowed to the Morgan partners, put on his hat and walked out of the room.

About a year later Oppenheimer made his long-sought strike. In a very rich vein, he discovered the largest diamond ever found up to that time. He presented it to the Queen of England and was later knighted and became Sir Ernest. Before long he found a diamond almost as large which he sent to Margaret as a gift.

In the early 1930's, meanwhile, Margaret married Tony Biddle, who had been appointed Ambassador to Norway by President Roosevelt. Two or three years later he was transferred to Poland. When Hitler invaded Poland the Biddles and their staff made a unique escape in a cavalcade of Rolls Royces through Constantinople and eventually made it to London. Tony Biddle then became Ambassador to the Occupied Countries—all of them. After a ten-year marriage the Biddles were divorced and Margaret settled in Paris.

Most people in her position would have settled down into a comfortable, glamorous life as a socialite. But Margaret was never like most people. As the largest shareholder, she remained very active in the affairs of Newmont Mining. And she sought out and got the job as Paris editor of *Flair*.

It was during this period that Margaret and I became good friends. One day she invited me to pick her up and escort her to a dinner party at the home of the Duke and Duchess of Windsor. When I arrived at her house—a charming place on the Left Bank near the Chamber of Deputies with a walled garden in back—I was met by an attractive, muscular man who looked as if he might have played tackle for Notre Dame. He was wearing black tie so I assumed he was a friend of Margaret's. The butler said Mrs. Biddle was going to be about fifteen minutes late so I suggested to the stranger that we go into the library and fix ourselves a drink, which we did.

Fifteen minutes later Margaret came down the stairs, looking regal wearing the famous Oppenheimer diamond. Set in a pendant, it looked spectacular. I suddenly realized that the man waiting with me must be a security guard from an insurance company. I was right. His job was to

167

accompany Margaret whenever she wore this priceless piece of jewelry.

When Margaret and I got into the back seat of the Rolls, the insurance guard locked us in—the car was equipped with Yale locks—and sat up front with the chauffeur. The guard never left Margaret's side until he had delivered her safely into the Windsor drawing room.

When the three of us returned from the party, Margaret invited me in for a nightcap. "Excuse us a minute," Margaret said once we were inside. "You go into the library, Mike, and mix yourself a drink." She and the security guard went upstairs to deposit the diamond in a wall safe. The guard bedded down for the night right under the safe in a small anteroom to Margaret's bedroom. "Mike," she said laughing as she came downstairs, "not every woman can have a big, handsome specimen like that sleeping outside her bedroom whenever she wants him there!"

Mining, not parties, though, remained Margaret's principal love. Once, during a quiet dinner alone, during which we talked almost exclusively about her business affairs, she told me her associates at Newmont had just learned of some extraordinary rich mineral deposits in French North Africa. She said she intended to obtain for Newmont an exclusive concession for the mineral rights from the French government.

"How are you going to do that?" I asked her.

"I'm going to elect my own premier of France," she responded, in all seriousness.

I couldn't help laughing at the absurdity of the idea. But I had underestimated Margaret—and the political power that wealth can command. Though her French was rather skimpy in her early days in Paris, she managed to cultivate the friendship of the most influential politicians in France. Then she selected the most attractive, articulate, and intelligent among them—a man named Rene Plevin—and backed him with plenty of money. In 1950, Plevin was elected president of the Council of Ministers, as the premier was called at the time. Soon thereafter, Newmont obtained the mining concessions.

The LaCoz family, which owned the largest French mining company, was outraged. Having discovered the quid pro quo, they threatened to expose it unless they were given the concessions. Margaret shrewdly forestalled a public scandal by cutting the LaCoz family in on half the deal.

As business partners now, Margaret and the LaCoz family members sometimes saw each other socially. One evening Margaret was invited by the family to be their guest at a dinner at their home prior to the gala opening of the Paris opera season and to attend the performance afterward. During the performance, Margaret became very ill. As it happened, one of the members of the party was a doctor who was married to one of the LaCoz daughters. He agreed to take her home and put her to bed. The next morning, Margaret's maid found her dead.

168

Margaret's death made headlines in the French press. It was soon disclosed that the doctor had a rather questionable background and had been accused of murdering a sailor on the LaCoz estate on the Riviera about a year earlier. Yet no proof of foul play was ever uncovered and no charges were ever filed. After things quieted down, however, the LaCoz family was granted Newmont's half of the North Africa mineral concessions.

In the years after Margaret's death, I kept wondering what happened to her fabulous diamond. I talked with some of her friends and even some members of the family, including Morton Downey, her son-in-law. But nobody seemed to know—or at least was willing to talk about it.

THE WINDSORS REMEMBERED

I saw the Duke and Duchess of Windsor often, both in Europe and America, and over a period of years I got to know them well. In New York, my wife at the time, Fleur, and I gave several dinner parties for them. My impression of the Duke was of a man sadly lacking in judgment when it came to world affairs, British problems, or even simple human relations. But he had an incredible memory, especially for inconsequentials. He relished talking about his trips to India as Prince of Wales, for example, and could rattle off dates, the names of hostesses who had entertained him, even the names of guests at dinner parties that I'm sure had been long since forgotten by everyone else.

When it came to affairs that mattered he had no sense at all. During the war he became involved with the notorious Clivedon Set, the powerful little clique of British aristocrats working for totalitarianism in England, who would just as soon have welcomed a Hitler victory. The Duke seemed to be unaware that he was being manipulated by the group to further their interests.

The interests of the Duke and Duchess were limited to their rarified social world. Their life seemed to be a continuous battle against boredom which was often fought with frivolous entertainment. One of their diversions when they were in New York was to go to Chubby Checkers' dive on the West Side and watch the twist, the dance craze of the day. In fact, they occasionally had Chubby in to entertain their guests after a dinner party in their Waldorf Towers suite.

The Duke enjoyed the attention of the press, which was almost universally favorable even after his abdication. On one of his New York visits I invited him to lunch in the executive dining room at *LOOK*. I called for him at his suite and walked him back to the *LOOK* offices a few blocks away. He was wearing a raincoat which I casually threw over the arm of a sofa. When my secretary, Martha Stephens, picked it up to hang it in a closet she was startled to see that it was lined in mink. This was years before mink-lined raincoats became regarded as the height of chic

169

among the fashion conscious. At a luncheon the Duke managed to fascinate the *LOOK* editors with stories about his good-will travels throughout the British Empire when he was Prince of Wales.

I visited the Windsors in France one year at the old mill which the Duchess had bought and converted into a charming country house. I was amused by what she had done with the private quarters.

For herself, she had laid out a huge bedroom, with an enormous bed, a tremendous bathroom-dressing room, and an elegant salon. Down a narrow hallway toward the back of the house and two or three steps down, were the Duke's quarters. About one-third the size of hers, they consisted of a bedroom and bathroom-sitting room. Part of the suite was directly over the kitchen. But I really don't think this arrangement bothered the former King of England. He remained very fond of the Duchess during all the years of their marriage until his death in 1972.

A DUET WITH TRUMAN

I did not support Harry Truman when he ran against Tom Dewey in 1948, but as I got to know him better over the years, my respect for him grew. One evening during the Truman Administration, he attended the annual formal dinner of the Gridiron Club, the exclusive organization of top Washington journalists. Richard Wilson, head of the Cowles Washington Bureau, was president of the Gridiron Club that year and he informed me that Truman would drop by the reception that the Cowles papers always gave after the dinner at the Statler Hotel.

The President was scheduled to close out the dinner with a speech, and after the speech, according to custom, the audience would be told to remain standing until the President and his party had left the room. Because Truman was to proceed immediately to the Cowles suite, I left the dinner before his speech to make sure I was on hand when he arrived.

A dozen waiters were busily administering the last-minute touches to several buffet tables and three bars when I arrived at the suite. Quite excited by the President's imminent appearance, they all lined up at the door, hoping for a glimpse and a handshake. I fell in at the tail end of the line. When Truman walked in the door, he greeted each man with a warm word and a firm clasp of the hand. But when he got to me, he gave me just a cold stare and no handshake.

From the receiving line of waiters, Truman marched straight over to a baby grand piano set in an alcove. None of the other guests had arrived, and he began to play a piece of classical music that was unfamiliar to me. Could he have mistaken me for a maitre d' he didn't like? That was impossible, for we had met several times since he had become President. Truman had been known to snub people who had not supported him politically, and I figured that must have been the reason for the chilly

170

reception. I couldn't just let it end there, and I followed him to the piano and sat down beside him.

He continued playing the piano and, without looking at me, asked, "You play the piano?"

"I took lessons about forty-five years ago, Mr. President, but there's only one piece left in my repertoire now."

"What's that."

"The Missouri Waltz."

Truman laughed. "When I'm through playing this piece," he said, "we'll do a duet."

He played through to the end of whatever it was and then inquired, "What key are we going to play it in?" I told him, and off we went into a duet of his famous theme song.

"Who are you?" the President, obviously pretending not to know, asked when we finished our performance.

"I'm Mike Cowles, Mr. President, one of your hosts."

He gave me a long hard look. "I know you think I'm a son of a bitch," he said. "I know you are a son of a bitch. Let's go to the bar and have a drink together."

We got up from the piano bench. The President put his arm around me and we walked over to the bar. The room was still empty except for the two of us, the waiters, and the bartender. Truman asked for a bourbon. The bartender poured a very generous drink. "What do you think I am, a child?" the President chided. "Pour me a man's drink." The bartender poured some more, a lot more. "That's more like it," Truman said approvingly. I asked for a Scotch highball and we clinked glasses. People were at last beginning to arrive and that was the end of our conversation.

One summer during the mid-1960's, long after Truman had left the White House, my wife Jan received a call from Truman's daughter Margaret. Margaret and her husband Clifton Daniel had a summer cottage near ours in Mt. Kisco, New York, and were good friends of my wife. Margaret's parents were coming in from Independence, Missouri, for the weekend to see the grandchildren and, since her house was quite small, she wondered if we would be willing to host a dinner party.

Jan said we would be delighted. We were already expecting one weekend visitor, Charles Goren, the world-famous bridge expert.

It was a beautiful party. Conversation was animated and interesting. Halfway through dinner, Truman asked my wife, although he was really addressing all of the eighteen people at our table, "How many around this table have been divorced?" My wife looked from couple to couple and, to her chagrin, had to admit that everyone, with the exception of Bess and Harry Truman, had gone through a divorce.

While the President held forth on the evils of divorce in a rather loud voice at his end of the table I enjoyed a quiet conversation with Mrs.

Truman at my end. I found her unpretentious and charming. At one point she leaned toward me and whispered, "I can't wait to get back to Independence. When I tell the girls at the bridge club that I'd actually met Charlie Goren they'll be thrilled!" I was amused to hear this from a woman who probably met most of the important people in the world during her years at the White House.

After dinner, while the guests were gathering for coffee in the living room, I guided Mr. Truman and three other men into a small library for coffee and brandy. When we were comfortably seated I steered the talk toward politics.

"Now that you're above parties and politics, Mr. President, do you think the country might just be in the mood for a Republican president in the next election?" At the time, it was universally accepted that Lyndon Johnson would be running for a second term—and would almost certainly be elected.

Truman eyed me suspiciously.

"You know them all, Mr. President," I persisted. "Which Republican do you think would be best for the country?"

Truman took a moment or so to think about this and then decided to answer the question. And he did, in his customary, blunt, honest way. "Well, Mr. Cowles, I always liked that Rockefeller boy. If he could get the Republican nomination, he'd be a helluva candidate. In fact, I think he'd win and make a goddamn good president!"

THE LION OF JUDAH

One day during Eisenhower's first administration, possibly 1953 or 1954, I had a phone call from Secretary of State John Foster Dulles asking me for a favor. Haile Selassie, the ruler of Ethiopia, was coming to New York and the State Department was trying to line up private hosts to entertain him. I had never especially admired Selassie and his ostensibly benevolent but too often repressive brand of despotism that did little to lift his country out of a state of appalling poverty and illiteracy. But I agreed to help, and when Selassie arrived in New York, I called on him in his Waldorf Towers suite to inquire if there was anything I could do to make his trip more pleasant. I was received graciously if briefly but with such pomp and circumstance that, when I prepared to leave the room, I was quietly advised by an aide I was to walk backwards so as not to turn my back on the Emperor.

Just as I reached the door, however, Selassie suddenly remarked that he had heard of a famous New York restaurant called "21." Would it be possible, he asked, for me to arrange a luncheon there for him and his entourage? I assured him I would be honored and he chose a time a few days later.

I went right over to "21" to talk to Mac and Jack Kreindler, the restaurant's owners. They were clearly nervous about the idea. In those days, few if any blacks had crossed "21" 's hallowed threshold. The Kreindlers certainly harbored no racial prejudices, but they were worried about the possibility of an "incident," as they called it. "Nonsense," I told them firmly. "This is a luncheon for an Emperor and his royal party." I proceeded to order the best table in the upstairs dining room. The Kreindlers promised to do their best.

I rode with the Emperor from the Waldorf to "21" with the rest of the party of twelve in limousines behind us. Word of the event had spread, and when we arrived a crowd of spectators had gathered in the small reception area in the front of the restaurant.

At the end of the meal, I introduced the Kreindlers to the Emperor who complimented them on the excellent food and service. Everything went off beautifully. And, of course, there was no "incident."

Years later, I visited Ethiopia with my wife Jan, and the last day of our trip we obtained an audience with the Emperor. It was like a scene from an old MGM spectacular. There actually were lions chained to the entrance gates of the palace. Jan and I and a few other visitors were ushered by a large group of retainers into a throne room more than sixty feet long. At the far end sat the Lion of Judah on a tall throne. A fair number of women—wives and daughters, I guessed—were seated along the wall. Two small chairs stood alongside the throne for those whom the Emperor would be addressing directly. The visitors were instructed to advance one by one along a carpet stretching the length of the room, stop about twenty feet in front of the throne, and then bow to the Emperor. We were then to step to one side until everyone had been introduced and wait our turn to be summoned to one of the little chairs.

When my turn came to talk to the Emperor, I reminded him of the luncheon at "21." He responded warmly. But without warning, his tone changed. He launched into a loud and angry tirade against the United States. Why hadn't we stopped Mussolini when he invaded Ethiopia? The United States would never be a great power, he went on, until it did something about stopping imperialism.

I couldn't think of an appropriate response, and so I just sat there until he had finished talking and then made way for the next visitor.

A SPEECH BY NEHRU

Winston Churchill once remarked that the single most important fact about India was that everyone in the government and the Civil Service spoke English and no Russian. I mentioned this to Prime Minister Nehru during a one-and-a-half-hour interview I had with him in 1952 during a visit to India. Nehru remembered Churchill's observation. But he reminded me quite pointedly that officially India was bilingual—Hindi and English.

It was a pleasant interview. We chatted about a number of other subjects for a while until a secretary came in to remind him that he was due in Parliament in about ten minutes. The Prime Minister graciously invited me to ride with him to the Parliament building. When we arrived he arranged for me to be seated in the distinguished visitors' gallery. The press gallery was packed with about thirty or forty journalists.

The proceedings were conducted entirely in English until Nehru finished answering questions from the Opposition. But then he announced he had a few further remarks to make and switched to Hindi. As he talked, most members of the press, who apparently did not speak Hindi, slowly drifted out of the chamber. And, to my astonishment, so did about three-quarters of the M.P.'s, at lease some of whom probably didn't speak Hindi either.

I later learned that this was the first time Nehru had used Hindi in Parliament in many months. Nehru had always been sensitive to criticism of India's close ties to England and the English-speaking, and I felt quite certain that his short speech in Hindi was for my benefit.

KHRUSHCHEV—"AN OLD SPARROW"

I had two encounters with Nikita Khrushchev under quite different circumstances. The first was during his 1959 tour of the United States when he addressed the Economic Club in New York. One of the major points of his speech was that it was of the utmost importance that a better understanding be established between the American and Russian peoples. But his tone throughout seemed tough, combative, and uncompromising. During the question period, I rose to ask him about freedom of the press and freedom of information.

"Why is it, sir," I asked, "if that is your feeling you will not allow your people to listen to a broadcast from the United States, if they wish, and why is it that you do not allow periodicals, magazines, and newspapers to be distributed freely throughout the Soviet Union, and why is it that when the Soviet journalists resident in the United States are allowed to send any dispatches they want without any interference from the government or anybody else, why do you insist on censoring the dispatches of American correspondents in the Soviet Union?"

Khrushchev responded that the circumstances of the American invitation for his visit included an agreement "that our discussions will not bear on the internal affairs of either country."

"Answer the question!" several people in the audience demanded.

Khrushchev was obviously annoyed. "I am an old sparrow," he said, "and you cannot muddle me with your cries. . .I come here as a representative of a great country, a great people who have made a great revolution, and no cries. . .can do away with the great achievement of our people."

174

Shouts of "Answer the question!" became more insistent.

"I will reply to the question when there are no interruptions. The reply is this: The question of what is listened to or read should be decided, not by any outside government. . .but by our own people and by the government." That was as much of an answer as he was willing to give.

Three years later, in April 1962, I had an exclusive, three-hour interview with Khrushchev in Moscow. It took place in the same third-floor room in the Kremlin where Joe Barnes and I had met Joseph Stalin in 1942 during the Willkie trip. Accompanying me was Edward M. Korry, my assistant and formerly *LOOK's* European editor. Also present were an official of the Soviet foreign ministry, a translator, and a stenographer.

As we entered the 40-foot-long office, whose three windows faced the upper part of the Kremlin walls a few feet away, Khrushchev was standing beside his desk at the far end. After an exchange of greetings, we took seats at a long, felt-covered conference table, just beyond which was a glass cabinet holding four ears of corn—a fitting symbol of his peasant origins and his continuing strong interest in improving Soviet agricultural performance.

He was very cordial. One reason might have been that the Cowles newspapers in Des Moines had spearheaded an intensive drive to establish good agricultural relations between the U.S. and the Soviet Union. But he also appeared anxious to erase the popular American picture of him as a loud-mouthed, unruly, vodka-swilling Communist tyrant—a picture derived in large part from his bellicose, shoe-thumping performance at the United Nations General Assembly session in 1960. In answering my questions, he did not retreat an inch from such well-known demands that Western troops would have to quit West Berlin for there to be any real peace in Germany. But he chose his words with care, prudently avoiding giving any offense to Americans, voiced his respect for President Kennedy, and sought to explain his belief in the evolutionary triumph of Communism while at the same time paying tribute to American achievements. He seemed to be trying to convey the impression of a statesman sensitive to the responsibilities of heading the second most powerful country in the world with the potential to destroy much of the world.

As I noted earlier, I was struck by the immense contrast between Khrushchev and Stalin. Stalin was basically a man who distrusted other men, who had no confidence in the future and whose dour cynicism stamped his every action. The present ruler was an extrovert, a realist and an optimist, who genuinely believed that the lot of the average citizen can and must be improved. Whereas Stalin clamped a lid of terror on the U.S.S.R. because he was deeply suspicious of the motives of his allies, his fellow Russians and even his closest associates, Khrushchev had confidently opened Soviet society to the winds of change. Few other world leaders were spending as much time in grass-roots traveling, and his journeys around the Soviet Union had made him conscious of people's needs, desires, and foibles. Khrushchev, of course, remained a dedicated Communist who was mistrustful of the West. But I had the clear sense I was also talking to a pragmatist who had learned from his travels and was willing to listen to other points of view and explore new ways of doing things.

Much of our conversation covered such current political matters as a possible summit meeting with President Kennedy and the future of Germany and Berlin. In light of future events, though, his comments on Soviet agriculture and its problems were especially noteworthy. He talked at great length about Stalin's "ignorance of questions of agriculture" which had had "many harmful consequences" and the fact that Soviet farming was still experiencing "a period of difficulties of growth." Agriculture in Russia, he admitted, had failed to keep pace with the development of industry. While he felt that over time Soviet farming would produce big surpluses, it would take "much time and money" as well as a broad program to educate Soviet farmers on how to bring output to needed levels. "Enthusiasm alone is not enough," he said in one of his most revealing remarks. "Talk about Communism will not make the belly full. A man must eat, he needs clothes, he needs a flat, he needs many other things without which it is impossible to live."

Two years after our interview, Khrushchev was removed from power. According to informed speculation, one of the chief reasons was Russia's repeated failure to meet its agricultural goals. Khrushchev lived in obscurity in a small cottage outside Moscow until his death in 1971.

In 1969, my wife and I made another visit to Russia. While we were in Moscow, I was surprised to receive a call from Victor Louis inviting us to Sunday dinner at his dacha in Peredelkino, the exclusive writers' colony on the outskirts of the city. Louis is a somewhat shadowy figure of uncertain vested interests who has long drifted about in the world of foreign correspondents. Ostensibly, he is a correspondent for French, English, and Italian newspapers as well as an international literary agent. It is said that he helped smuggle the memoirs of Stalin's daughter Svetlana out of Russia. He appears to have intimate contacts with and access to the upper levels of the Soviet government, and many foreign journalists believe he is a special Russian intelligence operative.

Louis picked us up at our hotel in a four-wheel-drive Land Rover. He was as proud of it as a small boy with a complicated electric train. There was an elaborate world-wide receiver built into the dashboard and he asked me if I'd like to listen to the BBC. I said yes, and he twiddled four or five dials until the BBC came in as clearly as though we were on an English road. Would I like to hear Radio Luxembourg? A broadcast from Berlin? The sound came in perfectly from a half dozen countries as he twisted the dials.

When we drove up to his dacha, a large two-story frame house, I could see a Mercedes parked in the driveway and a Porsche in the garage. Nearby, three men were working on a large excavation for a swimming pool that he said he planned to freeze over in winter for skating.

Dinner was served by a friendly, plump middle-aged woman who seemed to have been the cook as well. After dinner my wife asked if she could see more of the house. Mrs. Louis showed us through various rooms until we reached a huge storeroom. It was lined with shelves stacked with thousands of cans of food of all kinds—American, British, and French. The cache seemed to reflect not only the frequency with which the Louises entertain at home but the frequency of Soviet food shortages.

Then Louis led me into his library. It contained a first-rate collection of Russian, French, British, and American books on a wide variety of subjects. Displayed on one shelf by itself was a large silver tray. Victor reached up and handed it to me. I could see at once that it was silver plate with bits of silver peeling off in spots. Engraved on the copper underneath the flaking silver was the inscription: "To the brave people of the Soviet Socialist Republic, and for their heroic efforts in World War II in defeating the imperialist government of Adolf Hitler, I bring the thanks of the people of the United States." It was signed by the Vice President, Richard Milhous Nixon. Nixon had presented the tray to Premier Khrushchev during his 1959 visit to Moscow during which he and the Russian leader had conducted their famous "kitchen debate."

"How in God's name did you get your hands on this?" I asked with astonishment.

"Well, Mr. Cowles," Louis replied, "you see Khrushchev had a dacha just a few miles through the woods from here. Now that he is no longer in power, he is a sad and lonely man. I visit him every week or so, whenever I can. When I was there a few weeks ago he took the tray down from a shelf in his library and said, 'Look, Victor, look how chintzy these capitalist countries are. Nixon brought me this tray as a present from America. Just look at it—nothing but silver-plated and badly silver-plated because it's worn out already. I don't want it. If you want it, take it!'"

When Victor got up to leave Khrushchev that day he just tucked the tray under his arm and brought it home.

BEN GURION'S VISION

In the past twenty-five years or so, my wife Jan and I were accompanied in our worldwide travels by our dear friends Marie and Ed Swenson of Miami, Florida.

Marie and Ed are remarkably public-spirited citizens. They founded a girls' school in Miami and have taken a leading role in dozens of worthy community projects in Florida. Ed, an investment adviser, generously

177

devoted more than two years of his time recently to a large, and highly-successful campaign to increase the endowment of Yale University, his alma mater.

In 1963, in the company of the Swensons, we drove south through the dusty town of Beersheba and into the Negev desert to visit Israel's first Prime Minister, David Ben-Gurion, on his kibbutz, Side Boker.

I shall never forget my first impression of this distinguished world citizen. Small and powerfully built, with his famous mane of white hair, he lived unpretentiously in a little frame cottage, the essence of simplicity. I couldn't help but contrast it in my mind with all the trappings we generally afford our own former heads of state.

Frequently during our meeting, his wife, a former Brooklyn school teacher, would shout from the adjacent kitchen, giving her views on the matter at hand.

At the time of our meeting, Israel was spending perhaps forty percent of her budget on her military establishment; on what Ben-Gurion called "security." He genuinely feared an Arab attack on Israel and, while he admitted that the United States would eventually come to Israel's defense, he worried about a massacre before such help might arrive.

Ben-Gurion, with a quickness of mind that belied his age, argued persuasively that the greatest thing the United States could do for Israel and for peace in the Near East would be to give Israel an adequate quantity of defensive weapons and simultaneously say to Israel, and to the Arab world, that the United States would not tolerate any changes in Israel's boundaries and would move instantly against any aggressor, including Israel itself.

Ben-Gurion thought that sometime during the next decade or two the Soviet Union would evolve into a freer society and that then, perhaps, one or two million Jews from Russia would want to migrate and would be permitted to migrate to Israel. Holding out a welcoming hand to oppressed Jews everywhere in the world, he nevertheless was concerned about the integration problem that created. Large numbers of Jews were emigrating from North Africa and the Yemen and they spoke different languages and had different cultural backgrounds than the refugees from Eastern Europe who built Israel.

A VISIT TO VIETNAM

In *LOOK's* issue of May 14, 1968, we published an editorial (one of the few we ever published) in which we concluded that "the most important national business before us in this year of political debate is to wind up our involvement in the Vietnam war as quickly and as honorably as possible, and to go on from there to the creation of a world order in which America's ingenuity will truly serve the cause of peace."

I had not always thought that way concerning our involvement in that war. Neither, as history has shown, had millions of other Americans when we sent military advisors, and then our first troops, to that remote place on the other side of the world. Fears of a Communist takeover, followed by a Red conquest of all of Southeast Asia—the so-called "domino theory"—permeated our thinking, and a quick ending of the matter with an infusion of American power seemed in order.

Such was my thinking when, on March 5 through 8 in 1965 I visited Vietnam in the company of Ed Swenson of Miami. We arrived when the first contingent of U.S. Marines was landing at Danang. Members of the Joint Chiefs of Staff were present for that occasion.

General William C. Westmoreland included me at a dinner party he gave on the evening following arrival of the Joint Chiefs, and I was seated next to Robert G.K. Thompson, a British Brigadier General who established a reputation as an expert on counter-insurgency through several years spent in chasing the Huks out of Malaysia. He was present as head of a small British Advisory Mission in Vietnam and three months later was knighted by the British government.

General Thompson told me that U.S. troops in Vietnam did not know how to fight in a guerrila war. Your weapons are too heavy, he said, and your troops expect at least one complete meal each day from their commissary. He said that he had learned from his experience in Malaysia that the only way to fight a guerrila war was to send out groups of no more than twenty men who might have to survive in the jungle by their own resources for days or weeks without any contact with their army headquarters.

I should have paid more attention to what General Thompson told me that evening.

Later, General Westmoreland asked me to stay behind for a private talk. He asked me to go to Washington on my return and lobby to get him an additional 50,000 men immediately; that if he had those reinforcements he could win the war in the following six months. Westmoreland not only got those reinforcements (with no lobbying on my part), but several hundred thousand more men, and the war went on for eight more years, with the last of our G.I.'s leaving in 1973, and our Embassy evacuated in 1975.

Slightly more than a year after my visit, on May 21, 1966, *LOOK's* correspondent in Vietnam, Sam Castan, age 31, was killed while covering action in Vinh Thanh Valley. I shall never forget the words cabled to us in New York by one of Sam's fellow correspondents:
"Sam was an inspiration for those of us searching for some truth in this Babel of conflicting reports. He was one of the most respected journalists here, sensitive to the unbelievable complexities of politics and war. He was not a war hero, but he was among the bravest war correspondents in Vietnam."

DICK NIXON, A FRIEND, AND THEN. . .

I met Dick Nixon fairly early in his political career when he was a young Senator from California. One day in 1952 he called and asked if I could come to Chicago to join him for lunch at the Blackstone Hotel the following week. I agreed, and we spent quite some time alone. He impressed me as being an attractive, vigorous person. He also was extremely ambitious and anxious to get on the Republican ticket with Eisenhower in 1952. I thought it was a good idea.

During his years as Vice President, I got to know Nixon well. Each year I hosted a stag dinner for him at the Waldorf in New York attended by the heads of large corporations. My reason for hosting the dinner was a selfish one. I was working very hard to increase *LOOK*'s advertising volume, and I knew that business leaders enjoyed the opportunity to get acquainted with top political figures, especially one who was regarded as a likely future President. Nixon, for his part, enjoyed the opportunity to become acquainted with potential campaign contributors, and he always helped me complete the guest list.

Under the format we estalished, no *LOOK* business was discussed. Nixon was allotted about twenty minutes to say whatever he wanted about politics, economics, foreign affairs, or whatever. He then would answer questions from the audience for about forty-five minutes. Afterwards, he would stay around for about an hour, visiting informally and having a nightcap with the guests.

In 1962, following his overwhelming loss for the governorship of California, Nixon moved to New York, where he became a senior partner in the law firm of Mudge, Rose, Guthrie & Alexander. But he was a political animal to his fingertips and I was sure that the law firm was only a launching pad for another try for the White House. I went to his office one day in 1963 with a proposal for our mutual benefit.

"I think you're going to try for the nomination again, Dick," I said. "I believe foreign affairs are a big issue in America today and it seems to me that whichever candidate shows a good solid grasp of international matters stands a good chance of winning. How would you like to take a trip around the world for *LOOK*, the same sort of deal we made with Adlai Stevenson?"

Nixon listened intently, almost avidly. I told him he could take along a secretary, a researcher, and a press secretary, if he liked. "When you get back, you and I could sit down together and decide if we have one big story, or two or three smaller ones about world problem areas. We'll pick up the tab, and I'll pay you $25,000."

Nixon got up and came around his desk. He grasped my hand. "Mike," he said, "that's just wonderful. You're the best friend I have in the world."

The deal was sealed, I thought.

But Nixon kept postponing his departure, pleading engagements

180

here and there. One morning I picked up *The New York Times* and saw a small story that Richard Nixon was undertaking an around-the-world trip for *The Saturday Evening Post*. *The Post* was in serious financial trouble at the time, and the Curtis Publishing Company had been spending millions of dollars in trying to keep it alive.

I was infuriated. I immediately called Rosemary Woods and told her I wanted to see her boss that day.

"Impossible, Mr. Cowles," she said. "Mr. Nixon's calendar is filled up."

I became insistent and she fit me in at six o'clock that evening in his office. Dispensing with the amenities when I arrived, I threw the clipping on Nixon's desk.

"What about this, Dick?" I asked.

"What about it?" he responded.

"You will recall," I said, "that three months ago I made this suggestion of a trip around the world and you told me that I was the best friend you had and that you'd be eternally grateful to me for making this trip possible, and now I read that you're going to make the trip for *The Saturday Evening Post*."

"That's right."

"For God's sake, why didn't you call me and discuss it with me before you agreed to an arrangement with *The Saturday Evening Post*? I feel you have double-crossed me."

"*The Post* offered me $50,000 in cash," Nixon said, "and you only offered me $25,000, so I am going to go for *The Post* and there isn't a damned thing you can do about it."

"Dick, you've lost me permanently," I said. "There's a flaw in your character. You seem to feel you have no obligation to people who have helped you. If somebody else comes along and offers you more money, you forget your old friends."

"I'm sorry you feel that way, but I'm busy," Nixon replied, and ushered me out of his office.

Years later, after Nixon had been elected President, my wife and I were invited down to the White House to attend a dinner at which four or five veteran White House correspondents were to receive the Medal of Freedom from the President. At one point, Jan and I found ourselves next to Arthur Krock, the long-time Washington columnist for *The New York Times*, who was one of the recipients. Spurred by the dinner's ostentatious trappings, including a band of buglers from the U.S. Marine Band, we got into a discussion of Nixon and particularly his preoccupation with money.

"Mike," Krock said, "money is going to be Nixon's Achilles heel. He is brighter than most Presidents we have had, and he might become a superior President if only he could get over his fixation that he needs a lot of money. Why don't you get some of your multi-millionaire Republican friends to open a bank account in the Riggs National Bank in

Dick Nixon's name and give him two or three million dollars with no strings attached. Be sure the rich Republicans pay the gift tax so there'll be no scandal of any kind. I think if Nixon had a couple of million dollars in his own name he might then become a really outstanding President."

As far as I know, no one ever followed through on Arthur Krock's suggestion.

A NUDE SWIM WITH JOHNSON

My acquaintance with Lyndon Johnson was very slight during his term as Senator and Vice President under Jack Kennedy. At occasions such as Gridiron dinners, we would greet one another with a handshake and a few casual words, and that would be the extent of it. It came as something of a surprise when, just two months after Johnson has been sworn in as President, I received a called from Pierre Salinger, whom he had kept on as press secretary. Salinger said the President would like for me and the editors of *LOOK* to come down to Washington to have lunch with him. I naturally said we would be delighted. On a cold, but sunny day in January, 1964, I, together with Dan Mich, *LOOK's* editor, and Bill Arthur, the managing editor, went to Washington where we were joined by Dick Wilson, Cowles Publications bureau chief, and Fletcher Knebel, *LOOK's* Washington correspondent.

There was about three-quarters of an hour wait in the Cabinet room, which is not unusual since all Presidents run behind schedule, and we were ushered into the Oval Office. The President immediately began to address me as Gardner. After five minutes or so, Salinger wrote a little note and put it on the President's desk. I became "Mike" for the rest of the visit.

We chatted for a short while until Lyndon got up and announced, "Let's go over to lunch." We left the executive wing and walked through the garden on the south side of the White House. Suddenly, I felt a wallop on the back that almost knocked me over. "Mike," Lyndon said, his arm resting now on my shoulder, "your figure is as bad as mine. I'm not going to feed you until we have a swim."

We had reached a door between the executive offices and the main part of the White House. Lyndon opened it and we walked through a small gymnasium that John Kennedy had installed. At the end of a corridor, we entered a rather elegant dressing room with a few lockers and some benches. The President disappeared through another door, leaving us standing there wondering what to do next.

Suddenly there was a bellow from the adjoining room. "Mike, what's the matter with you? Are you afraid to see me in the nude? Come on in here and get undressed with me!" I walked into the President's dressing room and glanced around. There were no trunks and no towels. But there was the President, undressing, so I began to follow suit, lagging one

182

garment behind. Like most males of his age, Lyndon was not a very prepossessing figure in the nude.

As he and I walked toward the pool, with the rest of our now fully naked entourage following, Lyndon said: "I kept on Jack's lady doctor. She makes me take a swim twice a day. I swim slowly so let's get in and swim alongside so we can talk." As we swam back and forth, Lyndon recalled that the pool was built for F.D.R. by 10-cent contributions from school children a quarter a century ago. He recalled that Jack Kennedy swam in the pool often because the warm (92 degrees) water had a therapeutic effect on his back injury. At the end of the third lap, he let out another thunderous bellow which seemed all the more thunderous in that hollow chamber: "Pierre, get our guests a drink!"

"I don't know what they like, Mr. President," replied Salinger, who was in the water with the rest of us.

"They're damn Yankees," came the response, "just get them some Scotch. I'll have a double bourbon."

Pierre climbed out of the pool, telephoned the order and in about three minutes a black man, wearing white gloves, brought in the drinks on a little silver tray. As we stood in the shallow end of the pool, Lyndon began telling corny jokes about events in small Texas towns during his various political campaigns. We all laughed dutifully. Ten minutes later, Lyndon ordered another round of drinks. And so there we were: a group of grown men of assorted shapes without a stitch of clothing gathered in the White House swimming pool in the early afternoon with a second stiff drink listening to the President of the United States recount stories of the good old days. I had made a fair number of trips to the White House in my time, I reflected as Lyndon talked, but there had never been a scene to equal this.

We got dressed, towels having been deposited in the dressing room, and went to lunch, a pleasant affair during which Lyndon did most of the talking. He got a big kick showing us a snapshot of Pierre riding on a jackass at the L.B.J. Ranch. Several times he reached into his coat pocket to display proudly the nation's latest economic statistics.

At about three-thirty I began to feel we were over-staying our time. "It's been absolutely delightful, Mr. President," I said, starting to get up, "but we really should leave."

"Oh, not at all," the President said. "Sit down."

Fifteen minutes later, I started to make departure sounds again. "We really must not keep you any longer, Mr. President."

"Well, you can't go until you see Lady Bird," he insisted. "She's most anxious to see you." I had met Lady Bird only once before in my life.

Lyndon got up from the table and I had no alternative but to follow him. While the rest of the group toured the building with Pierre, the President and I got into his private elevator and rode up to the bedroom floor. As we walked down the hall, Lyndon began bellowing, "Lady

Bird!" There was no response. We kept walking and Lyndon kept opening doors without knocking and hollering, "Lady Bird!" Finally from down the hall came a faint sound. We marched toward a door and Lyndon burst in. Fortunately, Lady Bird, who was dictating to a secretary, was fully dressed. She also was furious.

"Lady Bird," the President said, ignoring the expression of rage on her face, "here is our dear friend Mike Cowles. Do you remember we were talking about him just two, three nights ago, saying how long it had been since we'd seen him? Well, here he is!"

It took Lady Bird a minute to adjust her face to an expression of warm welcome.

Taking me by one arm and his wife by the other Lyndon led me further down to the hall to the Lincoln bedroom. When we entered, Lyndon said, "Mike, I want to show you the plaque that Jackie had had cemented over the fireplace." With his index finger gliding along under the words, Lyndon read: "In this bedroom slept Abraham Lincoln." After that inscription were the dates of Lincoln's inauguration and his assassination. Below this was a second inscription: "In this bedroom slept John Fitzgerald Kennedy and his wife, Jacqueline," followed by the date of Kennedy's inauguration and the date of his assassination.

When he finished reading the plaque, Lyndon poked me in the ribs with his elbow and said, "Jackie didn't give Mrs. Lincoln much billing, did she?"

Later, we joined the rest of the group on the famous White House balcony—the "Truman Balcony"—with its superb view of the Ellipse, the Washington Monument, and the Jefferson Memorial.

"Mr. President," Fletcher Knebel said, "you have been President only a few weeks, following a great tragedy. It has been said by other Presidents that the White House is a lonesome place. Do you find it so?"

"Fletch," the President said, "when I was Vice President I used to go once in a while to one of those many lunches up on the Hill with the old gang I worked with for so many years. It was 'Lyndon' this and 'Lyndon' that, but the last time I went it was 'Mr. President' this and 'Mr. President' that. When I asked that it still be 'Lyndon,' someone said it isn't the same anymore. 'It isn't Lyndon. From now on, it's Mr. President.'

"Yes, I do get lonesome," Johnson conceded. He recalled how his great friend and patron speaker Sam Rayburn spoke to Harry S. Truman when F.D.R. died. Vice President Truman was in Rayburn's office when the word came.

"'This is the last time I ever will call you Harry,' Rayburn said. 'You will go to the White House, and you will have advisers. They will build you up and tell you how right you are, and what a great man you are. And, Harry, you and I know that is not true.'

"Fletch," the President said wistfully, "I only wish Mr. Sam was around now. I could just pick up the phone and Mr. Sam would come arunnin'."

THE GOLDEN YEARS

Shortly after Dan Mich returned to *LOOK* from *McCall's,* he called a meeting of the entire editorial staff. His message was very simple: "We're going to be the best and I am here to help you achieve the best." And it was effective. After years of wrenching managerial upheavals, eroding editorial quality, sagging morale, bruising circulation battles with *Collier's,* and the distressing failures of *Flair* and *Quick*, a discernible spirit of optimism began to permeate the organization. Soon that optimism turned to enthusiasm and we were on our way toward *LOOK's* golden years.

It took time, of course, to get the badly enervated machinery up to full speed and peak performance, to refill the empty pipeline of ideas and reestablish the flow of ideas into the magazine. But as ideas were encouraged and accepted, writers and photographers returned to the field. With his widespread contacts throughout the world of literary agents, book publishers, and outside writers, Mich reopened sources that had all but dried up during the years of trouble. No longer did I face blank pages as deadlines approached.

Mich made some immediate important additions to our staff and roster of contributors. He hired Gurney Williams away from *Collier's* to be *LOOK's* humor editor. He felt that there was always need for a touch of lightness in a magazine and Gurney was one of the most respected editors of humor—cartoons and verse—around. In our issue of July 27, 1954, "LOOK on the Lightside" began as a regular feature, and cartoons, including the very popular "Brother Sebastian," were interspersed throughout the magazine.

Also in 1954, Dan signed a contract with Dr. Norman Vincent Peale to do a regular one-page column entitled "Norman Vincent Peale Answers

Your Questions." Initially, we had to dream up the questions, but not for long. Peale, who had recently published his best-selling book "The Power of Positive Thinking," was at the height of his popularity, and questions were soon arriving by the sackful. Peale and his wife Ruth spent many hours during their travels coming up with helpful answers.

Mich made major strides improving *LOOK*'s perennially problematic art direction. Allen Hurlburt, Merle Armitage's successor as art director, had very nearly quit during Dana Tasker's regime, and if I had not secured Tasker's resignation when I did, we might have lost Al without knowing just how good he really was. Under Mich, Al flowered and the magazine's design became better than it had ever been.

It was enhanced by some far-reaching innovations in printing. In 1956, we began using a new method of paper coating known as "Trail-Blade," conceived by Marvin Whatmore. Under previous methods, paper had been coated by rollers, which left peaks and valleys where the rollers pulled away from the paper. Marvin reasoned correctly that if the coating were applied with a knife, the way frosting is to a cake, the coat would be smoother and the quality of the photographic reproduction much improved. In 1957, we completed our gradual shift from Alco Gravure, the company that had printed the *Register* and *Tribune* rotogravure section and *LOOK* during its early years, to the huge R.R. Donnelley & Sons facilities in Chicago. In 1960, we introduced *LOOK*-Kromatic printing, a high-speed color printing technique that requires no plates and combines the best features of letterpress and gravure. This gave *LOOK*'s color reproduction an appearance of unparalleled (among major magazines) richness. I shall never forget demonstrations by our advertising salesmen comparing *LOOK*'s reproductive quality with that of our competitors—the rendition, for example, of the diamond in the Cadillac emblem in *LOOK* as compared to the same ad in *LIFE*. There was really no comparison.

Mich perfected a remarkably smooth and effective story production process. In contrast to many large publications, especially the Time Inc. magazines, which featured rather rigid, formalistic, and hierarchical systems, *LOOK* was quite informal and fluid with only the minimum amount of structure necessary to keep the mechanism operating efficiently.

The mechanism was overseen by the editorial board, consisting of the editor, managing editor, assistant managing editors, art director, picture editor, special departments (food, fashion, home living) editor, and the editorial production assistant, who also served as recorder. The board met once a week but sometimes more often if events warranted. Staff members would sometimes be invited, especially if they wanted to make a personal pitch for a story.

Editorial board meetings were aimed at stimulating, weighing, and selecting ideas. Members would collect and cull ideas from a myriad of sources and bring the best ones, along with their own ideas, to the meetings, where everyone's suggestions would be subjected to hearty and sometimes heated discussion. All suggestions would be acted upon, though sometimes they would be sent back to the originator for refinement or further development. The board would discuss who should do an accepted story, but almost without exception the person suggesting the story would be the one to get the assignment. Exceptions would be when it was felt that someone else would be especially suitable for the assignment, or when the person suggesting the story already was overloaded with assignments. Knowing that you would get to do the story you suggested was a great impetus to submitting well-thought-out ideas. (It was interesting to observe the number of story ideas presented in January suggesting trips to the Caribbean or Florida.) Professional free-lancers always were given the stories they suggested except on the rare occasions when they wanted only a fee for the suggestion.

Most stories, except for long text pieces and investigative reports, were the product of a writer-photographer team who worked closely together. While the writer interviewed the subject of a story, for instance, the photographer would be taking photographs of the individual. The team members kept in close touch with *LOOK's* managing editor to keep him informed of their progress and any problems, such as the need to change the story's focus. After their return from the field, the writer and photographer would work with the editors and the art department to go through the photographs and select which ones best told the story. From perhaps a thousand or more pictures, it was not unusual for only a dozen to "make the book."

After the writer had completed the text for the story, a layout was made to the specific space that the editors thought the story warranted or was available in a particular issue. To accompany the picture positions sketched by the art department, the writer, in conjunction with one of the senior editors, would prepare text blocks, picture captions, and headlines. All stories were laid out to avoid requiring the reader to "jump" to the back of the magazine, as one must do in reading most page-one newspaper stories. Jumping, we felt, was discouraging to the reader and disturbed the "flow" of the issue.

Depending upon its interest value and timeliness, and the editorial mix of articles in the issue it was being considered for, the story could be scheduled immediately—perhaps in a somewhat different layout configuration depending on the space available in the magazine—or placed in a "futures box" for possible later use. It might also be "killed" if the editors felt it had lost its timeliness or had not turned out to be as compelling as the editors thought it would be. *LOOK's* killed-to-published ratio was low because enough controls were built into the system to assign only the best ideas and halt a story in progress if it didn't appear that the results would be worth the effort.

Once all the pages for an issue were pasted up—in other words, reproductions of all the pictures had been cut to size and pasted on page-sized sheets along with hunks of dummy type indicating the placement of text, captions, and headlines—the entire issue, including advertisements, would be mounted in consecutive page order around the walls of the editorial conference room so that the editorial board could visualize the page-by-page sequence of editorial features and advertisements.

When the entire issue was assembled, a "preview" meeting was held to decide whether content or copy should stay as it was or whether changes or substitutions were needed to improve the issue's balance, effectiveness, or appeal.

This system also helped to prevent visual or copy clashes between advertisements and editorial features. For example, a full-page "bleed" ad photograph (no margins) opposite a similar "bleed" editorial photograph more often that not produced a clash which was confusing and displeasing to the eye. The ad would be moved—unless in the rare case that it had been sold in a fixed position, in which case the editorial feature would be moved so long as the issue's flow was not disrupted.

The final object of the preview session was to create an issue that offered a satisfying mix of long stories, short stories, serious stories, light stories, about a wide variety of subjects that would sustain the reader's interest from cover to cover.

GUESSES, HOPES AND DREAMS

While there were procedures and conventions, the whole editorial process at *LOOK* was ultimately highly subjective. Indeed, the subjectivity in a typical issue of *LOOK*—the extent to which intuition, instinct, hunches, and just plain guesses, hopes, and dreams played determining roles—was probably as great or greater than any magazine of its time, or of today. Magazines increasingly are the product of carefully set formulas. They are assemblages of very specific kinds of information organized in a very predetermined and predictable manner to be of interest to a very precise kind of audience. *LOOK* was still evolving during these early years after Dan Mich's return, but from the beginning he avoided formulas and published what he felt would interest, amuse, entertain, excite, educate, intrigue, and provoke the vastly diverse mass of people who were *LOOK's* readers.

Whatever Mich's formula or lack thereof was, within a year or two after his return *LOOK* was publishing some of the most noteworthy stories in its history. *LOOK* was among the first national magazines to chronicle gradually rising racial tensions in the South. In our March 22, 1955 issue, Hodding Carter, the great Southern newspaper editor, wrote "A Wave of Terror Threatens the South," which described the emergence of White Citizens Councils. Perhaps the most controversial story we ever published was in our January 24, 1956 issue. Entitled "The Shocking Story of Approved Killing in Mississippi," by William Bradford Huie, it gave a graphically detailed account of the murder of a young black boy named Emmett "Bobo" Till by two white men. Though the men had already been brought to trial and exonerated, Huie quoted them directly telling how and why they had committed the crime. Wire services reportedly refused to move it, for fear of libel suits, but did so after it had been read into the Congressional Record and had thus become public information.

Blacks were not the only minority whose plight we reported on. *LOOK* staff writer Thomas B. Morgan, Jr. and photographer John Vachon produced a powerful article called "The Sioux Indians: Their Plight is Our Worst Disgrace."

Perhaps the most acclaimed series *LOOK* ever ran was developed by Leo Rosten, whom I had met while we were both with the OWI in Washington and who for years served as *LOOK's* special editorial adviser. Leo, one of the most brilliantly creative people I have ever known and who is justifiably renowned for his many accomplishments—not the least of which was his delightful *New Yorker* series and subsequent best-selling book "The Education of H*Y*M*A*N K*A*P*L*A*N"—developed and edited a series on religions that started running in *LOOK* in 1952. By-lined by religious authorities in the various denominations, it covered and dealt in question-and-answer form with "What is a Jew?", "What is a Catholic?", "What is a Methodist?", and so forth. It was widely reprinted, and enjoyed excellent success as a book published by Simon & Schuster under the title "A Guide to the Religions of America."

Our foreign coverage during this period was especially commendable. In 1955, *LOOK* writer Chester Morrison and photographer Robert Sandberg went to Hiroshima to produce "Lest We Forget." "Today, Americans are accepted here—not with a warm welcome, exactly, but not with open hostility either," Chet reported. "Hiroshima has not really forgiven us for dropping the bomb (it happened to explode above the grounds of a hospital), and the lesson to be learned is that mankind, if he wills it so, is unconquerable." The same year, we published a 14-page takeout on "AFRICA: The World's Most Explosive Continent." The story included prescient reports by John Gunther, Adlai Stevenson, and Robert Ruark, with a preface by Ernest Hemingway. In our December 13, 1955 issue—at 192 pages the biggest in *LOOK's* history (at only 25 cents a copy!)—we published William O. Douglas' "Soviet Colonialism—Product of Terror."

In late 1956, we sent Edmund Stevens, our Moscow correspondent, and *LOOK* photographer Phillip Harrington to China. We knew this was in defiance of a U.S. government ban on visits by Americans to China, but we felt that the American people had the right to know what was going on behind the bamboo curtain.

We had hoped, perhaps unrealistically, that they would be able to get in and out of China undetected. But after they entered China, reporters in Hong Kong got wind of the story and filed news reports. All hell soon broke loose. The State Department charged that the presence of the *LOOK* team in China not only was against the law but was hampering negotiations for the release of ten Americans being held in Chinese jails. Because of the negotiations, we immediately instructed Stevens and Harrington to leave China, which cut their trip short by several weeks.

But the matter did not end there. When he returned to Moscow, Stevens was summoned to the American Embassy and told that his passport would be invalidated for all travel other than a return to the United States. Until this point, we had refrained from getting into a public battle with the State Department. But the threatened action against Stevens, and Harrington as well, was too consequential an issue to ignore. We retained counsel in Washington to represent Stevens and Harrington and announced that we were asking the State Department for an open hearing. The invalidation threat, we said, "involves important aspects of freedom of the press" and "leaves *LOOK* no choice but to challenge the right of the Department to dictate the movement of reporters on legitimate news-gathering assignments." The statement produced a flood of editorials in the press supporting *LOOK's* position and blasting the State Department.

The State Department was in no mood for a protracted legal fight on the matter and substantially softened its position. It said it would not invalidate the passports if Stevens and Harrington would promise not to return to China. We considered challenging even that stand, but then decided it would not be worth the time and money. We had made our point that the ban could be defied if one was willing to take the risks. Moreover, though their visit was cut short, Stevens and Harrington still had been able to accumulate a great deal of excellent material. Their article appeared in the April 16, 1957 issue—the first story on China by American journalists since the dropping of the bamboo curtain in the late 1940's. Aware that their ban on travel to China was untenable, the State Department later announced it would allow a select group of American reporters and editors to visit China. Ironically, though, China said it would not let them in.

Another measure of our growing editorial achievements was the number of awards *LOOK* stories were getting. In fact, *LOOK* became the preeminent award winner for editorial excellence of its time. In 1954, for example, our awards included the Public Service in Magazine Journalism Award from Sigma Delta Chi for the religion series and one for our cosponsorship and coverage of the All-America Cities program; the National Safety Council's Public Interest Award for articles in the safety field; the Benjamin Franklin Magazine Award for the best interpretation of the foreign scene) given for a series by Adlai Stevenson on a round-the-world trip *LOOK* sponsored), and the National Headliners Club Award for an article by Richard Wilson, chief of the Cowles Washington Bureau, titled "Is Nixon Fit to Be President?" (Dick determined that he was, at least *then.*)

By 1956, awards were coming in thicker and faster. Among the most significant were these: the National Brotherhood Award from the National Conference of Christians and Jews for our articles on racial, religious, and social subjects; the George Polk Memorial Award for outstanding magazine reporting (given for an article "A New Look at Americans," by William Attwood, then our national affairs editor, who later became editor-in-chief of all of Cowles Communications, and still later, publisher of *Newsday);* the Benjamin Franklin Magazine Award for an article by Roland Berg, our medical editor, on "The Truth About the Salk Polio Vaccine," which was judged the best article on science and health published in any magazine during 1956; the National School Bell Award, presented through the National Education Association, for an article titled "What is a Teacher?" written by George Leonard, a senior editor who later became our West Coast bureau chief, and photographed by Charlotte Brooks, and again, the Sigma Delta Chi Public Service Award for our "courageous and objective presentation" of subjects in the public interest, and the SDX award for the most outstanding magazine reporting, which went to Fletcher Knebel of our Washington bureau for his article titled "Crisis," dealing with President Eisenhower's heart attack. Fletch later went on to co-author the novel "Seven Days in May" with Charles Bailey, later editor of *The Minneapolis Tribune*, and to author "Night of Camp David," and "Vanished," among many other novels.

"OUT OF THE SHADOW"

Some of the lesser known awards were the most meaningful to us. Managing Editor Bill Arthur tells the story of the night that he and *LOOK* senior editor Jerry Astor accepted an award for an article published on retarded children in our issue of February 9, 1953, by Astor, with photographs by Phillip Harrington, titled "Out of the Shadow." The ceremony took place at the old Astor Hotel in Times Square at a gathering of the New York chapter of the National Association for the Help of Retarded Children. Up to this point, retarded children had, indeed, lived in a shadowland. When we decided to do a story on the subject we had great difficulties in finding a family willing to bring their child out of the shadows for photographs. Robert Seaman, a *LOOK* advertising salesmen, heard of our problems. "I have a son who is retarded," Bob told Bill, "and my wife and I are willing to let you photograph him for your story." We did, and the result was the first mass circulation national magazine story on the subject. Bill tells me that his eyes filled with tears at the ovation the award ceremony got that night at the Astor. Most of those present were the parents of retarded children.

LOOK's performance during these years was mostly the result of the calibre of people we had gathered under the direction of Dan Mich. But it also derived from the fact that we were always operated as the underdog to *LIFE*, the "Big Red One," as we called it, two blocks to the west on the Avenue of the Americas.

It was hard *not* to be an underdog to *LIFE*. With mammoth Time Inc. behind it, *LIFE* had 251 editorial staffers, 317 "stringers" or part-time correspondents, and 28 bureaus around the world. It roamed the world and would send as many people as necessary anywhere to do any story for as long as it took. It had no qualms, for instance, sending a team to Africa for several months to do a story on elephants. Its forte, though, was breaking news, which it sometimes covered the way armies capture cities.

Perhaps the ultimate example of *LIFE's* flamboyant, uninhibited style was the coverage of Winston Churchill's funeral in 1965. The funeral was scheduled for a Saturday. To have the story in its issue due out two days later, *LIFE* chartered an entire DC-8 and outfitted it as a flying editorial office including darkroom, layout room, and research library. Exposed film from the team of sixteen photographers covering the event was motorcycled to the plane standing by at a London airport. As the plane flew to *LIFE's* printers in Chicago at 600 miles an hour, the film was developed and the story was laid out, written, and made ready for the presses. *LIFE* was on the stands Monday morning with 21 full-color pages on the event. The whole operation involved 40 people in London, another 40 in New York, and 34 on board the plane. The precise cost was never disclosed but must have been several hundred thousand dollars.

As a biweekly with less than half the staff and far less financial resources, *LOOK* would have been demolished if we had tried to go head to head with *LIFE* on big-budget stories like the Churchill funeral. But there were other ways to play the game. We liked to regard the *LIFE* staff—rightly or wrongly—as cocky, arrogant, and wasteful. If we couldn't outspend *LIFE,* we felt we could at least outwrite, outphotograph, outedit, and generally outhustle *LIFE*. If we couldn't be bigger than *LIFE,* we could at least be better.

And because we thought we could, I would argue—admittedly as a very interested party—that we very frequently were. I think our best stories tended to have an edge, an extra angle, a deeper insight, a special perception. But however one judges the competition, the fact of *LIFE* made us try harder and do better than we otherwise would have done.

TROUBLE AT *COLLIER'S*

While our competition with *LIFE* remained an uphill battle, our competition with *Collier's* and *The Saturday Evening Post* became easier and easier in the years following Dan Mich's return.

The reasons for the decline of a magazine are always complex and multifaceted. But on reflecting on the failure of *Collier's*, I think a predominant reason was the fact that Crowell-Collier for many years was run by businessmen who had little if any feel or understanding for the editorial side of the company. Magazines, of course, are businesses and must make a profit to survive. But making a profit is not just a matter of such things as clever circulation strategies, aggressive advertising sales, or superior printing technology. Much more important are the editorial sensibilities at work. When editorial quality declines, that drags down everything else. All of the circulation genius of a Shap Shapiro cannot rescue a badly edited magazine.

An editorial genius like Dan Mich makes a big difference. But to flourish the editor must feel the support and encouragement of the entire organization. He must feel that he is part of an organization that is dedicated not just to the accumulation of profits but to the production of a superior editorial product. The amazing success of the Time Inc. publications, in my mind, is attributable in large measure to the preeminent role within that organization of editors. Harry Luce was an editor first and a businessman second. Even today, on *Time* magazine's masthead, Time Inc.'s overall editor-in-chief Henry Grunwald is listed above J. Richard Monro, the company's president and chief executive officer. I feel *LOOK*'s success was due to our preoccupation with the editorial side of the company, our insistence that *LOOK* be vital, vigorous, and interesting, even if the costs involved did not always produce equivalent or greater profits. At *Collier's*, by contrast, I think the senior business executives had very little concern about the stories their magazines were running.

Advertisers are leery of being associated with a publication that is in trouble. The media director of Wells Rich Greene, the large advertising agency, once put it this way: "The internal political situation of a medium, or whether it is losing money or not, is not really any of our business. It ought to be that we are buying so much circulation at a price. But unfortunately, we all tend to make it our business. You have to understand this is a very frightened business. Our livelihood is at the whim of our clients, and we'll go a long way to avoid being criticized. Now there's nothing really wrong with advertising in the last issue of a magazine. But if we were to recommend a medium and it folded a half a dozen issues later, it might mean we were out of touch, that our judgment was wrong. Everybody likes to stick with a winner."

Collier's was beginning to smell like a loser.

And I think we played a role in adding to this impression. I have already mentioned how we got *LOOK* considered as part of the weekly category of magazines instead of as a monthly, how we exploited the Magazine Audience Group total audience studies, and how we used the killing of *Quick* to retain our circulation lead over *Collier's*. But an equally telling ploy was the reorientation of our comparative advertising in the early 1950's. Instead of comparing *LOOK* to the other members of the "big four" mass magazines—*LIFE, LOOK, The Post,* and *Collier's*—we began talking about *LOOK* as part of the "big three"—*LIFE, LOOK,* and *The Post.* We just ignored *Collier's* and tried to give the impression—one that had become quite accurate—that we no longer considered *Collier's* of any consequence.

In casting about for ways to save *Collier's*, Crowell-Collier executives approached us. I began having discussions with Paul Smith, the president, whom I had known for many years while he was working for the *San Francisco Chronicle* and who had been hired by Crowell at my recommendation. Also joining many of the discussions was J. Patrick Lannan, a Chicago businessman and leader of a group that had made a large investment in Crowell the year earlier. Smith wanted to arrange a merger between *LOOK* and *Collier's*. But he insisted that the Crowell-Collier stockholders get half the stock of the merged company. I kept telling Paul that *"Collier's* isn't worth as much as *LOOK* and I'd be a damned fool to make that kind of deal."

Finally, Marvin Whatmore and I worked out a much better deal: We paid $1,600,000 for *Collier's* name and Crowell-Collier's subscription selling divisions (which handled subscription sales for many other magazines). We also took over the *Collier's* subscriber list and assumed the obligation to fulfill the remaining portion of those subscriptions. On paper, this represented an $11,000,000 liability - in other words, it could cost us $11,000,000 to send *Collier's* subscribers copies of *LOOK* for the balance of their subscriptions. But we figured that the additional circulation would bring in more than enough advertising to offset the fulfillment costs.

Having made what we thought was a good deal, though, we were suddenly faced with the possibility that it could also become suddenly undone. Despite the $1,600,000 payment, Crowell-Collier was in imminent danger of bankruptcy. Under the bankruptcy law, any deal made within 90 days of a bankruptcy can be set aside by the courts and the assets involved restored to the bankrupt company. To give the company enough working capital to get through the next 90 days, we loaned it $1,000,000—secured by one of the company's large printing plants.

Looking back on the whole episode, I have only one regret. On the night I shook hands with Pat Lannan on the *Collier's* acquisition, he said, "Mike, give me another $1,000,000 and I'll give you the entire company instead of just Collier's." With Crowell-Collier close to bankruptcy, I said no. But I hadn't taken the time to see just how profitable the Crowell book publishing operations were. Those operations were later merged into Macmillan and became even more remunerative. That "no" to Pat Lannan cost me many millions of dollars.

196

I am consoled by the fact that purchasing *Collier's*, in effect, produced many millions of dollars for *LOOK*. In fact, that deal was the single most important transaction in *LOOK's* history. At the time, *LOOK's* circulation base was 4,200,000. Addition of the *Collier's* subscribers added at least another 1,000,000, which put us ahead of *The Post*, then at 4,850,000. At the time, only *LIFE* (at 5,600,000), the *Reader's Digest*, and *McCall's* were above 5,000,000. We offered the additional circulation to advertisers for the first six months of 1957 at no additional cost.

We were almost swamped with takers. During 1957, we carried 1,765 ad pages, 134 above 1956 and the largest in our history. Ad revenue jumped more than $9,000,000, from $34,350,878 to $43,461,430.

The advantages went beyond numbers. For some years, there had been a consensus that there was just not room for four major mass magazines, and that sooner or later one of the four would have to fold. The identify of the magazine that would have to fold varied from observer to observer and from time to time, but sometimes the betting was that it would be *LOOK*. In acquiring *Collier's*, we not only virtually ended this negative thinking about *LOOK* but helped erase, at least for the time being, the notion that the field was overcrowded.

THE *POST* GOES DOWN

As the 1950's wore on, everything seemed to be going right for *LOOK*. Our circulation guarantee was raised from 4,850,000 to 5,300,000 to 5,550,000, effective with the July 8, 1958 issue. Though 1958 was a recession year and halted our record of 18 consecutive years of advertising revenue gains, *LOOK* moved ahead of *Time* magazine for the first time and became the fourth largest revenue producer among magazines. In 1962, we finally passed *The Saturday Evening Post*, our revenues of $75,145,000 producing an $8,600,000 margin. By 1965, *LOOK's* revenues were double those of *The Post*. The change in a quarter century was startling. In 1938, the first full year that *LOOK* carried advertising, *The Post* was the unquestioned leader in the field. It carried gross ad revenues of $22,300,000 compared with *LIFE's* $6,500,000 and *LOOK's* $1,100,000. In 1965, *LIFE* was now the leader with $163,000,000, *LOOK* was second with $79,500,000. *The Post*, which at one time had been over $100,000,000, had now slumped to only $36,000,000.

It had been clear since the late 1950's that *The Post* was very seriously ill. The decline and eventual death of *The Post* and of the Curtis Publishing Company became one of the most thoroughly chronicled corporate collapses in history. It would be redundant for me to retell the story in any detail. Suffice it to say that Curtis' and *The Post's* problems were remarkably similar to those of Crowell-Collier and *Collier's*: a badly managed parent company, an outdated and confusing editorial ap-

197

proach, and a dizzying succession of managerial shifts.

The Post did manage to hang on until 1969, but without a fortuitous $24,000,000 boost in 1965 from the sale of its share in Texas Gulf Sulphur's famous Canadian copper strike, it probably would have gone under several years earlier.

Throughout the 1950's and well into the 1960's, we remained convinced that the problems on *Collier's* and *The Post* were aberrations, the product of specific mistakes by a specific group of managers and editors. If a magazine was well managed and well edited, as we were certain *LOOK* was, it had nothing to worry about. It would be several years before we realized that while *LOOK* was well managed and well edited, we had a great deal to worry about.

DAN MICH—A GREAT EDITOR

It is tragic that in our time several great editors of magazines have come and gone without leaving behind written memoirs or autobiographies. Perhaps, as is so often the case, the thought to do so simply did not occur to them. Or, more likely, they lived their lives so wrapped up in the daily effort, in their deadline-ridden schedule, that they didn't want to take the time to jot down, in one way or another, their recollections of the effort. The product itself became their legacy, not how the product was put together, how it was shaped and given direction, and why they did it the way they did it.

Such was the case of Daniel D. (for Danforth) Mich, whose name is inextricably entwined in the history of *LOOK*, from almost its beginning in 1937, through its years of trial and travail, to what I like to think of as the golden years that preceded and followed his death in November, 1965. As much as anything, *LOOK* was Dan's legacy. Its pages mirrored the man through the sixteen years he occupied the editor's chair. Dan's influence went beyond that, to the many editors, writers, photographers, and researchers who developed and flourished under his direction. And it continued after he was gone.

Dan Mich left us in perhaps the peak year of *LOOK's* success. It is appropriate before moving on to *LOOK's* traumatic last years to attempt a brief retrospective—not nearly as good as Dan would have done it, if he had had a mind to try, but a start nonetheless.

Dan's great genius as an editor, I think, was his ability to divine what was concerning or bothering Americans almost before they knew themselves. His editorial sense, like that of most great editors, was very instinctive and intuitive. As I have noted, he had no neatly packaged editorial formula—other than the notion that *LOOK* should give readers information they needed and wanted to know, which is really no formula at all. But when it came down to a particular story, he had a distinct idea of whether *LOOK* should do it and, if so, how *LOOK* should do it.

198

Dan felt a story should be an essentially personal experience both for the reporter and photographer and for the reader. He disliked the idea of mass media and mass audiences. "These expressions are prevalent in our modern folklore," he once said, "but I think few people try to figure out what they really mean. In a very real sense there is no such thing as a mass audience. If you are reading a magazine that has many millions of readers, you are part of a mass audience. No doubt about that. But you are reading as an individual something that has been prepared for you by another individual. So, in its real essence, mass communications boils down, as conversation does, to one individual talking to another."

He encouraged *LOOK* reporters and photographers to put themselves as individuals into their stories. George Leonard, for many years a senior editor of *LOOK* who became the magazine's west coast editor, once said that he "always suspected that if one of our readers went where we did and met the people I did, he would ask them the questions I ask and leave with the same ideas. There's a reason. Our method is personal. It permits, even encourages reaction. . . . If something's bugging you, you ask to write about it. There's an enormous gulf between polemic and insight. One is prejudice, the other's plowing harvest. . . . The *LOOK* writer first plows his fields. *Then*, when he writes, he may say, 'This is who I am, this is what I found, and this is what it means to me.' "

J. Robert Moskin, who served as *LOOK*'s foreign editor, tells a story which, to me, vividly illustrates the freedom to present views and insights that Dan encouraged among his writers: In 1962, the year after the Berlin Wall went up, Dan sent Bob and veteran *LOOK* photographer James Hansen to do a report on life in Berlin as a divided city. Both men had been there for *LOOK* in 1960 when Berlin was still united.

Bob Moskin, in particular, was shocked by the changes in the city and how the assurances he had been given in 1960 by American leaders and commanders there about American firmness in Berlin had been washed out by allowing the Wall to go up. When the team came back to New York, they put together a story that Bob titled "Retreat in Berlin." It ran in the January 15, 1963 issue.

Shortly afterwards, Bob was in Washington on another assignment and he had occasion to visit Pierre Salinger, who was then President Kennedy's press secretary. Salinger told Bob that the President had read his article but did not believe that the United States had retreated in Berlin. Bob told Salinger that he had written the article after he had been to Berlin personally and these were his journalistic conclusions. When Bob returned to New York he told Dan that President Kennedy had disagreed with the article.

"So did I," Dan said.

"That was the greatest compliment Dan could have given me," Bob said later. "He published my article even though he disagreed with it. That was what *LOOK* was all about. We were supposed to go out and find

199

the story and report what we found. It was as clean and simple and honest as that. No *LOOK* editor ever expected me to adjust my facts or conclusions to fit his preconceptions. In a very vital sense, *LOOK* was a reporter's magazine."

The object of all the rewriting, to Dan, was clarity. He liked graceful writing, clever writing, imaginative writing, creative writing—but only so far as it enhanced comprehension and did not produce confusion and bewilderment. He hated rhetorical flourishes that were designed more to impress than to inform. "I would never write down to anybody," he once said, "but I would try always to make myself so clear that nobody could misunderstand me. I would realize that mass communications means communication to a great variety of people. I would take to heart the quotation:

" 'It isn't hard to make yourself clear to a Harvard professor. No matter how you stumble or how badly you express yourself, he is fairly certain to understand what you are trying to say. It is the person without education or an elastic mind who must have everything said to him clearly and succinctly. Yet never can the story be so childish that your more sophisticated readers will be offended.' "

Mich was a complex man. In his earlier years he was known as "Red." His hair was then flaming red and he had what was commonly known as a redhead's temper. I seldom saw it triggered, but it was well-known among the staff that any display of incompetence was a sure way to pull the trigger. But his devotion to those who worked for him, or counted him as a friend, was deep.

A PASSION FOR HUMAN RIGHTS

He was driven by an absolute passion (there is no better word) for human rights—for the lone man, the underdog, the people society neglects. Once he got a letter, pencil-written, almost illegible, from a member of a black congregation of a small church in Louisiana. The church had been destroyed by fire, ignited by the Ku Klux Klan, and the members were struggling to rebuild. "Please help us," the letter said. Dan sent a check for $100 immediately. And he did the same the next year and the next.

Speaking before the Anti-Defamation League of B'nai B'rith at a meeting in New York on December 6, 1958, Dan declared that "We are told on all sides—sometimes by men of good will—that our race problem is very difficult and complicated. We are told by some that it cannot be solved in less than a century, by others that it will take a thousand years. I, for one, don't believe we will be given a thousand years to solve it—not even a century. In the world of today, a year is what a century used to be. I agree with those who say that the solution will be difficult and complicated. But I do not believe that the ISSUE which causes the problem is complicated at all. It is one of the simplest issues of all time,

200

easily boiled down to this simple question: Do we, or do we not, believe that every American is entitled to the same rights and privileges as every other American? To make it even shorter, do we believe in treating our fellow man as we expect to be treated?

"That is the issue, the *whole* issue. It is, if you like, a moral issue—and no amount of legalistic doubletalk can make it any different."

Dan was a courageous editor. Under him, we gave extensive coverage to civil rights (which I prefer calling human rights) and birth control long before most other magazines took these difficult subjects on. Our stories often produced angry reactions from readers—and from advertisers. But this never bothered Dan or me. "Magazines," Dan once said, "must deal with the tough and controversial issues of our time." And then he added: "The hottest places in hell are reserved for those who, in time of moral crisis, maintain their neutrality."

The article that best exemplifies Dan's courage, though, was one we published in our March 19, 1957 issue. It was titled "Death of a Man," in which Lael Tucker Wertenbaker recounted the agony of her author husband, Charles, who, doomed by cancer, decided to meet his fate on his own terms. Dan wrote an editors' precede:

"This is a shocking story, a heartbreaking story of pain and love and death. . . . No article in years has caused so much debate among our editors and such soul-searching about the decision to publish. Some will attack us for printing this. Some will applaud us for 'courage,' some will criticize Mrs. Wertenbaker for the part she played in helping her husband to do what he deeply wanted. Some will praise her for a decision no woman should be asked to make. And some will see in this tragedy the double tragedy of 'those of us who do not seek God.' It is not for us to judge. To us, this is too honest and human a document to be denied the dignity of print."

Dan was right: no article had ever created such controversy among *LOOK*'s editors. Debates over whether to publish or not to publish went on for days. Perhaps, in the context of today such contention would not occur; but in 1957, attitudes were considerably different. Magazine readers were not accustomed to words such as these, written by Charles Wertenbaker himself:

"The problem with death is to recognize the point at which you can die with all your faculties, and take a healthy look at the world and the people as you go out. Let them get you in bed, drug you or cut you, And you become sick and afraid. If you wait too long, you may be reduced to something less than a man who could swim out to meet death."

Dan was an avid sports fan, with a particular love of baseball. He had developed the interest as sports editor from 1924 to 1927 of the *Wisconsin State Journal*. One morning I spotted him in his office at *LOOK* wearing a baseball catcher's face mask and a cap with the letter "P" on it. He was holding a sign reading "I am a Pirate fan." On the preceding day,

Pittsburgh had once again locked up last place in the National League.

Dick McCarthy of *LOOK*'s Detroit advertising staff, himself a dyed-in-the-wool baseball fan, would challenge Dan to a baseball quizfest at *LOOK* ad sales conventions. It usually ended in a standoff. Both could tell you Ty Cobb's lifetime batting average, or who the catcher was for the Cincinnati Reds when Johnny Vandermeer pitched his back-to-back no-hitters.

He became a friend of Jackie Robinson and arranged for *LOOK* to publish exclusively Jackie's announcement of his retirement from the Dodgers. The story, of course, made Page 1 in many newspapers around the country, and caused quite a furor among baseball writers and, in particular, among writers who covered the Dodgers.

He was a devotee of Dixieland jazz, and for hours on end would listen to his record collection featuring Bix Biederbeck and others on scratchy recordings, inherited for the most part from Jack Guenther following Jack's death in 1947 in an airplane crash in Bryce Canyon, Utah. Jack had been *LOOK*'s managing editor under Dan from 1944.

His awareness, and knowledge, of the problems of publishing magazines was keen, leading to the leadership role he took, along with Ted Patrick of *Holiday*, Ted Weeks of *The Atlantic*, Wade Nichols of *Good Housekeeping* and Bob Stein of *McCalls*, in establishing the American Society of Magazine Editors. "Unlike newspapers," he told the *LOOK* ad staff in 1962, "every major national magazine competes with every other major national magazine—and thus cooperation within the magazine industry, to sell magazines as an industry, is mighty hard to come by.

"Trying to get advertising dollars switched from TV to magazines has been largely futile, and therefore all of us in the magazine business have spent at least 90% of our time selling against other magazines—and in the process we have by no means conveyed an image of growth and prosperity for the magazine business generally."

He would talk to the ad staff about the editorial product because they had to sell it to advertisers. But he never let advertising salesmen and advertisers tell him how to edit *LOOK*.

On December 11, 1964, Professor William E. Porter of the School of Journalism, University of Michigan, came to New York to speak at a meeting of the American Society of Magazine Editors. Two things in that speech made a deep impression on Dan. He later told me about Professor Porter's story concerning Forest Evashevski, who at one time coached football at the University of Michigan. Evashevski had been a member of the staff for a college all-star game. His assignment was to coach the punters. On the squad were a couple of young men who could regularly kick the ball around fifty yards. Porter had asked him how he went about coaching those guys. Evashevski had replied:

"Easy. I just kept yelling 'kick it farther'."

"If I tried to give you advice about your job," Porter had said to his audience of editors, "I'd simply have to say 'edit better.' "

This approach, of course, was not news to Dan. "Nothing we have done in the past will ever be good enough again," he once told the staff, and throughout his career he encouraged the staff to believe this.

The title of Porter's speech was 'Why Aren't You Home Writing?" In it he had bemoaned the fact that "honest-to-God-editors" did not seem to be leaving a record of how they did it.

"I would like to think that there are some contemporary editors putting down, on paper or tape, some account of their involvement in these, our times," Porter said. "I wish DeWitt Wallace were doing it. And Henry Luce, and Dan Mich, and Gerald Piel, and Herbert Mayes, and Arnold Gingrich, and Ed Thompson, and John Fischer, and Sid Kirkpatrick, and a good many others. I'd like to think they were, but I doubt it."

That affected Dan. On his return to the office from that meeting he immediately began to collect material for an autobiography, or perhaps a memoir. He wrote to friends in Madison and Des Moines. He began to cull his files.

A few months later, Dan dropped the project. He never gave a reason why, but I suspect he felt it would take too much of his time from editing.

And so we will never have much of a record of how Dan Mich did what he did—only a few anecdotes, recollections of associates and friends, and scraps of quotations from speeches. But we do have the issues of *LOOK* that he edited. We know what Dan Mich did and we know that, in the ranks of editors, he stood in the front line. He was among the greats.

LOOK—THE EXCITING STORY OF PEOPLE

Casting *LOOK* as a "conversation" of "one individual talking to another," as Dan Mich put it, had much to do with *LOOK*'s popularity during the Golden Years. Everyone at *LOOK*, and I as much as anyone, was fascinated by people. For many years, *LOOK* officially defined itself as "The exciting story of people; what they do, what they feel, what they want, what they think—an ever-changing story told with warmth, understanding and wonder." We believed in people, in their ability to confront and deal rationally and effectively with problems if presented with information about what was going on.

Because we believed that people could make a difference, and because we talked directly and frankly to the individual reader, reaction to our stories was frequently very intense. It was often the sort of response you might expect if the reader had been told the story during a face-to-face meeting with the writer and photographer. I never ceased to be amazed at the impact some words and pictures on a few pages in *LOOK* could have.

I remember a story we did in our December 26, 1967 issue entitled

"The Hungry World of Teresa Pilgrim." In words and photographs, it depicted the life of a six-year-old black girl who epitomized about 500 poverty-stricken people in Yazoo City, Mississippi. Our young writer, William Hedgepeth, a Georgian, asked little Teresa what she expected for Christmas. "We don' get much of th' wonderful things folks eats," she said. "Onc't," she said, she got a "norange" for Christmas.

Immediately following publication of that story contributions of more than $2,000 were sent to our offices in New York from all over the nation, earmarked for Teresa and the rest of Yazoo City's hungry. In Yazoo City itself letters arrived for the Pilgrim family at the rate of 150 a day along with money, packages of food, clothes and toys. The postmaster reported that *LOOK* readers who weren't sure how their communications and packages should be addressed wrote "See article in December 26 issue of *LOOK* magazine" on the outside, or pasted the article on the package. A doctor living near Detroit rented a truck, loaded it with food and clothing, and drove to Mississippi during the holidays to distribute the gifts from himself and his friends.

The Mississippi Council on Human Relations reported that a post-Christmas party was held for the families of Yazoo City at which 12,000 pounds of clothing, 12,000 pounds of food, and some 15,000 toys were distributed—all sent as a direct result of the *LOOK* article.

Few subjects we wrote about elicited the intensity of feeling as civil or human rights. Whenever we published an article about the plight of blacks during the 1950's or even the 1960's, we knew in advance to expect hundreds, even thousands of the most violent letters calling us "nigger lovers" and everything else you can think of. This was a time when the very thought of black equality, or even justice, was abhorrent to large segments of the population, and of our readers. There were advertisers who steadfastly refused to use *LOOK* solely on the basis of its human rights coverage.

The condemnation we received from readers on this subject often seemed to be more intense than the praise, which was why I was especially proud when in 1966 *LOOK* won the first National Magazine Award for "outstanding editorial achievement." The award cited us "for skilled editing, imagination and integrity, all of which were reflected in its treatment of the racial issue during 1965." The National Magazine Award, administered by Columbia University's Graduate School of Journalism, was given to us *before*, not *after*, the violent summer of America's cities in 1967.

Whenever we published an article on birth control, we expected, and we got, scathing letters from a broad segment of Catholics and the most vicious kind of letters from hundreds of Protestants castigating the Catholics for the Church's stand on birth control. Even raising, the subject was anathema to a great many thousands of people at the time, and in some respects it still is. I recall a time when a Catholic group

204

methodically contacted our advertisers, asking them to boycott the pages of *LOOK*. It was a precarious—to say the least—period in our history, but I was certain that world opinion was moving toward acceptance of at least discussion of birth control, so we kept right on.

Readers were also quick to second-guess us on our coverage of virtually any issue. Most often they accused us of ignoring certain topics—usually for allegedly nefarious reasons or because we were "afraid." But sometimes they claimed we gave some things too much coverage. One example was the Kennedy family, and we were often labeled a house organ for the Kennedys. (I should mention that our sales always shot up when we put a Kennedy on the cover.)

On the day President Kennedy was assassinated, *LOOK* was on the newsstands with a picture story titled "The President and His Son." Photographed by Stanley Tretick and written by Laura Bergquist, it was one of the most appealing picture stories every produced. Kennedy was absolutely delighted with it and had taken that particular issue of *LOOK* on the plane to Dallas with him.

A BLURB—TOO LATE TO RECALL

During the first few days that issue was on sale practically all of the letters we received concerning it blasted us for "too much Kennedy." And, while the tide changed by-and-large to commendations, there still were a number of people whose hatred of Kennedy was so intense that they still couldn't resist lambasting us for the feature.

At the time of the assassination, the following issue of *LOOK* had already been printed and was in the distribution chain to newsstand wholesalers and retailers and to subscribers and was too late to recall. On its cover was a blurb reading "Kennedy Could Lose." The story inside, based on a poll of voters in an Iowa area that had become a bellwether for future elections, said simply these voters would not re-elect Kennedy if the Presidential election of 1964 were held today. We quickly had stickers printed and asked dealers to place them over the blurb. Many did, but even then many readers peeled them off and wrote letters castigating us for our "lack of feeling."

While we were always interested and frequently astounded at reader mail, we avoided making the mistake of concluding that it represented anything of a true measure of reader opinion. We never used it as a guide to the kinds of stories we ought to publish. At best, the letters were a rough and often inaccurate gauge of public sensitivity and prejudice. In 1958, we published a story entitled "Democratic Forecast: A Catholic in 1960," Half the people who wrote to us denied vehemently that a Catholic could ever become President of the United States.

Often our letter writers were not responding to a particular article or even to *LOOK* itself. They simply wanted some kind of help or wanted to offer their services. Anne Celli, of *LOOK's* public relations department, deserved some kind of medal for the heroic job she did over so many years in coping with mail from our readers (all letters were answered).

Whenever we reported on a "new cure" for cancer or arthritis or any kind of new way to deal with a problem, we were beseiged with thousands of letters saying "Where can I go for treatment", "To whom can I write?" We were not just writing stories. We learned we were providing counsel. We were having the impact of a doctor or a psychiatrist on some people's lives. And some of the things people would do after reading our stories, literally involved questions of life and death. We had to accept that responsibility.

And so we tried to be as cautious and precise as we could so as not to build up false hopes. If we were writing about a new development in medical research, we would be careful to make very clear, if it were the case, that the development had only gone through limited laboratory tests and while it *might* prove to be an important cure much more work needed to be done to be sure. It would have been wrong to ignore promising experiments. Publicity of new research often helps secure the assistance of others who are working in the same area. But it would have been just as wrong to give the impression to readers that the answer to all of their ills was about to arrive at their local pharmacy.

LOOK also went out of its way to be absolutely accurate in everything it printed—not just stories about cures but even the most inconsequential facts. Particularly during our later years we maintained one of the most elaborate copy-checking departments of any magazine. Each article, each photograph, each caption, each headline, was meticulously examined by someone in this department for accuracy, and for legal and ethical implications. If a writer said a particular photograph was of a ketch, instead of what is really was, a yawl, the copy checkers were expected to catch the error. If they didn't, we heard from the boat lovers, en masse.

We committed our share of bloopers—some of them real beauties—but I was rather tolerant about most of them. I realized that 100 percent accuracy is impossible to achieve. The best that can be hoped for is to achieve a commendable batting average, and when an error is committed to acknowledge it publicly and promptly.

In my experience, magazine readers, even more than newspaper readers, take particular delight in spotting errors and in letting you know about them. Perhaps this is because of the slickness of the pages, or the periodicity, or the price. But whatever the case the slightest error would bring in a flood of letters.

Once we published a cartoon by Tom Henderson that showed some scientists haggling about who was going to erase a blackboard full of complicated mathematical formulas. Our copy checking group never imagined that anyone would scrutinize the formulas for accuracy and

206

didn't bother to check them. But for weeks, putative mathematical geniuses peppered us with letters concerning what they perceived to be errors in the formulas. When we printed one of these letters, we received another batch of letters alleging that the letter writer was wrong in his mathematical analysis of the alleged error in the cartoon. It didn't seem as if the matter would ever end.

During its 34 years, *LOOK* strived to bring to a great mass of people some clarification and interpretation of important events and issues in an extremely complex world. And we were always gratified to know that the readers were listening to us, that they cared about what we were talking about just as much as we did, and that it was a rewarding "conversation" for both sides.

A DIVERSIFICATION PROGRAM

By the end of 1966, when *LOOK* had completed 30 years of publishing, the company not only had outgrown its second name—Cowles Magazines, Inc.—but also its third—Cowles Magazines and Broadcasting, Inc.—and had become Cowles Communications, Inc., which our directors felt more properly described our areas of activity.

We also changed from a small closely-held company to a large public corporation whose stock was traded on the New York Stock Exchange.

Our 1966 annual report declared that the most significant achievement in our 30th year was our continued diversification within the broad spectrum of communications, and listed the following breakdown of our properties:

CONSUMER MAGAZINES: LOOK; Family Circle; Family Circle-Britain (part interest); Family Circle-German Version (part interest); Venture, The Traveler's World; The Insider's Newsletter.

BUSINESS MAGAZINES: Magazines for Industry, Inc.

BROADCASTING: KRNT-TV (Des Moines, Iowa); KRNT-Radio (Des Moines, Iowa); KRNT-Theater (Des Moines, Iowa); WESH-TV (Orlando-Daytona Beach, Fla.); WREC-TV (Memphis, Tenn.); Community Antenna Television (part interest, Winter Haven, Fla.).

NEWSPAPERS: The San Juan Star (Puerto Rico); Gainesville Sun (Florida); the Ledger (Lakeland, Fla.); Suffolk Sun (New York).

3-DIMENSIONAL PRODUCTIONS: Visual Panographics, Inc. (XO-GRAPH).

EDUCATION: Cambridge Book Co., Inc.; College Publishing Corp.;

The Cowles Comprehensive Encyclopedia; Publications of the Book Divisions.

PUBLICATION SALES OPERATIONS: Civic Reading Club, Inc.; Educational Book Club, Inc.; Home Reader Service, Inc.; Home Reference Library, Inc.; Mutual Readers League, Inc.; National Organization Service, Inc.

Most of these properties were the result of a major diversification program begun in 1959. *LOOK* was doing very well, and I felt that we had enough talent within the organization to build a communications complex that would range far beyond just one general circulation magazine. To accomplish this, I knew, Cowles Magazines would have to become a publicly held company. Going public would not be an easy step—psychologically and for many other reasons—for a company that had always been privately owned. But since we did not have sufficient cash to make a major expansion, we would need to use stock. And making acquisitions with stock is difficult for a private company mainly because of the complexities in establishing the stock's worth. Stock acquisitions are easier for a public company because the value of the stock is set daily by trading in the stock market.

In order to go public, though, I knew we had to make some initial diversification ventures to broaden our base beyond *LOOK* and the subscription subsidiaries we had picked up from Crowell-Collier. Investors are often leery of one-product companies.

Our initial move was to begin publication of *The Insider's Newsletter* in April 1959, our first new publication since *Quick*. I had long been fascinated with the economics of publishing newsletters such as the *Kiplinger Report*. Though they carry no advertising, they cost very little to produce and often can be sold for more than a much bigger and thicker magazine like *LOOK*. *The Insider's Newsletter*, which was published in separate sections for men and women, was a kind of *Quick* in newsletter form, a potpourri of interesting information including a behind-the-scenes look at the news and advice on investments, health, and the like. It cost $18 a year while *LOOK* sold for only $4. By 1961, it had achieved a circulation of 51,000.

Our second new venture was the *San Juan Star*, the only English-language newspaper in Puerto Rico. The *Star* came into being almost by accident. I had been on vacation in Puerto Rico on two or three occasions and I was fascinated by its rapid economic growth. One day a representative from the Puerto Rican Government's "Operation Bootstrap" came to see Marvin Whatmore and me to convince us to start a motion picture studio operation on the island. His selling ammunition included glowing accounts of scenery that made Puerto Rico ideal for movies requiring tropical settings and details on the very favorable weather, an important factor in movie production.

I was intrigued, and we decided to go ahead. We set up a wholly-owned subsidiary named Studio City, Inc. (later renamed Cinestudio de Puerto Rico, Inc.) to produce movie and TV films.

In the meantime, however, in one of the many talks we had with Governor Munoz about the proposed motion picture operation, I had mentioned that Puerto Rico badly needed an English-language newspaper. Governor Munoz said he agreed completely and advised me to see a fellow in Puerto Rico named Bill Dorvillier, who had been trying for two years to start an English-language daily. "He's trying to get my old political rival, Luis Ferre of Ponce, to put up the money," Governor Munoz said, "and I'd much rather see you than Ferre provide the capital." The next day we met with Dorvillier. The upshot was that we went into the newspaper business instead of the movie studio business.

A group of us from New York went to Puerto Rico for the launching of the *Star* on November 2, 1959. I'll never forget the horrendous problems we had getting the first issue out. For one thing, everyone in San Juan naturally assumed that the newspaper wouldn't come out on November 2nd as it was supposed to because, they said, nothing in Puerto Rico ever happens on time. Unfortunately among the people who assumed that the *Star* wouldn't appear on time were a number of advertisers who wanted to schedule insertions, and so it was impossible to know how big the paper really had to be.

Even worse, most of the compositors setting type for the paper neither spoke nor read English. And some of the people who were proofreading and trying to correct errors couldn't speak Spanish. The result was that the first issue of the *Star* probably had more typographical errors per page than any newspaper ever published. Despite this inauspicious beginning the *Star* won a Pulitzer Prize for material published during its first year, specifically editorials on the Catholic Bishops advising their parishoners on abortion, written by Bill Dorvillier, the editor and publisher. The *Star* was the youngest newspaper ever to win such recognition.

In 1960, we arranged with *The Register* and *Tribune* to merge Cowles Broadcasting, which owned a KRNT-TV and KRNT-Radio in Des Moines, into Cowles Magazines. With this merger, we changed our name to Cowles Magazines and Broadcasting. I felt we now had a sufficiently broad list of properties to go ahead with the public issue. In August 1961, we filed a registration statement with the Securities and Exchange Commission covering a proposed offering and announced that Goldman, Sachs & Co. would head a group of underwriters who would offer stock to the public later that year. On October 23, 1961, we sold 350,000 shares, which represented about 13 percent of the company. The price was $14.50 per share, which gave us proceeds, less the underwriting discount, of $4,690,000.

Our growth for the next few years was so rapid that sometimes I was hard-pressed to remember the names of our major subsidiaries.

In August, 1962, we announced the purchase of the *Gainesville (Florida) Sun*. The purchase came about through my son-in-law Jack Harrison, who was then married to my daughter Lois. After I married my present wife, Jan, I had started spending a good deal of time in Florida, where we have a home on Indian Creek Island. I had heard through a Florida broker that the Fort Pierce *News-Tribune* could be purchased. Having become sold on the Florida economy I bought the *News-Tribune* personally—not as an investment by the corporation—and Jack Harrison moved to Fort Pierce to become the publisher.

Jack and I were astounded at the money to be made through sound and responsible editing and management of a small paper like the *News-Tribune*. I had never fully realized before how good the arithmetic could be. So we searched around for more. One day Jack phoned to tell me that the Pepper family, publishers of the *Gainesville Sun*, had had a big row, and that the property could be purchased.

I immediately flew to Gainesville with Marvin Whatmore and Jack Harding. Luther Hill, one of our directors who lived in Naples, Florida, joined us and was violently opposed to buying the *Sun*. The company's books were in horrible shape, he pointed out, that it was difficult to project anything with accuracy. Despite his opposition, I made an offer of $2,000,000 and concluded a deal very close to that figure. In the end, that property provided us with the highest return per dollar of investment of any of our properties. In 1963, we bought still another Florida paper, the *Lakeland Ledger*.

WE ACQUIRE *FAMILY CIRCLE*

Perhaps our single most important acquisition, in October, 1962, was that of *Family Circle*, which later became the largest selling women's magazine. I had been looking longingly at the magazine for years. I was fascinated that month after month, seven million women would push their carts through the aisles in supermarkets and reach up at the checkout counter to put *Family Circle* on top of their groceries. I would take out my pencil and attempt to figure the net *Family Circle* could get out of such circulation without the horrible expense of securing and maintaining subscriptions. But I never got around to talking with P.K. Leberman, who was then publisher and majority stockholder of *Family Circle*, about the possibility of acquiring the magazine—even though I had known P.K. through an old friend Niles Trammell.

Then one day Roy Quinlan, who put out a weekly publication called "The Magazine Industry Newsletter," came in with a presentation he had prepared on what a desirable property *Family Circle* was. Without thinking more about it, I told him to go ahead and set up a lunch with

210

Leberman. Several weeks later, when we were in the middle of negotiations to acquire *Family Circle*, Quinlan came in and wanted to know who was going to pay his "finder's fee." Feeling like a fool, I ended up paying a finder's fee for a property I had been interested in acquiring for years.

I had also eyed WREC-AM and WREC-TV in Memphis, Tennessee, for years. Luther Hill and I had bought them from Hoyt Wooten for *The Des Moines Register* and *Tribune* in November, 1958 for $6,000,000 cash. However, Hoyt then discovered that most of the $6,000,000 would have to go for taxes. He personally had founded the stations, and the way the business was set up, the $6,000,000 sale price could not have been considered a capital gain. Thus I let Hoyt back out of the deal. Four years later and after Hoyt had gotten some expert tax advice so that the purchase would be a capital gain, the deal went through. In the meantime, however, the price of television stations had skyrocketed, and we had to pay $2,000,000 more for the WREC properties than *The Register* and *Tribune* had agreed to pay in 1958.

In 1963, we announced the start of a new travel magazine, *Venture, The Traveler's World,* whose first issue was dated June, 1964.

During the next three years—from 1963 through 1966 we set up a subsidiary, Visual Panographics, Inc., to market XOGRAPH products produced by a 3-D printing process developed by Marv Whatmore in cooperation with Eastman Kodak; got into international publishing for the first time with the purchase of a 50 percent interest in Standbrook Publications, Limited, publisher of *Trio*, a monthly women's magazine distributed in supermarkets in England—and renamed the magazine *Family Circle;* started—through Standbrook and the firm of M. DuMont Schauberg in Cologne—a German version of *Family Circle;* acquired WESH-TV in Orlando-Daytona Beach, Florida; acquired a 70 percent interest in Universal Cable Vision, Inc., a company formed to construct and operate a community antenna television system in Winter Haven, Florida, and adjacent communities; established a new daily newspaper, the *Suffolk (New York) Sun* to cover the Eastern end of Long Island; acquired the College Publishing Corporation, which published test preparation books on a variety of subjects; got into the business magazine field for the first time with the acquisition of Magazines for Industry, Inc., publishers of nine highly respected business magazines, three annuals, and a newsletter. And that's where we stood as we completed our first 30 years. There were later acquisitions, including the *Ocala* (Fla.) *Star-Banner; Modern Medicine;* the Dental and Journal Lancet groups of publications; Bettendorf Publications; and the Dairy Industry Division of Miller Publishing Company.

Since Cowles Magazines and Broadcasting had gone public in 1961, our stock had been traded in the over-the-counter market. But we were anxious eventually to obtain the prestige and visibility of a listing on the

New York Stock Exchange. We finally met the requirements. On May 10, 1966, the Big Board listing became effective and what became Cowles Communications began trading with the ticker Symbol CWL.

THE MANCHESTER BOOK

Entering our 31st year in 1967, *LOOK* published in its January 24 issue the first of a four-part serialization of William Manchester's book, *The Death of a President*, about the assassination of President Kennedy. It was the most famous and widely read series *LOOK* ever published. One study showed that nearly 70,000,000 Americans read at least one of the four installments, constituting the largest audience ever for four consecutive issues of a magazine.

Manchester's story was extraordinarily compelling. But the story behind its publication in *LOOK*—a widely publicized and often unpleasant dispute between Jackie Kennedy and *LOOK*—had some quite compelling qualities of its own, especially for those of us with the misfortune to be directly involved.

The story behind the story began in late 1963 and early 1964 when the Kennedy family decided they wanted a definitive authorized book about the assassination. Some members of the family, as well as family advisers, were familiar with the earlier works of Manchester and it was decided by Jackie and Bobby Kennedy that he was the man for the job. Although Manchester was under contract to Little, Brown for another book, this company graciously released him to Harper & Row, whom the Kennedy's had chosen as publishers. Harper & Row had published John F. Kennedy's *Profiles in Courage* and Robert Kennedy's *The Enemy Within*, and the Kennedys were on friendly terms with Cass Canfield, chairman of the board at Harper & Row, and its chief editor, Evan Thomas.

In accepting the assignment, Manchester signed a "memorandum of understanding" that granted the Kennedys manuscript approval before the book could be published. This memorandum would be the focal point for all of the controversy that followed.

On July 18, 1966, *LOOK* and five other magazines received a copy of the still incomplete manuscript from Don Congdon of the Harold Matson Company, a literary agency representing Manchester. In an accompanying letter, Congdon explained that the book was being offered in competitive bidding for first serialization rights and that the deadline for such bids would be 5 p.m. July 29.

Bill Arthur, *LOOK's* editor, immediately turned the manuscript over to Mike Land, a *LOOK* senior editor charged with the reading of such submissions. The reaction of Land, and of Arthur, who read the manuscript the next day, was so enthusiastic that I took it home to read. We were unanimous in our belief that it was one of the most powerful narratives of our time and that *LOOK* should enter into the bidding race.

212

In plotting our strategy, we decided a little lobbying wouldn't hurt. Knowing that Bobby would be involved in the final selection, we asked our Washington bureau chief, Warren Rogers, who was a friend of Bobby, to meet with him to convey our great interest. And, knowing little about Manchester himself, Arthur drove to Middletown, Connecticut, and spent an afternoon visiting with the author in his office at Wesleyan Univesity.

Shortly before 5 p.m. on the 29th, a Friday, Arthur and *LOOK*'s managing editor, Robert Meskill, hand-delivered our bid to the Matson office. Never before had we bid so much for a manuscript: $305,000 for first serialization rights in the United States and Canada, plus $100,000 (through our Des Moines Register and Tribune Syndicate) for worldwide first serialization rights. We were told we were considerably under the top bid, which was from *LIFE*. I immediately authorized Arthur to cross out the $305,000 and make it $505,000, and to cross out the $100,000 and make it $150,000. That totaled $655,000 and I was, to say the least, somewhat nervous.

Congdon informed Arthur that, to be fair, *LIFE* and the other magazines would be given another 24 hours—until 5 p.m. on Saturday—to submit a second bid of their own.

During the day on Saturday, Arthur learned that George Hunt, *LIFE*'s managing editor, was aboard a sailboat somewhere on Long Island Sound, that he had no ship-to-shore communications facilities, and that he was not due to return to port until 6 p.m. We decided we might be able to forestall further bidding by *LIFE* by getting the matter resolved before Hunt got back. (We learned later that *LIFE* had upped its initial $500,000 bid to $550,000 on Friday, but had asked for an extension of the deadline until Monday in order to get its executives together for a further reappraisal.)

Arthur called Congdon and said, "We believe we are entitled to a final decision by 5 p.m. today."

The strategy worked. At 5:15, Congdon called Arthur. "*LOOK* has the book," he said. Bill called me. "We got it!" he said excitedly.

I was excited too. But I called Congdon to tell him I still wanted to hear the news directly from either Bobby or Jackie. Bobby soon called, said he was at the tennis court with Jackie at Hyannisport, and that they were both very pleased that *LOOK* and not *LIFE* had won the auction. Bobby later said the same thing to Manchester. "*LOOK* has been so nice to the family," Bobby told Manchester, "and Henry Luce has been such a bastard."

Everything seemed set. Manchester turned in the final version of the manuscript, which was far better than I ever dared hope. Cass Canfield was equally elated. Manchester had produced a superb job. We finished our copy-editing and the printers began to set type for the first of what were to be seven installments. *LOOK* men who handled foreign serial

213

rights were busy selling rights in 42 countries.

Then one Sunday morning I got a call from Jackie inviting me to come to Hyannisport. I instantly sensed trouble, but I tried to sound matter-of-fact. "Sure, Jackie, I'd be glad to," I said. "When would you like me to come?" She named August 24th, the following Tuesday.

"Would you mind if I brought Jack Harding, the *LOOK* general counsel, with me?" I asked.

"Fine," she said, "because I expect to have my lawyer here too." Now I *knew* there was trouble.

Jack Harding and I arrived at Hyannisport on a beautiful late-summer day. Jackie was at the airport to meet us, dressed in a flowing Pucci dress and sandals. I did not know Jackie well, but had met her socially about a dozen times. She greeted me warmly and I introduced Harding. We had not been aware of it but a lawyer from Judge Simon Rifkind's office, Jackie's lawyer, had been on the plane with us, along with a few Kennedy friends. It was quite a crowd. I offered to get a taxi for Harding and myself but Jackie insisted that we would all get into her car. One of her friends drove and I sat in the back seat with Jackie on my lap.

AN AWKWARD SILENCE

The Kennedy compound was about five minutes from the airport. After a brief tour of the house, we joined the rest of the group on the terrace. Drinks were served and consumed in an awkward silence until Bobby came up from the bay with *his* lawyer. So there we were, out on the terrace of Jack Kennedy's house—Jackie with her lawyer, Bobby with his lawyer, and I with the *LOOK* lawyer. I think there were two more men, one of them a public-relations man for Bobby Kennedy.

Bobby was obviously in charge of the proceedings. He started by saying that Mrs. Kennedy (he always referred to Jackie as Mrs. Kennedy in formal situations) was worried about how the book was going to be handled by *LOOK*. Of course, he said, Jackie had manuscript approval of the syndication editing of the Manchester manuscript.

"No, Senator," I interrupted. "The manuscript as written by Manchester was put up for competitive bidding and *LOOK* won. You called to tell me how pleased you and Mrs. Kennedy were that *LOOK* had bought the serialization rights. There is nothing *at all* in our contract with Manchester about manuscript approval by anyone."

"However," I added, "we will be perfectly willing to consider any legitimate complaint you or Mrs. Kennedy may have. But I must correct what you have just said. Neither you, nor Mrs. Kennedy, nor anyone else has the right of censorship over the *LOOK* excerpts. I think that should be clarified right from the beginning."

Bobby didn't utter a sound. Jackie, who was sitting beside me, took over. She exploded with an almost childlike tantrum. "I don't care what

214

the contract with *LOOK* says!" The famous whispery voice was loud and clear. "*I* have the sole right to decide what is published by *LOOK* and what is not published by *LOOK*," she went on. "And nothing is going to be published that I don't approve of. And that's that. Have you got that straight, Mike?"

"That is not in accord with the contract *LOOK* made for the Manchester book," I insisted. "We have exclusive rights to publish in our magazine whatever part of the manuscript we wish to use."

Jackie suddenly jumped from her chair, pointed her finger at me and screamed hysterically, "This will only be published with my approval! If you go ahead without it I'm going to destroy *LOOK* and, furthermore, I'm going to destroy you, Mike!" She burst into tears and ran into the house.

There was a shocked silence. After a few moments Bobby said quietly, "Mike, I don't believe anything constructive can be accomplished here today. Let's go back to New York. I have to get back to Washington. Perhaps two or three days from now we can get together again."

The meeting broke up. Jackie suddenly appeared on the terrace, composed and cool, but said nothing further. We all sat around uneasily for a bit then I said, "We'd better go." Bobby, who was taking the old Kennedy family plane, offered to drop Jack and me at La Guardia. We bade Jackie a polite farewell.

Once we were airborne, Bobby asked me to sit with him. What Jackie was mostly upset about, he told me, was that she had suddenly realized that since *LOOK* was a bi-weekly and was going to run seven installments, it would mean fourteen weeks of anguish for her and especially the children, who would be hearing about the tragedy for weeks on end from their playmates at school.

"Would you consider cutting the number of installments from seven to three?" he asked me.

I said I would. "If it will make Mrs. Kennedy happier and settle the dispute, we'll compromise and make it four installments, provided *LOOK* can use whatever number of words it decides upon in each installment."

The Senator seemed pleased. "That's great, Mike," he said. "I appreciate it very much. It'll make my problem much easier." Bobby's "problem," presumably, was placating Jackie. Jack Harding and I were greatly relieved that the matter had been amicably settled.

Two days later, however, everything unraveled again. At Jackie's behest, Judge Rifkind went into court to obtain an order enjoining *LOOK* from distributing any part of the Manchester manuscript. While our lawyers argued with Jackie's lawyers—and the press gleefully put the story on page one day after day—we faced a growing risk of serious financial loss. It was getting close to press time. If we went ahead and printed eight million copies of *LOOK* with the first installment and Jackie

215

was successful in preventing its distribution, we would be unable to collect any of the newsstand or advertising revenues but still would have to pay the printing bill. Altogether, *LOOK* stood to lose three or four million dollars.

Cass Canfield was also concerned. Under our agreement with Manchester, Harper & Row could not publish the hard-cover book before the first serialization appeared. If Jackie could stop us, she might be able to stop Harper & Row from publishing.

The most maddening and frustrating aspect of the dispute was that we could not determine exactly what was bothering Jackie. I had agreed with Bobby to cut the book to four installments, but that obviously had not satisfied her. We guessed there must be something in the manuscript that bothered her, but we couldn't seem to find out what that might be.

While the lawyers continued to argue, I arranged some meetings between our editors and Cass Canfield and Evan Thomas, to discuss what modifications we might make to appease Jackie. We all agreed that the gory details describing the two or three minutes after the shooting could easily be omitted.

In order to have Manchester available to approve any editorial changes, and to protect him from the ruckus, we put him up at the Berkshire Hotel, across the street from the *LOOK* building. The Kennedys found where he was. Apparently concerned that he might be making some kind of private deal with us behind his back, Bobby and a couple of his aides showed up one day and began pounding on Manchester's door demanding entry. It was like a scene from some Grade-B movie. Manchester did not answer and they didn't get into his suite.

CONFLICTING ASSESSMENTS

Gradually, from different sources, I began to find out if not what Jackie's precise problem was at least *why* she was having a problem. She had never read Manchester's manuscript. She had refused from the beginning to do so because it might revive memories of those terrible days. Bobby had declined to read it for the same reason. Instead, they had given it to several family friends, including Ed Guthman of the *Los Angeles Times* and John Seigenthaler of the *Nashville Tennesseean*. The assessments from this diverse group had been often conflicting, to the point that even before we saw the manuscript Manchester had become exhausted, bewildered, and angry trying to reconcile the diverse editorial instructions.

Among the group of advisers was Pamela Turnure, Jackie's longtime and trusted secretary. I never found out exactly what Turnure told Jackie. But based on the events that followed I think Turnure must have expressed the opinion to Jackie that she did not come off very well in

216

Manchester's description of the period immediately preceeding and following the assassination. It was this, I think, that must have caused Jackie to try to claim control over the *LOOK* installments and to try to stop publication.

The only way to resolve the dispute was to get Jackie to read the *LOOK* installments herself and specify which parts she didn't like. I got her to agree to meet on a Saturday at Sullivan & Cromwell, the law firm representing *LOOK*. The firm's offices were near Wall Street, which normally would be deserted on a Saturday and free from discovery by the press. I told Jackie she could read the dummies at her leisure and discuss her objections. I also decided to bring along Bill Attwood, editor-in-chief of Cowles Communications. Attwood, whom President Kennedy had appointed ambassador to Guinea and later Kenya, had long been close to the Kennedy family and might be useful in putting Jackie at ease.

The meeting started at eleven o'clock, with Jackie arriving pretty much on time. Wall Street was absolutely deserted. Bill and Jackie went into a private office with the pasted-up proofs. I sat in an outer office together with the high-priced lawyers and the inevitable Kennedy public-relations man. Twice, Jackie, who was a chain smoker, and Bill sent out for cigarettes. About two o'clock Jackie said she had finished the manuscript and had to leave for an appointment uptown. The Kennedy public-relations man took her aside and told her: "The television networks and the newspapers have found out you are down here and when you go out you're going to have to face those TV cameras."

Until that moment Jackie seemed to be perfectly calm and at ease. Now she reached for a handkerchief and clutched it in her hand. She went down in the elevator with the p.r. man and walked out into the street holding his arm. She began to weep and, dabbing at her eyes with the hankie, told the television audience that she was being put upon by *LOOK*. I have forgotten her exact words, but she made it clear, between sobs, that *LOOK* was trying to dishonor the name of her late husband by what they were about to publish.

After Jackie's departure Bill Attwood sat down at a big round table with Judge Rifkind and me. All of the legal bickering and controversy at last came down to three changes which Jackie wanted made in the Manchester material *LOOK* was going to publish:

1. Manchester had written, accurately, that Jackie and John Kennedy had quarreled and slept in separate rooms the night before the assassination. She wanted this changed to say that they had slept together.

2. Manchester had written, accurately, that she had taken an hour to fix her hair and apply her makeup the morning of the assassination. She wanted this cut.

3. Manchester had written, accurately, that Jackie did not have enough

courage to tell her children their father had been assassinated and that she made the governess break the news. Jackie wanted this changed to say that she had broken the news to the children.

After Attwood relayed these three demands I saw the problem was not insurmountable. I offered Judge Rifkind my proposals: "I'll take the responsibility of handling Manchester on the 'sleeping in separate rooms' point. We'll just cut it and the reader will not give a thought to whether or not they slept together the night before the assassination. But we are not going to say something that is not true."

"On the second point, we can simply say she wanted to look her best that day and there will be no mention of time span."

"The third point is a difficult one. It will be a distortion of history but I'll try to persuade Manchester to angle the story so that it suggests that the children could absorb the shock more easily hearing it from their governess rather than from their mother. I'll ask him to do it so that Jackie doesn't appear in a bad light."

Judge Rifkind approved my suggestions and agreed to get Jackie's consent.

On Monday morning, as R.R. Donnelley, the *LOOK* printers in Chicago, were already grinding out installments for our upcoming issues, Judge Rifkind called to suggest we meet at the Century Club at five o'clock. When Jack Harding and I arrived the judge was waiting for us with another man, I believe a Kennedy lawyer. The judge was in a most genial mood. "I've worked it out with Mrs. Kennedy," he said. "She agreed to drop her suit against *LOOK* on condition that *LOOK* make the three changes we discussed."

In all, we had to cut or change about 800 words.

One interesting footnote to this episode: In the midst of the turmoil, when Jackie was trying to restrain the publication of *LOOK*, she placed a call to Stan Tretick, a *LOOK* photographer covering the White House, and invited him to her apartment. The Kennedys thought Stan the best photographer ever assigned to them and they loved him. Jackie told Stan she was planning a trip to Cambodia to visit the ruins of Angkor Wat. "You're my favorite photographer," she said, "and I want you to come along on the trip. Go back to the office and tell Mike that if he'll give you the assignment, I'll give you an exclusive photograph of me, in color, standing in front of the ruins. It would make a great cover for *LOOK*."

I think I understand the kind of woman Jackie had become. As one of the most glamorous of Presidential wives and as a result of being constantly exposed to the glare of publicity, mostly favorable, Jackie adapted quickly to the role of royalty and all its prerogatives—with grace perhaps—but no humor and not much perspective. I like Jackie despite everything. But I feel a little sorry for her.

218

THE ENDING OF LOOK

The most difficult day in my life was Thursday, September 16, 1971. That was the day we announced that *LOOK* would cease publication with the issue dated October 19, 1971.

For about five years, I had been fighting a battle against increasingly hopeless business odds. In retrospect, 1966 was *LOOK's* high-water mark, the peak of its prosperity. After that began a deterioration toward disaster that I was able to delay but not prevent.

When *Collier's* had folded in 1956, most magazine executives tried to convince themselves that its demise was a fluke, simply the product of poor management. In fact, and many of us privately admitted it to ourselves, there were more fundamental forces involved that affected all mass-circulation, general-interest magazines. No fluke, the end of *Collier's* was a harbinger of things to come. It had fallen first only because it was the weakest of the mass magazines. The rest of us would live longer, but not forever.

The most fundamental of the fundamental forces, of course, was television. Television was slowly but inexorably supplanting our economic, if not our editorial, reason for being. All of the mass magazines had the same business strategy: Through our very broad editorial approach and our relatively low subscription rates, we tried to assemble the largest number of readers possible. We then marketed this audience to national advertisers of high-volume consumer products from automobiles to laundry soap to life insurance.

This strategy was highly successful for many years. Magazines such as *LIFE* and *LOOK*—with their large page size, expensive paper, extensive use of color, and worldwide staffs—were very expensive to produce. But we easily covered these costs with abundant advertising revenues, for advertisers wanting to reach a mass audience had nowhere else to go.

Until television. As television entered more and more homes, advertisers discovered that it could deliver an even larger mass audience at lower cost, many of them believed, with more effectiveness.

As television gradually became the most pervasive mass medium, the nature of the magazine business changed. Readers became less attracted to broad, picture-oriented, general interest magazines and we kept having a harder time keeping our circulation up and had to resort to more discounting. With television increasingly serving their mass entertainment and information needs, they began to prefer magazines that served more narrowly defined special interests: cooking, science fiction, health, family finance, science. The only unaffected general interest magazines were publications such as *Time* and *Newsweek* that have a very precise focus and role, in the newsweeklies' case to provide for a well-educated audience a tightly compressed account of the week's news and other current events and trends.

The new sharply focused magazines made good economic sense, too. Readers were willing to pay much more for them. And so were some kinds of advertisers. Television is an effective advertising medium for mass-distributed goods such as automobiles, soap, and other packaged goods. But it is not as efficient for more specialized products and services consumed by relatively narrow groups of people such as health-food buffs, yacht owners, dentists, or just educated people with a high disposable income. The proliferating sharp-focus magazines were just what advertisers with more targeted needs wanted. Though they had a relatively small circulation, the advertisers knew that a large percentage of their readers would be interested in what the advertisers were trying to sell.

During *LOOK's* first 30 years, I think the country needed magazines that were "the exciting story of people," to quote *LOOK's* slogan, or whose goal was "To see life, to see the world, to eyewitness great events," to quote Henry Luce's original definition of *LIFE*. Readers needed a few magazines run by creative, imaginative editors who took the broadest possible view of their role, who would take on any story that seemed interesting and important. Readers needed a few mass magazines to define where we as a nation were and where we were going. But as people spent more and more time in front of the television set and more and more time with publications catering to their own special interests, the need for mass circulation, broad-appeal magazines could not help but decline.

LOOK—"BIGGER THAN *LIFE*"

All of us in the mass magazine business tried to resist if not ignore these new realities, especially our growing competition with television for advertising. In *LOOK's* circulation battles with *Collier's*, *The Post*, and then *LIFE*, we kept believing that gross numbers still mattered. I remember my elation when *LOOK's* circulation passed *LIFE* in 1962 ("*LOOK* is bigger than *LIFE*," our ad campaign stressed) and my depression when *LIFE*, by purchasing the failing *Saturday Evening Post's* subscribers in 1969, jumped back into the lead.

Perhaps belatedly, we tried to change our strategy. In April, 1970, we reduced our circulation from 7,750,000 to 6,500,000 and announced that 80 percent of the lower circulation would be concentrated in the top 60 metropolitan markets that had the most appeal to advertisers. We came up with a novel program called Top/Spot which matched census data with Zip Codes to isolate 1,200,000 readers with high median incomes. We then tried to market these "upscale" readers to advertisers of so-called "quality" goods. We were trying to market *LOOK* less as a mass magazine and more as a class magazine.

None of these moves, while helpful, was able to arrest the alarming

220

slide in our ad revenue. Peaking at $80,133,200, it dropped by 1970 to $62,828,700. In 1969, for the first time in 22 years, *LOOK* lost money. In 1970, the losses exceeded $5,000,000 before taxes. We launched a massive cost-cutting program to cut *LOOK's* expenses but hikes in postal rates and other costs chewed up the savings so laboriously and painfully achieved.

But I remained determined to keep *LOOK* alive. Despite the broad economic forces working against us, I kept thinking that if I could just keep *LOOK* going we would hit upon some way to solve its problems. On October 17, 1969, we suspended the *Suffolk Sun,* a decision that was especially painful since my son Pat had been the publisher. Though the paper's losses had been reduced and its editorial quality improved, we were not in a position to keep investing money in it while waiting for it to move into the black. To cover *LOOK's* losses, I began selling some of the other pieces of Cowles Communications such as the *San Juan Star,* the Cowles Book Company, the Magazines for Industry group of trade publications, and our interest in the German *Family Circle.* Our biggest deal was with the New York Times Company, which was anxious to become more broadly diversified. In return for 2,600,000 shares of Time Class A stock (worth more than $50,000,000 at the time), and the assumption by the Times of $15,000,000 of Cowles long-term debt, we transferred to the Times in April 1971 *Family Circle* magazine, the Modern Medicine and Dental Survey Group of domestic and international publications, our three Florida newspapers, the Cambridge Book Company, and WREC-TV in Memphis. In 1970, I had been quoted in the press as saying, in response to a question about *LOOK's* future, "My heart is in *LOOK*—it's my baby. I founded it 33 years ago. I'd sell everything to keep it going." And that was the truth.

These transactions substantially improved our balance sheet. But they did nothing to arrest the rumors of *LOOK's* imminent demise that were becoming increasingly widespread on Madison Avenue. Like *Collier's* and the *Post* before us, we had acquired the smell of a loser, and there was nothing I could do by this time to change it. Everything I did to prolong *LOOK's* life reinforced the impression of last-minute desperation.

By September 1971, the awful reality of the situation was becoming oppressive. Advertising sales, which had seemed to be improving slightly at the beginning of the year, were now falling below 1970's depressed levels. Our annual automobile issue, dated September 21, had only three pages of automotive ads as against the twenty to thirty pages during more prosperous times. "It can't be," I kept telling myself. But it was.

It was an impossible situation. As I put it later, "When it came time to make this decision, I thought back over *LOOK's* thirty-five years of constructive, responsible, and award-winning journalism and my heart said, 'Keep it going,' but my head said, 'Suspend it.' And, there was really no other way."

On the evening of September 15, I called in each of our top executives, one by one, and told them "Tomorrow I am announcing that we are ceasing publication of *LOOK* with our October 19 issue."

I shall never forget their reactions. The struggle—theirs and mine—to keep *LOOK* alive had been lost. The end had come.

The next morning, I assembled our staff. "I don't think any of us has anything to reproach ourselves with," I said. "Obviously readers want and like *LOOK* since the response to our subscription and renewal offers is as good as or better than at any time in our history. Although down, our advertising sales are good by almost any comparison with other media. On the business side we have tried, and succeeded in achieving dozens of ingenious ways to save money. However, all of this has been more than offset by forces outside of our control."

LIFE did not escape these forces either. After our announcement to fold *LOOK*, the publisher of *LIFE* commented with seeming confidence that "*LIFE* goes on." But on December 8, 1972, Time Inc. was forced to announce that *LIFE* would be suspended with the last issue in 1972. *LIFE* lost $30,000,000 during its last four years of operation. Time Inc. revived *LIFE* in October 1978. But the new *LIFE* resembled the old in little more than name and an interest in good photography. A monthly with a much smaller circulation, much smaller staff, and much higher subscription rates, it concentrates on feature stories instead of the news. While it is a very beautiful looking magazine, to my mind it lacks the free-wheeling zest of its predecessor.

LOOK was also revived, but less successfully. Daniel Filipacchi, publisher of *Paris Match*, acquired the *LOOK* logo from Cowles Communications and invested a reported $25,000,000 in a new *LOOK* that made its debut on February 19, 1979. The new *LOOK* was less like the old *LOOK* than it was a trendy mixture of *Paris Match, People* magazine, and *Rolling Stone*. In fact, its editor and publisher for a brief time was Jann S. Wenner, *Rolling Stone's* founder and editor. After considerable editorial turmoil and losses said to be $1,000,000 a month, *LOOK* closed down again after its August issue.

Hardly a day passes now that I don't think of the old *LOOK*. I think about the thousands of articles we published over those 35 years, the great and near-great with whom we dealt, our millions of loyal readers.

I think of our request of the eminent historian, Henry Steele Commager, that he write his answer to the question: "Is Freedom Dying in America?", and of his response in the pages of *LOOK:*
"Do we need to proclaim once more the most elementary principle of our constitutional system: that in the United States, the people are the masters and all officials are servants—officials in the White House, in the Cabinet, in the Congress, in the state executive and legislative chambers, officials, too, in uniform, whether the National Guard or the police?

"History celebrates not the victors who successfully silenced dissent but their victims who fought to speak the truth as they saw it."

I think of a letter we got as a result of the story we published under the title "How Can You Tell If Your Child is Taking Drugs?" It was from a New York mother.

"This morning," she wrote, "I ran a quickie errand to the corner convenience store.

"'Have you seen the cover on *LOOK?*' I asked the grocer."

"'No,' answered the busy man.

"I grabbed a copy off the rack and slid it across the counter to him. 'See how young she is,' I exclaimed, pointing to the cover photograph of a young girl.

"'Looking up with a nice smile, he agreed.

"'Now look at this,' I said, pointing to the caption about her taking drugs.

"He read it, picked up the money, rang the cash register. When he dropped the change in my hand, he looked up—and his eyes were filled with tears.

"Of all the troubles in a troubled nation, this self-slaughter of our young is surely the heartbreak. Surely, they mean enough to us to warrant a thorough revamping of our values—such a jolt to the status quo that we see it for what it is—and rout it forever."

I think of *The New York Time's* editorial requiem for *LOOK:*
"For more than three decades *LOOK* sought to appeal to thoughtful Americans concerned with understanding and helping to solve the country's problems...It will be remembered as a civilized magazine, faithful to the conviction that an alert and informed public is the best insurance for a sound America—A magazine neither complacent nor despairing, but never given to easy tolerance of the intolerable."

I hold my head high.